SPICELAND QUAKER TRA
1940 – 1946

Cups Without Sa

Front Cover: From a watercolour: Courtesy of Spicelander H. Godwin Arnold, BArch, ARIBA, FSA: *Spiceland in the Snow*

Back Cover: Blackborough Church, Beacon Hill and Lord Egremont's House (on extreme right) [Spiceland] from Hutchinson's *Watercolours Illustrating Popular Pastoral Scenes* (1854). Courtesy of Devon Record Office

TO

John and Margaret Hoare — The First Wardens of Spiceland
My Wife Marjorie — Who Shared the Experience With Me
All Spicelanders
The People of Blackborough
The Blackdown Hills

SPICELAND

QUAKER TRAINING CENTRE

1940 – 1946

Cups Without Saucers

by
Stanley Smith

William Sessions Limited
York, England

ISBN 1 85072 064 9

Acknowledgements

To the excellent Spiceland Artists: Peter Reddick for his specially researched series of line-drawings, and Godwin Arnold for the reproductions of his three watercolours.

To Tim Evens — for his encouragement to "keep writing", for reading the finished manuscript and for the helpful suggestions and corrections which I was happy to accept.

To the Editor of *The Countryman* for permission to use two incidents in Chapter 18 which were published in 1951.

To the Devon Record Office for permission to use the Watercolour of Blackborough.

To the Hulton Picture Library for permission to use the pictures comprising plates IV, VII, VIII, IX, XI, XVI, XVII and XVIII.

Printed in 10 on 12 point Plantin Typeface
By William Sessions Limited
The Ebor Press, York, England

Contents

Illustrations

PREFACE

This is a book about Spiceland — the Quaker Training Centre for war relief workers which was established on a spur of the Blackdown Hills at Blackborough in the County of Devonshire between March 1940 and December 1945. It is not a history. It is based on archival material — Minutes, Correspondence, One hundred and four editions of the wall magazine, *Wallpaper*, published between January 1941 and January 1943, and News Letters edited by John Hoare and circulated to all Spicelanders — which came into my possession when I was Secretary to the Spiceland Trust from 1947 until 1967. But it is also based on my vivid personal memories — supplemented and amended by those of my wife, and of many other Spicelanders with whom we have maintained contact, and who have talked and written to us over many years. My intention was to write a book that my family could read and, hopefully, understand. Marjorie and I spent a brief working holiday at Spiceland in May 1940, and returned to take the full training course in January 1941. Almost by accident — certainly not by design — we remained there until the spring of 1946, became the longest resident Spicelanders, and eventually the repository of its written records. It seemed sensible to provide a copy of the book for the Society of Friends archives, together with the other written records. Some who have read parts of the book have expressed the hope that it can be made available to a wider Quaker readership, and, because it treats, in a minor fashion, of a period of history now fifty years away, a readership beyond that. Maybe.......

In the main the book is an incomplete story about what a relatively small group of people, holding minority views, did during the second world war, and in part about how their actions affected the people around them. Where I have expressed views or opinions about religion in general, the Society of Friends in particular, social conditions, or politics they are mine and must not be taken to represent the views of anyone else. The name Spiceland conjures memories for many people. For some it is an old and attractive Quaker Meeting House at Five Fords halfway between Culmstock and Uffculme and in the middle of nowhere; but to over three hundred pacifist men and women it means Blackborough House where, under the wardenship of John and Margaret Hoare, there flourished a remarkable community which established traditions of service and cemented bonds of friendship in an atmosphere which had deep spiritual roots but which was free from pious expression. That is my Spiceland.

Stanley Smith, Peterborough.

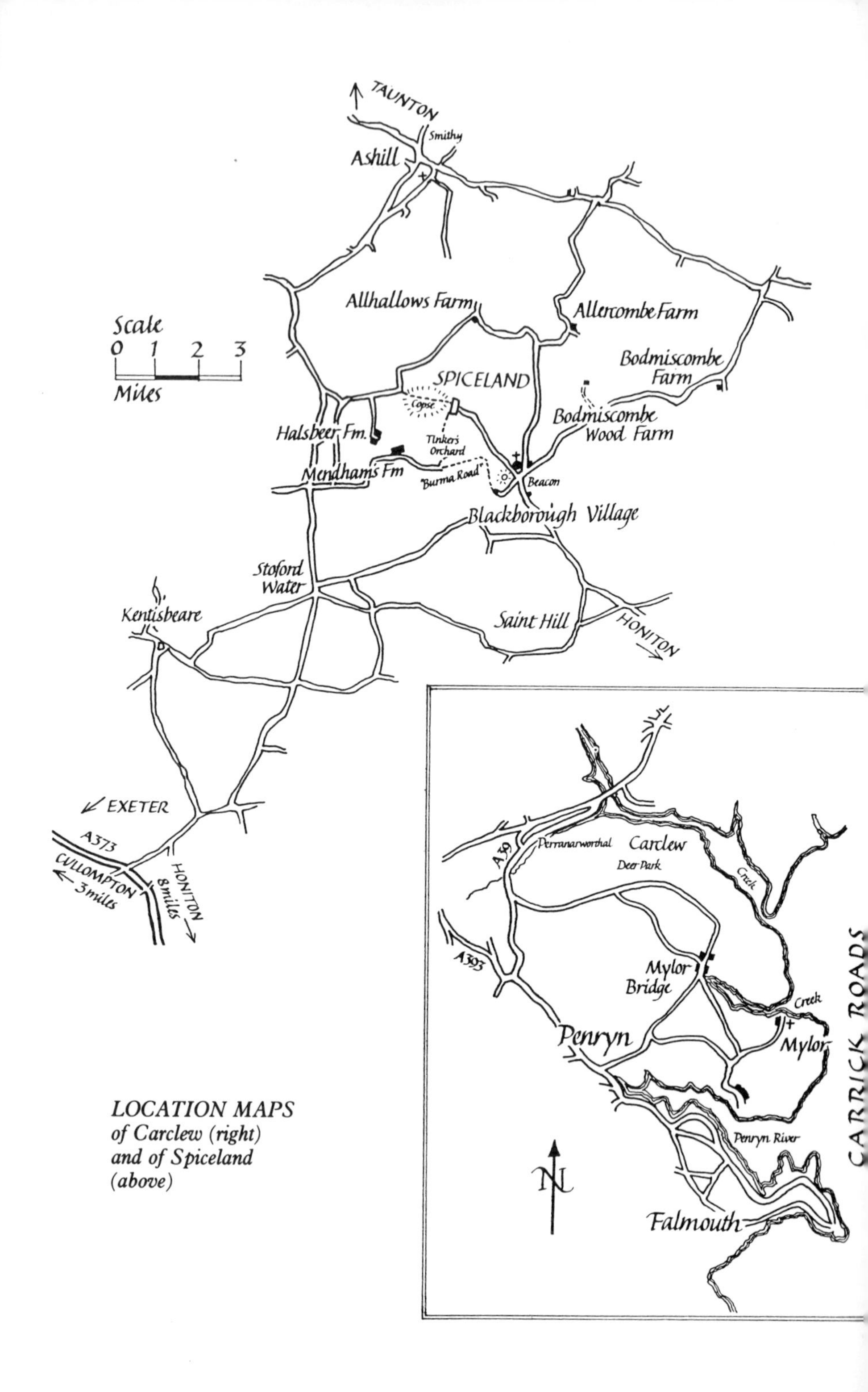

LOCATION MAPS
of Carclew (right)
and of Spiceland
(above)

CHAPTER 1

Tea With Mrs. Mendham

On a lovely summer day in August 1945 Marjorie and I left the big house and walked across the lawn to Mendham's Lane. On one edition of the Ordnance Survey it is shown as Mortimer's Lane and on another as Ballyman's Lane, but to us and to all Spicelanders it was Mendham's Lane because it led to Mr. Mendham's farm, and we had been invited to tea by Mrs. Mendham.

We walked slowly in the afternoon sunshine. An overgrown hedge hid the house and the vegetable garden, while a neglected copse containing a few fine trees screened from view the walled garden which lay sheltered someway down hill from the house. On our left was Big Field. Big, that is, by our standards. Something over eleven acres and described locally as a sideling knap, which meant that it sloped in more than one direction. It was steep and pear-shaped, narrowing towards the bottom of the hill where it was less steep. The bottom four acres had been fenced off and were growing a good crop of potatoes, but the upper, steeper, acres were poor hill pasture.

The lane veered to the right and bordered a small field known as Tinkers Orchard. In 1941 we had grubbed up the old, fallen, and neglected fruit trees with the savage brambles that had embraced them, so that we could plough the small patch of little more than an acre. For many years before that the orchard had been used as a free-range poultry run and the soil was splendidly fertile. We had grown artichokes, potatoes, green stuff, wheat and, now, a mixture of winter oats and peas. The wheat had grown six feet tall in the nitrogen rich soil. Tinkers was never less than bountiful.

The Big Field gave way to a smaller four-acre field called the Lower Path Field. It was bright green with the seedlings of Scotch Yellow turnips sown as a catch crop after a failed wheat crop. The hedge was pure hawthorn and had been a tangled mass twenty to thirty and more feet high in 1941. We had cut and layered it, a very painful occupation, and had been rewarded with new vigorous growth and a carpet of white violets which had lain there dormant for many years before responding, with shy beauty and heavenly scent, to the spring light.

Here was a junction with an old coach road which had run from Blackborough Church, through the estate, to Kentisbeare village. It had fallen into disuse and become overgrown; hollow in some parts, the banks had crumbled and fallen so that it was no longer recognisable as a road. In 1940 parts of it had been cleared to gain access to some of the fields and, when its character as an old road had been established, and then identified as such on an old map, it became known affectionately as the Burma Road.

Our walk of a little over half a mile took us to the farmyard gate. The cow byres were on the far side, the hay barns to our right, and the farm house, with Mrs. Mendham standing in the doorway, on the left. Although we had been neighbours for five years we had never before met.

Mr. Mendham I knew well and met frequently. He was over eighty and had retired from a prosperous hair dressing business in Totnes to fulfil a lifetime longing to become a small dairy farmer. He was broad shouldered, pink of face, and had a plentiful crop of thick grey hair which may have been a tribute to his skill as a hair dresser. He had more than once told me that my hair would stay with me and always added, with a slow smile, "They say you can't have brains and hair too." Then he would walk away, pause, and return to whisper very confidentially "But I always say that it is no good thatching an empty barn." He never tired of this little joke and would deliver the last phrase with great enjoyment and a chuckle as if his own life had proved something. That day he was not in sight, nor was their daughter Topsy whom I also knew well and who worked hard on the farm and for the Baptist Church in Cullompton. Topsy had once asked me to go and talk to the church fellowship about the life of George Fox, the founder of our Quaker Society. I had taken with me, for an outing, a thirteen year old girl, orphan of the London bombing, who had spent some recuperating months at Spiceland. Gracie had said that the only Fox she knew was Twentieth Century Fox, and I like to think that seventeenth century George would have enjoyed that.

Mrs. Mendham invited us into her parlour. She was formal and friendly. The table was laid with a pretty cloth, bone china tea set, thin bread and butter, home made raspberry jam, chudleighs — a home-made scone buttered and topped with jam and Devonshire cream — and a vase of freshly gathered garden flowers. Although it was summer a log fire burned in the hearth and a steaming kettle was suspended from a hook; a kettle from

Mendham's Farm

which a pot of tea was soon made.

The formality ended. The unaccustomed food was enjoyed, the tea cups were emptied and refilled several times. We were asked about our small son, where we came from, and all the other small matters which are the important things in a country no longer at war. For that was the reason why Mrs. Mendham had invited us to tea; it was her way of saying that the war was over and that life as she had known and lived it was to begin again. The cloth and china had been put away for the duration; like most of our neighbouring farmers the Mendhams had not made cream during the war. All the surplus milk had been sent to the dairy. For her, that day, making chudleighs and cutting thin bread and butter had been fun. We sat back from the table. I caught Marjorie's eye and followed its direction to my cup, which was resting, not in its pretty saucer, but on the cloth! For five years we had dined off bare wooden refectory tables and drunk from thick white cups with no saucers. The occasion had been too much for me, and I resolved that if ever I should write a book about those years that I would call it — Cups Without Saucers.

We strolled back up the lane, soaking in the late afternoon sunshine. We passed through the gate, on to the lawn, under the shade of the great Cedar tree, and on towards the house.

Blackborough House was built in the late 1830s for the Fourth Earl of Egremont and was of brick covered with a cement rendering. The bricks were made on site, and the woody dell to the right of the main entrance was probably the pit from which the clay had been dug. The clay was not of good quality, the bricks were soft, and the cement rendering was wholly necessary if unbecoming. A pillared loggia, now roofless, but still standing, surrounded the main elevation.

The third Earl had several children but omitted to marry their mother until years after the children had been born, and as a result, the title passed to a childless cousin and died with him. The third Earl, whose principal home was at Petworth in Sussex, spent a fortune on breeding horses good enough to win the Derby, and the fourth Earl spent another fortune on building houses of which Blackborough was but one.

It was really two houses, built back to back with two main entrances. The Earl, when in residence, occupied one and the Rector, whose living was in the gift of the Earl, lived in the other and used part of the generous accommodation to house the village school.

At some time between 1914 and 1918 the lead was stripped from the roof and sold and, after the war, the estate farms were sold to raise more money. The house stood open to wind and weather.

Eventually a Church of England Committee bought the house with about thirty odd acres of land and re-roofed the main building with slates. They established a Wayfarers' Home for travelling men who, as well as finding rest and refreshment, could receive training in gardening, printing, wood and metal work and other useful skills. One of its wardens was George Seaver, a member of Scott's Antartic expedition and the biographer of Edward Wilson. I think that the biography was written at Blackborough and, in our time, one of the rooms had a carved wooden plate "Seaver's Room."

The war of 1939 so reduced the number of travelling men that the Home fell into disuse and was offered for sale. In March 1940 the Society of Friends leased the property to establish a training centre for war relief workers. They renamed it Spiceland.

I have been told that the house was built during the worst period of English architecture but, whatever the critics' verdict on the style and appearance of the exterior, the main rooms were large, of good proportions and good to live in.

In December 1940 John Hoare wrote: "It is disconcerting to be told by a visitor that his first feeling on seeing your home was one of surprise that so isolated a house should have been bombed. Apologetically we explain that the best aspect of Spiceland is not seen as one comes down the drive, and the colonnade that looks like an unlovely Italian ruin at close quarters has some architectural dignity from a distance. We try to divert the visitor's eye from the windowless walls of the billiard old room to the glorious views all round, where, beyond the wide valley to which the thirty acres of garden, grass and copse slope down, he can see range upon range of hills and the distant heights of the moors.

Even when we get him inside there are awkward moments. We lead him through stone-flagged passages into a cavernous hall. We show him dormitories variously named Bohemia, Sidcot and the Manor House in which most of our family sleep on double-decker beds; but it is into the living rooms that we take him with most confidence. The dining room is a pleasant south facing room, so is the Common Room next door. Our best room is on the first floor, the library and Quiet Room which we built for ourselves. This we use for special purposes, for our morning quiet time, for our meetings for worship. Here too visitors occasionally talk to us and we discuss in family enclave those matters that are the concern of us all and that cannot be talked out briefly at the end of a meal."

As Marjorie and I walked into the house on that August day — not a momentous day nor a day of decision — I felt that we had crossed a watershed; that we were nearing the end of something, which to most of those who had spent some time — short or long — as part of it, had been a community. A community with a pattern of service and strong bonds of friendship. But in more than one sense it did not end, and has not ended. This book is part of the story.

CHAPTER 2

Carclew

In the spring of 1939 the British Government introduced conscription for military service in time of peace. The Act of Parliament contained a conscience clause, which enabled objectors to state a case. It also made provision for tribunals to consider grounds of objection, to grant exemption, prescribe alternative service, or to dismiss an application altogether.

The Society of Friends has a historic testimony against war — born out of the experience of its members during the Civil War of the 1640s. The testimony's first expression was in the refusal of its founder, George Fox, to accept a commission in Cromwell's army. "I told (the commissioners) I lived in the virtue of that life and power which took away the occasion of all wars....." The corporate expression was in a declaration made to Charles the Second after his accession — "We utterly deny all outward wars and strife and fightings..." But there is a more positive expression which was written in 1660 and attributed to Margaret Fell "We are a people that follow after those things that make for Peace, Love, and Unity....."

The Society of Friends has no credal basis of membership, believing that its members must be open to new light and to be sensitive to the times in which they live. In every generation some Friends have thought that a particular war was, for them, an exception; but the Society as a whole, in facing the challenge of its days and years, has upheld its testimony against all war.

In 1939, as in 1916, some Friends felt that they must testify against the right of the State to impose conscription; they refused to register and, in time, served prison sentences. Others accepted the principle of alternative service, but felt that they should be free to choose what form of service they should give; some of these refused direction and also served prison sentences. Many accepted the direction of tribunals and some, because they were not called up for military service, were free to choose. Because freedom of conscience is important to all, Friends uphold one another in which ever form of witness or action an individual may decide to take.

At the time of the Conscription Act, and still in time of peace, a number of Quaker groups were looking to give practical expression to their concerns. The Friends Peace Committee was, in addition to its work for peace, looking at the possibility of providing acceptable alternatives to military service. Another committee, active in giving help to people under threat in Germany and its occupied countries, had to guarantee that refugees admitted into Britain would be given training or work of a nature acceptable to the Government — all too often this was not the sort of occupation which the refugees had followed at home. Other Friends had been active in providing training and work for unemployed people. The Friends Home Service Committee, which is responsible for nurturing the spiritual life of Quaker meetings, was exercised by the difficulties facing widely scattered and very small gatherings of Quakers living in the west country; they wished to establish a Centre which could be a focus for Quaker life in Devon and Cornwall. These groups explored the possibility of coming together in a joint enterprise. They were joined by the International Voluntary Service for Peace (IVSP), some of whose members were also Quakers, who wanted to set up an international work centre in Britain.

A Cornish Quaker, Arthur Pearse Jenkins, who was an estate agent, had come into possession of Carclew — a country mansion which had been extensively damaged by fire. There was a considerable estate but, of the mansion, only the servants quarters could again be made habitable. A.P.J. had arranged a sale from which the purchaser withdrew in circumstances which made him feel bound to accept personal responsibility. The house and estate, some two miles north of Penryn, were in surroundings of great beauty and the estate included tree plantations, a deer park, and some farms.

The scope for rebuilding and restoring the parts of the building which were still standing, and the opportunities for agriculture and horticulture, opened up the possibility of providing, at Carclew, the means for teaching new skills and giving fresh hope and experience to men and women, in a setting which would fit the aims and needs of the interested groups.

An umbrella committee was formed which entered, in principle, into a long lease for the house and about forty acres of land but, because of the urgent situation of the refugees, they took possession and started work before the terms of the lease were settled and before any document was signed.

There were difficulties. A.P.J. was elderly and ill. The mortgagors of the estate prevented him from negotiating the generous lease that he wished. They were only protecting their own interests. A long lease with options to renew on favourable terms would prove embarrassing to them in the event of another sale of the whole property. They insisted that, if the property had to be sold, the lease must end. Negotiations dragged on.

The community soon encountered practical difficulties with the water supply which was erratic and metered. Alternative sources from a well and a reservoir were suspect, and a pump proved altogether too powerful for aged pipes. Dry and wet rot were discovered when work started on the building. Plans for agriculture were postponed because of the protracted negotiations over the lease, but the garden was cultivated and good crops of vegetables were grown. Rooms were made habitable and pleasant, and some refugees, sponsored by the Germany Emergency Committee and by individuals, arrived to take their place in the community.

IVSP maintained a flow of working parties of international volunteers who came, worked, went, and were replaced by others. IVSP also helped to finance some aspects of the project, but finance generally was on a shoestring. The Peace Committee provided most of the money and, in addition, made small loans. Some individual Friends also gave money, and made generous gifts of furniture and equipment. A number of professionals — architects, engineers and agriculturalists gave advice and encouragement, while the members of the community worked extremely hard for little or no financial reward.

The main loyalty of the IVSP groups, who came for short periods only, was to IVSP and its wider commitments. They had little time to get involved in more than their immediate jobs. The more permanent groups developed a strong sense of belonging to one another and to Carclew itself — the place. Another difficulty was that IVSP had a traditional approach to the division of labour, and expected men and women to accept traditional roles when tasks were allocated. This contrasted sharply with Quaker views on equality. "In the days of the apostacy" said George Fox in the seventeenth century, "women may have been subordinate to men, but in the New Age they are equal." There were tensions which peep through discreet minutes of the Carclew Committee.

Fifty inflation years later the sums involved in running the enterprise seem pitifully small, and the receipts and payments account for the period between Easter and July 22nd 1939 tells its own story:

PAYMENTS		RECEIPTS	
Equipment	£106.19.10	Peace Committee Loan	200. . .
Timber	23.19.10	Gifts	100. . .
Coal	4.16. 8	Refugee maintenance	3. . .
Housekeeper	4. -. -	Visitor's payment	3. .
Sundries	14. 3	Donations	11. . .
Provisions	55.10. -		
Cash to Wardn	52.10. -		
Balance in hand	66. 8. 4		
	£314. 3. -		£314. 3.-

Eventually a lease was signed, but the clause underlining the insecurity of tenure was included. Arthur Pearse Jenkins was almost too ill to sign, and soon afterwards he died.

The responsibility for the day to day work at Carclew had vested in temporary and changing wardens, but in December 1939 John and Margaret Hoare were appointed, and the committee had soon to consider one report from John Hoare on what he saw as the position at Carclew and, with it, a supplementary report from Hugh Flatt, the agricultural instructor, on the problems and opportunities for developing a farm and market garden.

John Hoare had been a young conscientious objector in the first world war and had spent two long years in prison — much of it for breaking prison rules which he thought were inhuman. After the war he was unable to return to Oxford University and complete his degree because his pacifism brought rejection by his College. He devoted himself to youth work in the East End of London where he worked as Secretary to the Highway group of six clubs for working class boys and girls — a position he held for twenty years. He met and married Margaret while they were both working for the Clubs, and their first child, David, was born in 1939.

John's principles as a pacifist and his belief in the importance of free speech and discussion as part of the Clubs development had, even in peace time, caused a rift between him and some of the Clubs well-to-do supporters. John became apprehensive that, in time of war, further trouble would develop and prove damaging to the Clubs and to his family. Although over military age, his memories of hostility and imprisonment gave him a great desire to help a new generation of conscientious objectors who might encounter similar situations. John and Margaret decided together that the time had come to give up their work at the Highway Clubs and they applied to take up the work of wardens at Carclew.

The winter of 1939/40 was bitterly cold — even in Cornwall — and only heroic efforts by the community — Margaret's words — kept everyone alive and happy with food prepared and cooked on an antiquated stove in the old servants' quarters.

As spring approached a number of the refugees found work on local farms where they "lived in" and the numbers of the community fell. Ideas for setting up a training centre for people willing to undertake the sort of war relief work which the Society had done during and after the first world war were already taking shape in people's minds, but the insecurities of Carclew rendered it an unsuitable place and a search was on for a better site. None of the sites considered was ideal, but two separate parties visited the house and land at Blackborough. John and Margaret spent two memorable days and nights talking with the wardens of the, now closed, Wayfarer's Home. They were still in isolated residence, and the ankle boots which they wore to keep themselves warm indoors were only one indication that life at Blackborough would also have its share of problems.

At about this time the committee reconsidered the purpose, and studied the outcome, of the Carclew project. Some extracts from the minutes are helpful indications of what was to follow:

".....John Hoare said that he found Carclew more of a refugee camp than he had expected or thought desirable.

The secretary described the growth of the Carclew idea from the concern of Friends to establish a centre helpful to neighbouring meetings, and of the Peace Committee to set up a peace service training centre..... of the wish not to set up a permanent agricultural community.....

.....the original ideas consonant with the present need for training young people for service as typified by the old Friends War Victims Relief Committee ..... training which would include land work, building construction, sanitation, languages, first aid, ...and would provide an opportunity for living a harder and more simple life.

......careful consideration to be given to the creation of a War Victims Relief Committee ..... Friends familiar with the work of the old committee to be consulted so that we may discover the right way to provide the service which those who train will seek to carry out."

At this stage IVSP withdrew from the venture to devote its energies and resources to its other activities. John and Margaret were asked to arrange for the removal of the community to Blackborough.

CHAPTER 3

Blackborough — Spiceland

Four miles from Blackborough House, half way between the villages of Uffculme and Culmstock, is an old Quaker Meeting House which stands in a field at a spot on the River Culm where there are five fords. It has the lovely name of Spiceland and its setting is one of great peace and beauty. The present building dates from 1815, but Friends have gathered for worship at this place since the latter half of the Seventeenth century. A member who owned this piece of land provided facilities for meeting in a time of persecution when Friends were willing to travel long distances to meet peaceably, and away from probable disturbance by the soldiery. An old minute records the appointment of Friends to look after "the children, the horses and the dogs." Spiceland is probably a happy derivation from "this piece of land."

The Culm valley was a centre of woolcombing, and a family of Cadbury is recorded as having lived in Uffculme in 1557. Three Cadbury brothers were active members of the Society of Friends in the time of George Fox. The last male member of the family moved away to Birmingham and founded the Cadbury chocolate business. Quaker families are still engaged in the west country woollen trade, but no longer in the Culm valley.

R.D. Blackmore, the author of Lorna Doone, spent his boyhood in the valley where his father was the curate of Culmstock. His novel Perlycross, which is his fictional name for Culmstock, is set in the valley during the 1830s and some of the characters in the novel are Quakers. He probably knew local Friends and the meeting house must surely have been in use during his time there.

By 1940 the meeting house was rarely used. There were no resident Friends, but Exeter Friends arranged occasional meetings in summer time.

Blackborough House itself stands over seven hundred feet above sea level on a spur of the Blackdown Hills. Its chimneys can be seen silhouetted against a hilly skyline from the Spiceland meeting house field. It is about sixteen miles from Exeter and about the same distance from Taunton. The nearest towns are Honiton, nine miles, and Cullompton, which then provided the nearest railway station, six miles. In 1940 one bus on Friday of each week left for Exeter from the village of Kentisbeare, two miles down the valley. The nearest active Quaker meeting was at Wellington — ten miles away.

In peace time Blackborough was isolated; in war time with petrol rationed it was very isolated indeed.

South western Friends, particularly those in Cornwall, were disappointed by the removal of a lively piece of Quaker work to a remote spot in north east Devonshire, but they accepted that the need for a suitable training base for relief workers was more important than that for a purely Quaker centre. The new site was near to the area covered by the Bristol and Somerset group of meetings and some of their members joined and strengthened the committee.

The new committee decided to appropriate the name of the old meeting house and Blackborough House became the Spiceland Training Centre but, more affectionately, and with common use, just Spiceland.

A relatively small team travelled from Carclew. John and Margaret with their small son David travelled in their Austin Ten. Josephine Noble and Joan Adamson travelled in Jo's Morris, and six men travelled by train to Cullompton and walked the six uphill miles to Blackborough carrying their personal belongings. They were glad to pause for breath near the top of the one in four gradient Ponchydown Hill and to ask the way from Douglas Holloway, whose farm, home and family were later to become very much a part of Spiceland's extra mural activities. What Douglas thought of his first encounter with three, obviously German, refugees and three English conchies is not known, but Hugh Flatt did record that one effect of the long walk was to cement an enduring friendship among the walkers.

Bert Baldwin must have travelled independently but he was certainly a member of the group which set about transforming the former tramps' home into a Quaker centre. Yet only three of the group were at that time members of the Society of Friends. In the early years of the Society there was no formal membership and to "profess with Friends" was to invite ignominy as well as share the joys of fellowship. In their attitudes to war, if not in matters of theology, the group professed with Friends and shared pain and joy.

The Carclew goats and chickens had been sold or given away, but the accumulated furniture and equipment travelled in a lorry. John Hoare was a

Quaker by convincement whose family had alternated between the Society and the Anglican church. His great grandfather had been a Quaker but his father was an Anglican bishop. Elizabeth Fry appeared in his family tree and her portrait on his study wall. Margaret was an Anglican who had read modern languages before working in East End clubland.

Hugh Flatt was another Anglican. He had a degree in Agriculture and a Diploma in Dairy Husbandry, and a particular concern to promote better understanding between town and country dwellers. He worked tremendously hard, not only at his farming, but also at making contacts and friendships with local farmers so that what was being done at Spiceland was better understood.

Hugh shared a room with Bert who, at that time, was a Christian Scientist. Born on November 18th, 1900, Bert reached his eighteenth birthday on Armistice Day 1918 and claimed that this event put a stop to the war! He developed an early interest in motors and engines, but then turned to woodwork and became a builder's foreman. He boasted that examples of his handiwork could be found in houses, shops, churches and pubs in Chelmsford, March, Welwyn Garden City, Wisbech and London. Early in 1940 he had volunteered to work with a Quaker team on building reconstruction in an earthquake area of Turkey, but the Turkish Government had withdrawn support for the scheme, and Bert came to Spiceland — to get "Construction" going and to teach the trainees skills of building and carpentry.

Josephine Noble was an "original." Born in Switzerland and educated by governesses until "finishing school" in Paris — she then studied "cordon bleu" cookery and ran a Home Service Bureau in Sheffield. She went to America with further study as the excuse and read nutrition and interior decorating at Columbia University. On holiday in Canada when war was declared she returned to England to work with refugees at Carclew. At Spiceland she taught basic catering, cooking and dietetics with enthusiasm, energy, and cordon bleu elan — to the delight and benefit of everyone. Jo gave her favourite occupation as talking about America, and her unfavoured occupation as talking about food. I never heard her say anything about America, but as I made frequent visits to the kitchen I often heard her talking about food. "The nicest way to lighten anything is to add more eggs — but you can't do that now, so you whisk like mad until your wrist drops off..." In post-war years she joined the Society of Friends and worked at the Quaker Centre in Paris, and for the Friends Service Council in European Affairs and in Morocco. Sadly, for everyone who knew her she died in her office at Friends House in London on the very day of her retirement.

Basil Goodey was a birthright Friend — an allrounder who could turn his brain and his hands to almost any task and do it well. After reading Biology at London University he volunteered for a spell of service at Carclew. He was mainly responsible for teaching outdoor catering and cooking in an open air field kitchen — a job in which he ingeniously and successfully combined his academic and practical skills, and made good, if sometimes unusual, use of whatever was available. His soups were a byword and a long running joke, but the occasions on which they were left uneaten were rare indeed, and then only when he had pushed the utility of left-overs beyond the bounds of acceptable imagination. His gourmet potential was realised when he found and identified the edible fungi Chanterella growing under some beech trees.

Bas had a discerning impish sense of humour which called for response from matching minds. Too often his best shafts missed their targets, but when the right tinder was available his sparks flamed into hilarity. When he was not engaged in teaching the art of outdoor cooking he would identify plants, insects, birds and other creatures to the enrichment of the general understanding of the natural world, and his knowledge of such matters was an asset in the garden.

Joan Adamson had been housekeeper at Carclew and the deep friendship and understanding which grew up between Joan and Bas while they were there, prospered so that, soon after the move to Spiceland, they married and, together, made a significant contribution to the development of that community. But their first love was for the Carclew where they had met, and which they remembered fondly as a response to human needs made freely in time of peace when other choices which could have been made, were put aside. Spiceland was to them eminently worthwhile, but a response to situations brought about by war and the pressure of mobilisation.

Joan was the doyen of the extensive laundry which became a feature of Spiceland life, and she taught generations of trainees how to care for, wash, and repair their sometimes inadequate wardrobes. These activities were presided over with a blend of vigorous authority, some humour, and in response to trainee feedback, a caricature of traditional pantomime.

Then there was Percy Pascoe, an over military age Cornishman, pink and cherubic in countenance, but suffering from indifferent health. He chose his own jobs and the times of doing them. He was painstakingly thorough, but slow. To be left to himself at eventide to make sure that the last glowing embers of a bonfire were dowsed before blackout was to hand him quiet happiness. He dined separately, was a convinced vegetarian who was always willing to stop what ever he was doing to talk about healthy eating, the value of Slippery Elm Food, the inherent dangers of cooking in aluminium saucepans — definitely a "bad thing" — and dozens of other topics. He could be lovable and maddeningly exasperating — never more so than when he slowly and deliberately beheaded just one of the thousands of thistles which grew, flowered, and seeded in the Spiceland fields — but he was just as deliberately part of Spiceland.

Of the three remaining Carclew refugees Karl and Johnny were young Germans who worked with Bert on construction and carpentry jobs, and Rudi was a considerably older Austrian. He had been an administrator of the Royal Parks in Vienna, but had now to turn his knowledge to the more physical task of reclaiming the Spiceland gardens. His hands had suffered torments which plagued his use of tools, and his mind, which liked everything to be precise and orderly, was tormented by the disorder of weeds and neglect; but a philosophic shrug of the shoulders, a slow smile, and some words of encouragement to himself as much as to others were never far away.

It is said that generals prefer to fight earlier wars than their own in the fond belief that the lessons have been learned. In expectation that Europe was where the new need would arise, the Spiceland committee thought about relief work in terms of the experience of work done by Quakers in Europe twenty years earlier. In fact the training course was developed on the spot, and was based on the more immediate challenge presented by the ruinous condition of the house itself, the opportunities afforded by the neglected acres, and the skills and experience of the available staff and trainees. In March 1940 nobody thought that the first need would arise in Britain — in bombed cities, in hospitals and among the children and old people evacuated from places of immediate danger to places of relative safety. Minds were firmly fixed on the Continent of Europe and a necessity to learn French and German.

Spiceland Friends Meeting House

CHAPTER 4

Settling Down

Jo Noble, looking back from March 1942 to March 1940 saw the two years telescope into a kaleidoscope of moving hands — dexterous, clumsy, smooth and workworn — mixing, stirring and whisking. She saw the hands developing into scenes and incidents, into living people and friends — separate and distinct, but strung together like beads on a common cord. To her, at that time, Spiceland seemed to have been there for ever, and the two years seemed like eternity.

Still looking back, she described her arrival from a Cornish spring to a bleak hill-top in Devonshire, where "winter lingered still with snowy footsteps." She described the first entry into the cavernous hall, with its structural darkness intensified by the black paint which covered every window in the house, and her persistent memories of feeling frozen and of living in Stygian gloom. So, removing black paint, making blackout curtains, and constructing blackout blinds provided the early tasks. Balanced precariously and uncomfortably on ladders and improvised perches people scraped and washed to let in the light, scrubbed and cleaned floors, arranged and re-arranged the furniture in a struggle to make rooms habitable and more pleasant to be in.

A party of boys and girls from the Quaker School at Sidcot in Somerset spent their Easter holidays lending a hand and, in their honour, the first dormitory was named Sidcot and a tradition was started of naming rooms to record memories and associations.

In that first month the staff had also to arrange the schedules of work for the training course and prepare for the arrival, in mid-April, of the first batch of trainees. A weekly staff meeting was held to consider reports and proposals, to decide priorities, to determine the allocation of scarce resources between the departments and to assess and promote the wellbeing of the trainees. John and Margaret, as Wardens, were responsible to the committee for the conduct of the Centre, but they introduced at these staff meetings the Quaker practice of reaching decisions by taking the "Sense of the meeting" after open discussion. The meetings held, without fail, on Tuesday evenings were known as the Semi-perms Meetings. With the intention of creating a single, perhaps singular, community the distinction between staff and trainees was minimal; the trainees, with some show of affection, preserved the distinction by calling the staff the "Odds and Ends", and the staff, to preserve their declared freedom to move away to other work, described themselves as the "Semi-perms".

The two superior Back-to-Back houses had been opened up into one large mansion with a possible sixty or seventy rooms. The two front doors opened into hallways which led to a single central hall soaring to the full height of the building and topped by large fan-light windows. Scraping the paint off these and fitting hinged blackout frames operated by sash cord and pulleys had been, quite literally, a tall order. Each hallway had a separate stairway leading to the first and second floors. The Rector's front door became the back door, his staircase gave access to John and Margarets' first floor flat, but beyond that it remained ruinous, leading upwards to darkness and, eventually, to the nest of a resident barn owl. Its cobwebbed and rickety bannisters, bordering uncertain treads, offered a beckoning invitation to a world of spooky fairytale and makebelieve. Outside this back door was a neglected circular lawn centred with a fine holm oak tree.

The eastern entrance was the Earl's, and Spiceland's, front door, and was approached from the main drive which divided round a white flag pole set in a circular lawn. To the south was a more extensive lawn once planted with fine trees including a Cedar and a tall Sequoia redwood which still stood.

The rooms on the south side of the house were large, and their windows commanded magnificent views. On the north were the kitchen with its large and reliable Esse stove, the laundry and wash house, the mens' bath, wash and shower room, and the construction room with its work benches and tool racks. The first floor southern rooms were also large. The windows overlooked the roofless colonnade of a vanished terrace. From cracks in its damaged masonry grew an assortment of twisted, gnarled, naturally bonsaid, trees, and a variety of annual weeds in season. Beyond this fascinating botanical display were those superb views — ever changing with season, light and weather. On first floor north was John and Margarets' home — "the flat", a large airing cupboard which was really a room and very much sort after in cold weather, and the womens' bath room.

On the second floor were smaller rooms which had no doubt been the servants' quarters, but on this floor the Wayfarers had made a Chapel, simply, but ecclesiastically, furnished with some very old heavy oak pews which had been brought from the Acland estate at Killerton. Quakers have no consecrated buildings and, once the Quiet Room had been constructed, meetings for worship, as well as other activities, were held there. The Chapel offered scope for three fairly easily constructed small rooms and a test case for solving serious differences. More orthodox Christians were loath to see the Chapel go, and there was much heart-torn discussion at many meetings before the idea of un unconsecrated Quiet Room was fully accepted, and the three rooms, named Faith, Hope and Charity were finally made.

After the black paint had been removed and replaced by more flexible blackout arrangements the Construction group found many small, and some major jobs, to claim their attention. Bert soon found that he had a longer list of things to do than he had materials or hands to do them with. Cupboards and shelves are seldom exactly where the users want them and most, if not all, trainees needed small simple jobs just to get the feel of using unaccustomed tools.

One urgent need was for a Common Room where the larger group could meet and circulate informally. The Wayfarers seemingly had no such need and a large derelict, but south facing, room on the ground floor was chosen. It was re-floored and the floor boards stained with Bert's own concoction of creosote, paraffin and oils before a hands-and-knees operation of sanding and polishing produced a clinically smelling but pleasing appearance. Trainees were then asked to submit designs for rebuilding the hearth and fireplace and, when Reg Rowntree was adjudged the winner, his reward was to be told to go ahead and do it. The result was a fine room with a fine hearth which became, as it does in any home, the focal place of the community's informal life.

The second major job came to pungent notice when Hugh, exploring the thirteen acre copse, discovered distressingly that the sewage system had been malfunctioning for some considerable time and had become an unpleasant and potentially dangerous hazard. Mickey Harkness, a trainee who was also an embryo architect with some practical experience, was entrusted with the design and supervision of the construction of a new drainage and septic tank system. The biology of sewage disposal and the engineering requirements of septic tanks became topics of conversation, while the digging of trenches, the careful laying of pipes and the construction of the tank itself became the practical outcome.

After the Common Room, a gutted area on the first floor was transformed into a Quiet Room and Library — the latter stocked with John Hoare's personal collection of books providing a wide range of reference reading and an even wider range of the world's literature. Except when used for meetings, a silence rule was gratefully accepted by all Spicelanders who could here be observed delightedly searching the shelves, lying sprawled in search of comfortable reading, sitting more circumspectly to write, nodding gently as a prelude to sleep and, sometimes, to sleep abandoned.

There was very little money. Feeding the community and buying materials for necessary construction work made first calls on what was available. The Wayfarers had planted a large area with autumn sown cabbages which were hearting well, even providing a surplus for sale — but there was very little else for immediate use. Hugh looked at the farm and garden and thought hard about ways and means for getting something growing quickly in addition to the inevitable long term clearing and digging. Rudi, who was to manage the gardens, remembered his well ordered parks of Vienna, and looked with despair as the warm and moist west country spring produced lush growths of weeds and an abundance of slugs and other pests to devour his gently nurtured seedlings. Rudi's response was drastic. He ordered more than enough of a poisonous compound with which to attack them. Although Hugh signed the chemist's poison book, Rudi's accent was enough to alarm some local residents. Tiverton's water supply reservoir was situate somewhere on the hill behind Blackborough and rumour did its worst. A public relations exercise became an urgent necessity.

Hugh made a series of visits to local farmers so that he could get the feel of the locality and, perhaps, arrange for some trainees to get, on nearby farms, experience of a kind which was not then available at Spiceland. His first visit found a farmer who was convinced that Spiceland was still a tramps' home, and nothing could persuade him to let any of the residents, "who were always looking for something for nothing," set foot on his land. Hugh continued to make patient visit after visit and eventually made friends with some while others remained critical or suspicious. Once made, the friendships deepened and had an effect on others, so that slowly, almost imperceptibly, Spiceland became a fringe member of the community of small villages and farms which occupied that part of the Blackdowns.

Of course there were some difficult characters on both sides. The local special constable had a German sounding name, Schwind, which may have made him more than usually sensitive. Dressed in a little brief authority he felt that he had to be particularly severe in dealing with blackout lapses or non-regulation cycle lamps. Some of the resulting minor clashes reflect no great credit either way but, when he left the area in 1942, he too had become reconciled with his eccentric neighbours.

Usable space in the house was at a premium and the farm records and account book were kept on Hugh's bed in the daytime and under it at night. The "cash in" entries were few and far between. In desperation, he began to finance the farm out of his own pocket with the help of a few small loans. Then a trainee lent him the princely sum of £300.; and, with first a cow and then a sow, Hugh was in business, and providing at long last experience with what he was wont to describe as the larger farm animals. This experience was intensified when, from a farm twenty miles away, he bought a spirited chestnut mare with four white socks and a white blaze on her nose — flaming June! Her dam was an Olympic jumper and her sire was a Suffolk Punch. She was what is known as a "half leg horse" — neither heavy draught nor light. She was young, she was strong and she could move. The journey home provided excitement for Hugh, and for the few people he met in the quiet lanes, as her high stepping and erratic progress taxed all his considerable skill as a horseman.

Now there was a horse but no cart. In Wellington there was an old established Quaker textile business, Fox Brothers, and Lloyd Fox had become the treasurer of the Spiceland committee. Although the firm no longer used horses Lloyd thought that there was an old cart somewhere in store and suggested that Hugh should collect it. It proved to be an old wool wagon of considerable size, stout construction and terrible weight. June could hardly move it unloaded on the flat and, when it had been horse and man handled at enormous cost in strained energy back to Spiceland, it languished unused and was referred to as the "Elephant Cart".

Construction turned from other tasks and built a light cart, low slung and sturdy, on an old car axle. This did yeoman service and was used in rough conditions and confined spaces where standard farm vehicles were a liability. The Kentisbeare wheelwright made a fine new tumbril, painted in bright blue and with the Spiceland name picked out in white paint on one of the panels. At £11. it represented tremendous value and was an eye catching morale boost for the farm group, who were further encouraged by the purchase of two more cows to feed on the flush of spring grass. All these acquisitions brought to vibrant life the small group of farm buildings which lay in a hollow to the north of the house — partly hidden, and approached by two steep and inconvenient trackways.

Horses need shoes. There were farriers at Kentisbeare and Ashill. The man at Kentisbeare had learned his trade in the army during the first world war and could not bring himself to shoe horses for "conchies". Bob Lake at Ashill never expressed strong feelings in favour or against anything or anybody. He was quiet spoken — a peaceable man who was generous with his time and his skills which extended far beyond shoeing. He just smiled and said "Horses have to be shod."

There is a tail piece to the story. Sometime in 1942, well before the end of the war, a Spicelander took a bridle for repair by the harness makers in Kentisbeare. While he was waiting for the leather to be stitched the farrier came in and passed the time of day. He recalled that he had once refused to shoe Mr. Flatt's horses, and said that if he were to be asked again "He'd not refuse, because he'd changed his mind about the folk at the House." He went on to say that he was not asking for the work "I know you be well suited, and I wouldn't want to change that — but I thought I'd tell 'ee."

The conversation in the harness maker's small workshop became general and soon the farrier was describing how he had won a big prize in the Irish Hospitals Sweep Stake. The sweep was illegal in Britain and he had to collect the prize money in person from an address near Regent Street in London. A whip round produced enough petrol ration coupons to make the journey by car. The prize was collected in cash, and the small happy party set out on the return journey in darkness and blackout conditions. They feared that they might be stopped and asked to justify their journey, and that if the real purpose came out, that the money would be confiscated. They were stopped, but their west country speech, more convincing than the implausible story they had thought up, got them through. Near Honiton they took to the lanes, lost their way and found themselves driving along the perimeter road of a wartime aerodrome. Challenged by U.S. sentries their nearness to home made the explanations sound convincing and they were allowed through only to run out of petrol when still a few miles from home. It was broad daylight when they arrived home with the winnings.

The tale, delivered in broad dialect, was long in the telling and contained much descriptive material. It was an adventure to be told and retold until it became part of village folk lore. For the Spicelander its significance was that he had been "included in."

Human values broke through in unexpected ways and places. The commandant of a small army unit who were manning a searchlight battery at the foot of Ponchydown Hill, was troubled by the problem of how to relieve boredom for men stuck in an isolated country lane far from the relaxations to which they would normally turn. Their leisure time was in daylight and he suggested some games of cricket and football, but Spiceland had no day time leisure, and it remains an interesting conjecture as to what could or would have come from such encounters. However, arrangements were made for the men to use Spiceland showers and washroom — despite the chronic water shortage — as a supplement to their more primitive wash bowl facilities. For some months, until the unit moved away, small groups of young men in khaki brought their soap and towels and were hospitably received.

Values of a different kind surfaced when Hugh, lacking the resources to fully stock the farm, entered into a joint venture with the local baker to rear and market some pigs. Before the pigs attained market weights, animal feeding stuffs became scarce and rationed. All the ingenuity of using swill and unmarketable potatoes — supplemented with boiled stinging nettles — could not hide the fact that the pigs were not thriving. The baker said, in a voice of hopeful enquiry, that he could get supplies through his trade connections — but they would not be legal and he supposed that Quakers would not go along with that? Half the pigs were sold at a loss while the remainder were kept and fattened. The baker shared the loss with very good grace and continued a friendly and understanding relationship.

Encounters like these were part of the process of getting to know and getting known. Spiceland was a place of mystery and curiosity — a talked about place. Mistakes were chuckled over, but things done well were noticed. The fears that it was a dangerous and subversive place slowly evaporated and opportunities for helpful involvement came along.

The arrival in April of fifteen trainees had increased the work force and the tempo. The expectation was still of working on the Continent and, in addition to the practical training, there were early morning and evening language courses. Long hard days gave trainees and semi-perms alike large appetites for food and sleep. A daily pattern of life emerged.

The day began at six-thirty but breakfast and milking parties were afoot well before then. Rising, and meal times, were announced by vigorous banging on a large and resonant gong made from the wheel hub of an old lorry. It was suspended from a bracket in the hallway and, using a home made but servicable, drum stick, ringers developed individual styles and patterns of rythm and created signatures in sound. A second ringing at a few minutes before seven speeded the sluggards to breakfast.

To be late for breakfast, or any other meal, was not a crime, but it was to be avoided if humanly possible. A small table bell graced the table at the south, window end, of the dining room and on this John, or in his rare absence, another semi-perm, struck a single note which brought instant quiet for a short period of silent grace. This was Spiceland's only ritual and was cherished as much by those who professed no faith as by those who did.

Breakfast was a good oatmeal porridge cooked slowly overnight in the large Esse oven. Sunday breakfast was an hour later and was the occasion of the weekly egg — sixty or more were timed perfectly and only specially ordered eggs were hard boiled. Everybody was given an empty cocoa tin into which was put half the weekly ration of sugar — the other half was retained in the kitchen. The individually labelled, easily recognised, cocoa tins adorned the mantel shelf near the dining room door. Jams and marmalades were rare but the kitchen sometimes produced a very palatable carrot marmalade, and unrationed but scarce spreads like pea-nut butter, ersatz chocolate spread or meat and yeast extracts were eagerly sought after on Saturday afternoon forays to neighbouring towns.

After breakfast a fifteen minute period of meditation, usually focussed on readings selected in turn by those taking part, was held in the Quiet Room.

Then it was work until a mid morning break — quickly dubbed the "Voor noons" to tie up with the similar break taken by local farmers — when bread and scrape taken from a bin placed near the dining room door helped to keep up strength and energy.

Lunch and the evening meal were gastronomic exercises and social occasions. Exchanges about the experiences of the day fused with discussion about the news filtering through from radio, late delivered papers and the personal news from home brought by the postman. Wit and humour blended with serious issues; fellowship and understanding developed between folk whose common ground was their objection to war, but who came from very different social, educational and occupational backgrounds. At the close of a meal John rose, struck the table bell to still the buzz of conversation, and made announcements about visitors, new arrivals, forthcoming events and shared any Spiceland news which had come to him during the day.

On weekdays work continued until an hour before the evening meal, but on Saturdays and Sundays tea and a slice of plain cake were served in the Common Room at four o'clock, and in fine weather, this was taken on the remains of the south facing terrace. There was always a feeling of gracious living when the company assembled informally and relaxed on the terrace. Often they were joined by the flock of Khaki Campbell ducks, useful egg providers and interesting characters in their own right. They may have come merely to share the warmth of the sun trap; some were certain that they were attracted by the strains of music wafting through the open Common Room windows; but all liked to think of them as part of Spiceland.

Weekday evenings provided time for farm lectures, language study groups, mathematics for fun, writing, reading, darning socks and repairing clothes — or whatever else were the current interests and needs. Late on Wednesday evenings there was a programmed service of worship for those who came from more orthodox backgrounds. Encouraged by Hugh, individuals were encouraged to choose and plan the services. More encouragement came from Brother Oswald — familiar Os — a lay brother of the Anglican order of St. Francis at Cerne Abbas who was released to work at Spiceland, and who never looked out of place as he moved about in his simple brown habit held together by a white girdle with three knots representing Poverty, Chastity and Obedience.

Friday evenings were special — Kultur flourished in the form of prose and poetry anthologies or play readings. There never seemed to be a lack of capable performers and impromptu organisers, and sometimes, when dramatic talent was around, the readings came very close to performance. Murder in the Cathedral, Back to Methuselah, and Lady Precious Stream remain vivid in the memory.

Saturday evenings were for more relaxed entertainment — a sort of variety show where people were invited to risk looking and sounding ridiculous for the general good. There were people who sang, others who recited or remembered monologues, juggled or conjured, groups who wrote and performed impromptu sketches, told stories ....

On special occasions, like Bank Holidays and Christmas, this form of entertainment was expanded into a very special effort, and the villagers were invited to join in the fun — which they did with marvellous enjoyment. Remember that they too were six miles from town, had no bus service and no petrol for jaunts. One original pantomime "The Babes of Bodmiscombe Wood or Jack and the Beanstalk" which drew freely on every pantomime plot and was firmly located in the surrounding countryside gave wondrous pleasure to the village children — it included a spectacular beanstalk which grew from nothing to full height in the twinkling of an eye — a cart rope dressed in laurel leaves and strong enough to climb!

Sundays also had their particular pattern. Weekend meals and essential farm work were carried out by rota groups. For the rest it was a time of rest and refreshment. A Quaker meeting for worship was held either in the Quiet Room or, in summer months, at the old Spiceland meeting house four miles away. The latter were picnic occasions preceded and followed by walks through some of Devonshire's most beautiful countryside. As we sat on the old benches it was easy to imagine that we had been transported back in time; but the worship was firmly rooted in the present, and Friends from Wellington, Exeter and Taunton who joined us helped to keep us there and dispelled any feelings of isolation.

Sunday evenings were given over to serious discussion — sometimes with stimulus provided by a visting speaker. Doubts and certainties were given full rein with endless permutations on how to advance the cause of peace in time of war. John presided over these discussions, rarely speaking himself, listening and encouraging general participation, never dominating but always helping people to face the consequences of what was asserted or denied.

Music formed an important part of the social life. In the early months this was hammered out on a honky-tonk piano of doubtful vintage on which some folk performed unenviably but with considerable skill. Community singing round this instrument was spontaneous, of variable quality, enjoyed by the participants, but not always by others within earshot. One trainee who could produce music from this instrument was Howard Jennings — a peace time cinema organist with an encyclopaedic repertoire ranging from Gershwin to Grieg from which he had nearly instant recall if aided by a few hummed notes.

Many months later — sometime in 1941 — a west country Quaker, Mary Cash, presented Spiceland with a Steinway Grand and a small organ. The Steinway was installed in the Common Room where a succession of talented performers enjoyed themselves and gave great pleasure to the rest. The organ was less appreciated. Its home in the Quiet Room inhibited its greater use, but Brother Os was one who would seize the opportunity afforded by rare occasions when that room was empty, to fill the house with reverberant sound.

There was a Common Room radio set and the nine o'clock news accompanied the serving of evening cocoa. Three other programmes attracted general audiences — Itma, the Sunday Afternoon Concert and the Brains Trust. The declared music lovers assembled for the concert and implored silence for the duration. Soon their eyes would close with rapt attention and concentration which gently softened into a more relaxed appreciation which the non-listeners mistakenly described as sleep. Joad, Huxley and Commander Campbell provided stimulus of a different order and provoked discussion which continued long beyond the end of the programme.

To live communally is not necessarily to live in community. Avoiding tension by trying to eliminate sources of difference reduces the opportunities for creative living and does not produce long term solutions. Differences may be buried, but go on smouldering until they flame into conflict — often sparked off by something of relative unimportance. Taking sides, or forming parties, has the effect of polarising differences in such ways as make acceptable solutions difficult to achieve and make imposed solutions almost inevitable.

When Friends are faithful to their method of taking decisions "by the sense of the meeting" and not by vote, their minutes accommodate minority attitudes and thought. They are made in the belief that the spirit of truth will be party to the deliberations and that all will have taken part in the exercise. For someone to withold part of the argument in the interest of preserving peace, or in fear of how it will be received, is to frustrate the search for the sense of the meeting. The Friend presiding over the meeting must help to create an atmosphere in which all aspects of the business can be presented. Even so human passion and frailty are parts of the process and can give rise to anguish and hurt in the search for unity.

There were, on occasion, strong differences among Spicelanders which did sometimes lead to misunderstanding and even quarrels. Spicelanders did not like one another all of the time; but arguments, whether they involved deeply held convictions, or were concerned with the comparative trivia of daily life, could be expressed and heard with respect and responded to with seriousness and humour. Business and discussion meetings always started with a period of silent worship and with good intent, which it was hoped would persist — "Faith is the substance of things hoped for, the evidence for things not seen." Decisions made in such fashion do not always come easily but are acceptable and rewarding when they do come. When the exercise ends in temporary failure it serves to emphasise how much more difficult it must be to reach good decisions when some of the participants are not seeking a common good but are striving to preserve "our interests" and have later to account to others for "our failure".

The religion of Jesus is not one of rules and regulations but of attitudes, and it is attitudes which have to change before societies become communities.

Community was never a stated aim at Spiceland. The prime concern was for the trainees — to give them experience and confidence, opportunities to acquire or develop skills, and to help them to find jobs and places where they could use them acceptably. The practical means for doing this was the restoration of the house, work in its kitchen, its laundry, the household generally, teaching the basics of first aid and nursing, and work in the gardens and on the farm. These tasks made competing demands on money, resources, and the time and energy available, and the demands had to be reconciled. Devotion to the tasks as ends in themselves could so easily have raised them to a greater importance than the people. By never losing sight of the prime concern for people, and by keeping the means subordinate to that concern, communal living became community.

CHAPTER 5

Change of Emphasis

In May 1940, when Spiceland was three months old and the first batch of trainees were less than halfway through their course, France fell and was occupied by Germany, and the British Forces escaped from the continent in fearful conditions. An invasion of Britain itself seemed to be more probable than possible.

This is not a book about the history of the war, but about the response which a minority group made to the war. In the context of those momentous events the effect on Spiceland was nationally insignificant, but they changed the experience of Spicelanders out of all expectation. Most of the trainees had volunteered with the intention of working behind the lines and giving support and succour to the victims of war in much the same way as had been done by the Society of Friends during and after the first world war. There was now no access to the continent and, until the air attacks on London and Southern England began in August and September, opportunities to serve in any way could not be seen. In the evenings there were involved discussions about how pacifists should respond to an invasion. A great divergence of supposed attitudes was revealed as they faced the difficulties posed for people who wanted to do "something" although that "something" was not fighting.

Out of these discussions came a wish to share their thinking with the Society as a whole, and John wrote a letter addressed to all Friends. The letter was dated September 3rd 1940 — a few days before the horrendous air attacks on the Thames and London — and it is reproduced here:

"Dear Friend,

This letter is being sent to you at the request of all at Spiceland because we are distressed to hear that there is real doubt in the minds of some Friends about the lines on which Spiceland is working. We have felt that a useful piece of service is taking shape, and that all developments have been natural modifications to meet changing circumstances, implicit in the original conception of Spiceland's war time service, and in no way incompatible with its possible service after the war. It is only with general matters of principle that this letter is concerned.

The opinion was strongly expressed in recent discussion here that the family feeling, esprit de corps, or whatever one may call it, that is inevitably fostered by living together in a place like Spiceland, is right and desirable, and is not in any way whatever a transfer of loyalty from some wider and more worthy communion. We are not less loyal to the Kingdom of God because we are members of the Society of Friends; rather do we find in the Society the right channel by which we can express in our lives that greater loyalty. Similarly, our loyalty to Spiceland makes us usually more able, and never less able, at this time to be loyal members of the Society of Friends, if we are members of it, and to the wider fellowship of Christian pacifists. Nor are we children, unable to break a connection, if in special circumstances our work required us to do so.

Nobody who comes to Spiceland can fail to realise that it is impossible for any committee to guarantee opportunities for service after three months or any other period. But Spiceland would not, I believe, be in existence now unless we had been able to say that genuine and vigorous efforts were being made, or were going to be made, to find such opportunities. It is only common sense that men with a keen desire for service and very limited resources (and most C.Os come within this category) cannot afford to expend time and money on coming to Spiceland in wartime simply because of the general value of that experience, but only if they can reasonably hope that they will be brought into more direct contact with the kind of opportunities for meeting real human needs that they desire and for which they are prepared to train themselves.

It seems to me on the one hand that a good deal of local initiative is necessary if we are to find where help is needed, and to deal with the requests for workers. The existence of a place like Spiceland must sometimes almost create a demand and often must bring requests for help direct to it; there are a number of useful men and women willing and able to go off and do a piece of work within a few hours, who can be personally recommended and who have worked together for a time. Such requests must of necessity be dealt with on the spot if they are to be properly and promptly answered.

On the other hand we know well, and are glad to know, that other groups and committees are also helping to solve, and in some cases on a larger scale, the two fold problem of responding sympathetically and practically to needs around us, and of helping C.Os and other pacifists to find work which is essentially disinterested and of service to others, and which at the same time gives them subsistence that they cannot provide for themselves.

It would seem to us most pitiful if for reasons of prestige, or because of difficulties of organisation that surely can be overcome, any of the groups who have this common purpose failed to give to the other groups or to receive from them the fullest possible help. We at Spiceland may have a field of service offered to us for which we cannot supply enough suitable workers. We may have in our group people who are unsuitable for the work that is offered to us who need to be put in touch with other opportunities. Other committees may have similar difficulties; if that is so, there does not seem to us to be any difference of principle to prevent genuine and immediate co-operation.

The more recent developments of the war have reduced the opportunities for service and have intensified the difficulties of many C.Os. It would, we believe, be an affectation to say that Friends should look only at the needs outside the Society; Meeting for Sufferings would never have had its name if the Society had refused to consider the personal needs of its own members. We are glad that Spiceland is one of the means by which Friends can help individual pacifists, especially C.Os, and we feel that this is a piece of service not unworthy of the Society. Those of us who are Friends are glad also that, although preference is given to the applications of Friends, we are able to welcome other pacifists.

It would be ungenerous to claim that this is merely a service rendered by the Society to people who are not Friends, though it would be worthwhile if it were only this. But in fact those who are Friends and those who are not, have a great sense of real unity and it would be impossible to say that either makes the more valuable contribution to the spiritual life or to the practical work of Spiceland."

The remoteness of Spiceland from Friends House in Euston Road, London, where the central committees of the Society operate, the distance from Spiceland of any large meeting of Friends, together with the formation of other Quaker committees in various parts of the country — all trying to express their concern in different practical ways, and all lacking effective means of communicating with one another are reflected in the pain which finds expression in that letter.

The Society of Friends is not a relief organisation; it is a religious society, and it had no standing machinery for doing relief work; before too long a special committee was set up to co-ordinate Quaker relief work and the Friends Relief Service was born. It was the fifth Friends War Victims Relief Committee to be set up since 1870 (its name was changed and shortened to Friends Relief Service in 1943) and while a few members had previous experience of relief work the great majority of those engaged in field or administration were Friends and non-Friends who had had no previous experience at all.

Soon happy and effective relationships were established and many Spicelanders found service in F.R.S. and many F.R.S. workers came to Spiceland for training and refreshment between jobs, or sometimes for recuperation from strain.

Winford Hospital, near Bristol

CHAPTER 6

The Winford Team

The first piece of work of importance came before the onset of the Blitz, and followed an approach made by Spiceland to Winford Hospital near Bristol, which produced a request from the hospital for a team of orderlies to undertake the background drudgery which enables a hospital to function.

Eighteen Spicelanders, some of whom had not completed the full course, but who would have dearly wished to do so, started work at the hospital on August 31st 1940. Later the team was increased to twenty-one, and was maintained for three and a half years. Many of the original team subsequently left to do other work and were replaced by other Spicelanders. After two years fourteen of the team, who had been stimulated by press publicity about the shortage of staff in sanatoria, decided to take up what they felt to be the more urgent and satisfying work of T.B. nursing. With the moral support of the remainder of the team, but to the regret of the Regional M.O.H., they went to the North Wales Sanatorium in Denbigh.

By that time Spiceland could no longer find enough trainees to maintain the team of twenty-one — a level which enabled twenty to be on duty and allow each man to have one week of leave in twenty-one weeks. In all sixty-one Spicelanders served in the Winford Team and they were joined by sixteen other C.Os at various times. In addition sixteen members of the Friends Ambulance Unit and its training group took part in the work.

The members were provided with board and lodging and ten shillings a week pocket money. From that ten shillings they made regular contributions to a fund called the Spiceland Pool which was used to help C.Os, unknown to them personally, who were in difficulty.

Winford was a civilian hospital but the heavy casualties sustained during the withdrawal from Europe resulted in service casualties filling an emergency ward with R.A.M.C. staff in attendance.

An unexpected test of conscience presented itself. Although it was confirmed that the hospital remained under the control of the Ministry of Health and that no preference was being given to service casualties, five men, after considerable individual thought and much group discussion, decided that they could not conscientiously continue to nurse Service patients. They were replaced, with great difficulty, by more men from Spiceland. In these early difficulties the temporary leader of the Team, Bill Sessions, had the unenviable task of explaining to the hospital authorities and to the Regional Ministry of Health, why some pacifists could look after soldiers and some could not!

The story of The Winford Team is told with a rich blend of humour and seriousness in a sixty page booklet of that name. It was written by Tim Evens and Stuart Walters, and brilliantly illustrated by Conrad Voss-Bark who were all members of the Team although only Tim Evens was a Spicelander.

John Hoare wrote a foreword to the booklet, which was published in 1945. Because the foreword puts the personal experience of the Team in a wider context it is reproduced here:

"As a mere collection of personal reminiscences this history would be well worth reading by those who belonged to or knew the Winford Team. But it is much more than that.

The pacifist in wartime makes a very bold claim and runs counter to the trend of thought and effort of the nation as a whole, and of most other groups of which he may be a member. His claim is not that he is a better man than others; it is that he has seen a better way of meeting and overcoming evil and of serving the ideals which he often shares with those who adopt other methods. He has not merely seen a vision but should be able to start living by it here and now. The consequent attempt to find practical service through which his conviction can be expressed may plunge him into deep waters.

Should he wait for the opportunity to do something big and costly, which will match the greatness of the truth he has glimpsed? It is often a bitter experience to find that the right course is shewn to him, not by any clarion call to service, but just by the pressure of circumstances on a mind that is determined to face the facts of life. Perhaps most of us pass an elementary test of our personal humility and spirit of service before we can become fit to take bigger opportunities.

Surely he must give his witness through dealing directly with people, not by grappling with boilers and "bumpers"? Yet most of us are not much good at influencing others by a frontal attack on their minds and characters;

our opportunity comes when we are least trying to create it as we share the ordinary things of life, and it often goes again without our realising what we have done or failed to do.

How much does technical efficiency matter? Well, we forgive ourselves much blundering and lack of real discipline because we know how good our spirit and intentions are; other people are much more censorious, and this is most discouraging.

Not least among the difficulties of the pacifist is that of living and working in a team, at very close quarters, perhaps with a score of other people, not for weeks but for months and years. It seems easy at first, especially for a great cause; but it proves before long to be a fine art which few of us have mastered.

These and similar problems are crucial for most C.Os. The members of the Winford Team had to find an answer to many of them, and I believe that they were unusually successful in doing so. Through good sense and good comradeship they grew into a real community; they won respect as workers from people who were not inclined to give any credit that had not been fully earned; the friendliness of their personal relations with patients and staff was obvious to anybody, and its effect must sometimes have been deep and enduring; the modest statement about their support for the Spiceland Service Pool conceals their very remarkable generosity to unknown fellow C.Os; and they clearly got a great deal of satisfaction and humour out of it all.

The incursion of many lively-minded amateurs into a rather rigid system tends to seriously undermine bad traditions, as happened when C.Os flooded into prisons for long periods in the last war. Over that part of their experience, as no doubt over others, the authors have discreetly drawn a veil. But perhaps the effect of a job well done, like that of the Winford Team, may be found later to have reached beyond the hospital where they actually worked and beyond the pacifist movement itself."

From the start the Team enjoyed a certain freedom and autonomy. They were engaged as a team and not individually, they were doing the work voluntarily because of the need for it, they worked for a nominal wage because they wanted, in respect of money, to make a sacrifice comparable with that of a common soldier, and they undertook to maintain the working team of twenty by deciding for themselves who should come and who should go.

In this way the stronger were able to compensate for the weaker, and the discharge of all duties was the responsibility of the whole. Jobs ranging from stoking to kitchen duties, cleaning to ward work, nurses' dining room duties to theatre orderly — this last could be the most demanding and most rewarding, and produced a feeling of satisfaction that other jobs could rarely supply — were arranged by the Team on a rotational basis and not by the hospital management.

Relations with the head stoker, the cook — mercurial in character — the matron and ward sisters were important and sometimes delicate.

Team decisions were determined by the "sense of the meeeting" and for much of the time a meeting for worship, short daily breakfast readings, and Sunday evening discussions were held in the Spiceland manner.

The ways in which men whose abilities were chiefly intellectual applied themselves to non mental work over very long periods, by developing techniques to a seemingly excessive degree, provided solutions to the performance of monotonous routines.

This could not have been easy for any and must have been very difficult for some. Richard Reiss, one of the Team who had a minor passion for photography, recalled that Fred Sanger asked to be photographed while washing lavatory floors. "I am going on to greater things than this, but I want to show that I can do this too." His future included two Nobel Prizes and an Order of Merit.

There was an off duty social life with readings of poetry, prose and informal talks by members of the Team about subjects of special interest. Occasionally something more ambitious like a play reading was attempted and, outstanding in the memory, was a reading of Milton's Comus which took place on a warm summer evening with the participants seated on top of the water tank. A Winford vocabulary developed and some "in" words changed their meanings with the passage of time. The word "tusker" started as an appellation for an agressive pacifist as opposed to a "blossom"; the verb meant "to attack" and the past participle came to describe the feeling of having been attacked or "ruined"; but eventually the verb came to describe lying in the sun in a sheltered spot and "tuskering banks" were places where one could withdraw to tusker. The water tank where Comus was read was one such place.

The Team's birthdays — in 1941 and 1942 — were the subject of special high tea celebrations followed by community singing of Winford songs which included a revised version of Green Grow the Rushes O, and the telling of traditional stories of Winford life — some true and some legendary.

Christmas and other festivals provided opportunity for sharing social activities with the medical and nursing staff. Full rein was given to latent talents for both writing and presenting "on stage" original and exciting material. It is curious how these activities echoed the similar pattern at Spiceland, and how the shared festivals complemented those which Spiceland shared with its village.

This account of social events and common interests reveals the pleasant, easy, side of community life. The real achievement was in shedding the priggishness of youthful idealism and learning to live together because of, rather than in spite of, differing educational and social backgrounds; and learning to accept criticism from non-pacifists at work and from one another in ordinary life.

The Team lived and worked together for over three years with little friction although they enjoyed little privacy. Frequently under strain and, occasionally, subject to anti-social behaviour, there were a few unwritten rules which, by general observance, preserved the community and contributed to what its members modestly claimed as a minor triumph of idealism and self control over apathy and selfishness.

The summer of 1943 revealed a strain on those Rump members who had remained after the departure to Denbigh, in October 1942, of the nursing team. They had rebuilt the team with the help of the Friends Ambulance Unit and others. They had borne the extra heat and burden of staff shortages during the rebuilding period; but they had also witnessed a deterioration of the Team, a deterioration which was apparent only to those who had known the Old Team. By conventional standards the work was being done well, but they experienced a falling away in levels of conversation, of manners, and of interest in communal activities.

Nevetheless, an ambitious Christmas pantomime was planned and it rivalled in excellence its predecessors.

The prospect in general was not good, but national events produced a local solution. Shortage of domestic staff in hospitals throughout the land was a subject of concern, and a Ministry of Labour investigation resulted in the direction of conscripted women to do the work. The Team informed the hospital that they were prepared to promote a gradual withdrawal to ease the Administration's problems of substitution. There was a curious inevitability about the fade out in 1944. The reduction was not planned but coincided with the expansion of the new domestic staff. So ended three and a half years of useful work.

CHAPTER 7

Response to the Blitz

The story of the Winford Team has been dealt with at length because it was the first work of importance to be undertaken from Spiceland. It was based on an attempt to serve by undertaking basic tasks; it was sustained over a long period; there was continuous contact throughout between Spiceland and The Team. This continuity was due, in part, to the team replacements which went from Spiceland, and in part to the return, for further training, or for refreshment and recuperation, of Team members to Spiceland. But it was also due to the exchange of letters between John Hoare and members of the Team — in particular those exchanged with Max Melling who was the Team's leader for two years. The letters reveal something about the forces at work, and the commonalty of the sense of community which developed in both places.

All Spicelanders acknowledge the existence of bonds between them which are as strong for those who spent short periods there as for those who spent longer; which have survived the separations of time, and have endured so that they are as strong today as they ever were. Certain it is that all who went there contributed in good measure and that all were receivers; the sum totals of the giving and receiving are greater than the sums of the parts and this is arrived at by general acknowledgement and not by arithmetic.

The Quaker practice of seeking the presence of God in meetings for worship and business, and of trying to find the sense of a meeting, does not encourage leadership of the kind described, wrongly, as charismatic. No one person can seek, or be given, overall control. John certainly presided over the community, and evidenced a charism, in the original sense of that word, as a grace given by God — never more evident than when he led the company into silent grace before meals, or when he spoke to the company with firm gentleness, laced with a rich vein of humour, at the end of meals.

He was a quiet person who never intruded on the lives of others. In personal matters he was always approachable, but could be disconcertingly slow to respond with words. He rarely offered solutions to problems, but prompted and encouraged people to find solutions for themselves. How much of his seeming disregard for time, as most of us use it, was the result of the prison experience which had undoubtedly shaped his own attitude to time, and how much was due to his own finely developed communion with the eternal, only John could say. If the spoken words came slowly and with seeming difficulty his written words came to the reader with revealing clarity. His correspondence with Spicelanders provided the material for a News Sheet which he edited and distributed to all of us so that our individual experiences became a shared experience, and our links with John helped to forge the bonds, and deepen the affection for the place associated with them.

The bombing of Southern England and the London Blitz which began in the late summer of 1940 changed the whole situation. The demand for workers soon outran the supply, and the involvement of Friends central committees and local meetings throughout the country established a network of Quaker work in which there were many and varied opportunities.

The evacuation of children and elderly people from the vulnerable city centres of population, to which so many had returned during the deceptively quiet months of the so-called phoney war, had revealed groups who were not suitable for billets in private homes. Many Friends Meeting Houses and other available properties were hastily converted for use as hostels while, in the city of London the Quaker centres for social work run by the Bedford Institute provided bases for relief work there.

This phase of the Spiceland story is best told and understood by piecing together some of the fragments used by John in the four issues of the News Sheet circulated between September and December 1940.

There was news from Spiceland itself, which continued to fill up with new trainees as quickly as others left. The comings and goings made it more difficult, but not impossible, to realise unity and the sense of family remained strong. There was news about the enlargement of the farm by renting an additional forty acres of derelict land at a nominal rent on the understanding that they should be cleared of thistles, brambles, ragwort and overgrown hedges, but with rights to plough and cultivate.

One group, working for the International Commission for Refugees, were in London — unpacking, sorting and distributing clothing and food sent from America. They had survived the air raids but were much in need of sleep. They described the collection of an American ambulance from the

Surrey Docks. It was not in running order and had to be towed behind a Ford V8 delivery van. Both vehicles had left hand steering which made traffic jams, bomb craters and unexploded time bombs difficult to negotiate. They described the thousands of refugees from Belgium, Holland, Spain, Germany and the East End of London all mixed together in London and receiving gratefully the clothing from America, which was in infinite variety. They were saddened by the sight of the terrible amount of damage which had been done in so short a space of time. Several other groups reported heavy engagement in evacuation work with no time to write in detail.

Harold and Janette Wheatley found themselves based in a Youth Hostel at Stratford on Avon and running a home for deaf children evacuated from Birmingham, while they maintained the youth hostel facilities in some stables.

In stark contrast, some wrote from the country about harvesting potatoes and other agricultural work. Architect, Mickey Harness, had been appointed by the International Commission to work on a refugee hutment project designed by Corbusier, but had to add that the start of the project was, frustratingly, very remote.

The second News Sheet opened with what John described as a few lines "in our chaste and classical editorial style" before passing on to news about old boys and old girls. "Yes 'old girls' is **absolutely right.** I saw a notice in the Times agony column only a day or two ago which said, after the name of a highclass girls school, 'Will all old girls please communicate with.....' In the Times, please note, so it **must** be right. Unless, of course, the headmistress concerned had seen it in our last issue and had said to herself 'In the Spiceland News Sheet please note, so it **must** be right'. In that case, I admit, my argument for its rightness is rather weakened." Dated? — but at that time relevant and appreciated.

The exodus of workers had, by then, been so great that Spiceland was well below maximum number but filling up again. John continued "Our financial position is precarious. Fifteen shillings a week does not pay for a great deal more than essential household supplies and food — not as we feed the hungry horde: in any case we do not want to lose so many good applicants who cannot pay the minimum charge and need a bursary fund. A great deal of equipment has had to be bought; building materials have cost us nearly £150.; fuel runs away with an amazing amount of money, especially during cold weather in this well aerated house. After our move to Spiceland we thought it best not to appeal publicly for support until we had established ourselves and shown that we were worth helping, so we were content to carry on for a time on loans and unsolicited gifts in cash and kind. This cannot go on and now, after six or seven months, we can and must blow our own trumpet and hand round the hat."

Michael Aitken found time to fill in some details about potato harvesting. "When you eat potatoes think of us with pity. Our operations begin at eight o'clock. George proceeds down the furrow with two horses pulling an infernal machine seemingly designed to scatter potatoes over as wide an area as possible. We each take a strip of about twenty yards, which has to be cleared before the reappearance of George, whose cycles take well under ten minutes. The 'tatties' are gathered in 50lb baskets the contents of which are then heaped into clamps. We continue with two breaks until 5 o'clock. The clamp digger is a sly old bird; he came round the first afternoon warning us 'never tell 'ee (George) the bloody right time — jest add o' five or ten minnits.' Many are the means used to slow down George's gyrations — from goading him into conversation or clogging the machine with potato haulms.

At five we struggle down to a sumptuous tea. The food is good and the place clean and attractive — decorated with Breton plates around the wall. The parlour is pleasant and comfortable and the farm buildings are built of solid granite. There is little place for sleeping, but I have found a corner in the loft where furniture is stored, and others have found similar niches."

Frank Kirby, based at the Friends Meeting House at Abingdon, and engaged on Thames Conservancy work wrote "…..my own job is not nearly as exciting as Winford or London. It consists solely of digging endless ditches for eight and a half hours a day — so I can't write very much about that! All I can say is that it is very hard work and keeps up a Spiceland appetite."

With work patterns at Winford well established the news is of steadily improving relations with the nursing staff and an actual sharing of off duty fun. One sister was overheard telling another of the good time they'd had with an added rider "You must come next time." This rapport paid off when new regulations were introduced barring orderlies from the operating theatre once a patient had been delivered. This caused great disappointment to the Team, but an approach to Matron which stressed their keenness and interest in surgery, touched her sensibilities, and the order was rescinded.

The story of one man's return trip to Cambridge — a journey of 300 miles — with a piece of cold fig pudding as his only luggage, but with a startling outcome that he had come back better off financially than when he set out, highlighted a new and growing method of travel described as hitchhiking. Should the technique be included in the Spiceland course? Ought a C.O. to accept lifts in army lorries or on the backs of soldiers' motor bikes? What about the doctrine of Ends and Means!

Two men working for the International Commission had been called to help with the evacuation of homeless people from the very part of the East London where John had worked between the wars. One letter describes a scene in terms which must have torn at his heart strings. "There are literally hundreds of homeless people in the East End now, and, of course, the number increases with every air-raid. The result is that large numbers are living day and night in air raid shelters, under railway arches and other places, in most insanitary conditions and without any kind of medical supervision or attempt to keep the diseased from the 'normal'. Many of them have been living that way for weeks. Most of them have only the clothes they are wearing and a blanket or two. There is no need for me to emphasise that aspect of the matter to you: you know that before the war conditions here were bad; now they are infinitely worse. The evacuation of these people has become a matter of the greatest urgency, both in order to alleviate their unfortunate condition and to prevent the outbreak of disease which, I am sure, will occur very soon unless drastic action is taken.

The Local Authorities are trying to evacuate the homeless, but with the best will in the world on the part of Borough officials, and the host of voluntary workers at such places as Paddy's Goose (where John and Margaret had lived), the present organisation can only be described as chaotic, chiefly because co-ordination between organisers in the evacuation and reception areas has been greatly hampered by the impossibility of making trunk or toll telephone calls. There are all sorts of circumstances which add to the confusion. For instance the billeting officer for Stepney Borough is Mr. James, the Town Clerk. The offices of his department at Wapping have been bombed and the department moved to the Peoples Palace — a great confusion there! When suitable parties of evacuees have been arranged there is considerable difficulty in finding the people concerned because most of them have no address — its just 'under the arches', and the Highway and district have to be combed by helpers before the party can be assembled. It isn't possible to send just anyone who wants to be evacuated because of the formalities with regard to billeting allowances. Although I understand that the authorities have now been instructed to interpret the legislation liberally, the actual letter of the Government's provision for billeting allowances covers only people from official evacuation areas; it does not provide for people who become homeless as the result of bombing!"

John, writing to Max Melling at Winford and responding to reported difficulties there, said "I have an immense respect for what Spicelanders are doing, and in many ways particularly for what the Winford Team are doing now that some of our people have gone to do more dramatic work in or around London — or at any rate work in more dramatic surroundings. I spent twenty years of work — or much more than work — of my whole life in helping to build up a fine club organisation that is now serving magnificently the district where I belong, where I have innumerable friends, and where there is probably more devastation than anywhere else in England. I simply ache to be with them, and find it very hard not to be bitterly rebellious just because it would, I think, clearly be wrong to throw in my hand here. Yet I have little excuse for not accepting serenely the truth, as I believe it is, that if one tries to insist on picking and choosing the way in which one will serve, there may be no opportunity of service allowed at all, or at any rate one will be unfit for first rate service...........

I am glad that the discussions about sticking to, or leaving, Winford have worked out satisfactorily as, on the whole, I gather they have. I hope that I was not very clumsy about it all. I had a kind of average uncomfortable time during the last war, rather more than average during my last year in prison: both inside and outside prison I felt a sense of utter boredom and wastefulness in the routine of the life I was leading. Of course the average was much more uncomfortable then than it is in this war. Nevertheless, it has not, I hope, made me into a kind of pacifist Colonel Blimp — 'Gad, sir, it would do these youngsters good to live through a bit of what I was put through.' But followed as it was by some harrassing experiences in East London, it may have made me too impatient with softness and vacillation in matters of principle (in myself I hope as well as in others). That may be quite justifiable in itself, but it is not justifiable when what is wrong, is not the wrong spirit, but lack of perception — inability to see that there is no real principle involved. One ought then to be patient and explanatory, and to remember that, even so, explanations will not carry much weight with people.........."

In November, Roger Warner — a peace time antique dealer — described his journeys as he switched his perceptive skills to buying equipment for hostels which were being set up in the country. He used travelling time on a bus from Coventry to Leamington to make notes of requirements and purchases — looking out of the window with unseeing eyes as he tried to master the art of writing on his knees in an unsteady vehicle. With half an hour to spare between buses before travelling on from Leamington to

Oxford, he went for a walk and returned to find two plain clothes detectives waiting to question him. His note taking as he passed through Coventry had been observed and reported as "suspicious". They asked for his note books and studied intently the prices paid for pots, pans and cutlery required for a hostel at Malmesbury. Then they asked for his identity card which they returned with the remark that one could not be too careful these days. They parted on good terms.

Once removed from the dangers of bombing, the hazards of living communally proved to be more than some evacuated mothers could accept. In daylight the irritations of shared accommodation were more irksome than quickly forgotten terrors of the East End. Spicelanders in reception areas soon found that dealing with mothers and children was even more demanding than dealing with authorities, or rationing, or the actual business of preparing meals and sleeping accommodation. But with the coming of the night the resumed noises of distant gunfire and bombing brought back old fears and, with the fears, acceptance of the inevitable. Eventually and happily these mothers also accepted a share in the chores and other responsibilities.

The International Commission Team were still coping with the distribution of supplies and clothes to the homeless and to refugees still arriving from the Continent, whilst living in bomb-damaged premises where they sustained life with the help of a primitive oil cooker. Leaking water prevented leaking gas from causing a catastrophe when the sound of running water wakened them to make an investigation which revealed the leaking gas! The later discovery of broken windows and an iron railing which had been severed by a flying brick, was less remarkable than the arrival of a paving stone which sailed over the roof of the house opposite and came to rest in the gutter of the house next door. The writer of this letter ended on the plaintive note that he would "dry up now" because no one was interested in other people's bombs.

Most of one team that had been helping to billet evacuees from a temporary dispersal centre on the edge of Epping Forest found that success left them with nothing to do, and they returned to Spiceland to complete interrupted training.

Those working in feeding centres in the East End found their daytime services in less demand as families either left the area or adapted themselves to changed living conditions. Refreshments were still needed in the night shelters, but introduction of a small charge was followed by a drop in demand. Improved sanitation and a supply of ground sheets and extra blankets had reduced fears about outbreaks of disease in these primitive surroundings, but as November gave way to December, memories of the hard winter of 1939/40 gave rise to some apprehension.

Charles Bubb and Hugh Brammer had started work on the conversion of some hop-pickers huts in Worcestershire for use by mothers and children from London. As they worked at the transformation, and saw the emergence of what seemed to them to be snug accommodation, they paused to reflect that their rose-tinted perception of what they had achieved from such basic foundations might not accord with the view of city mothers making a first acquaintance with rural England.

News from Blackborough was about fears for the water supply now that over sixty people were in residence. Dismissed in advance as "no good treatment" the application of a pressure pump to the aged pipe system — shades and memories of Carclew — had surprisingly produced a full tank, a full lower reservoir, and, even more surprising, the starting up of a new spring in the upper reservoir! The purchase of one hundred tons of farmyard manure for spreading on the cultivated land had triggered some foreboding in the minds of farm trainees, and a rashly untended bonfire had led to a summons for Brother Oswald for infringement of the blackout regulations. This news produced the wry comment that Brother Os could explain away his fine by demonstrating what the poverty knot on his Franciscan "dressing gown" was all about. In the event he **was** fined twenty shillings with costs, and Spiceland paid.

The December News Sheet acknowledged that Spiceland was really established — the earlier issues had been circulated by John, as he modestly explained, to save him much letter writing; but now it became an official Spiceland publication with a modest printing and postage charge of three pence. Just how much of Spiceland's periphery activity, like the News Sheet, was initiated and funded by John and Margaret as part of their unofficial and personal contribution, no one is ever likely to know.

The sixteen pages of news, although much of it was concerned with human tragedy, must have been, to them, a heart-warming reward for all their effort. The letters really were "letters home". The emphases were shifting away from the actual bombing — which in London had slackened but not ceased — to the sorting out and settling down of homeless people in new areas and improvised settlements.

A barn and squash court at Gerbestone Manor, the home of Lloyd and Griselda Fox, had become a childrens home. A meeting house at Woburn

Sands had become a home for mothers and young children. An empty, but partly furnished house in Gloucestershire, said to have been the home of Dick Whittington, had become a home for expectant mothers. A large house in Peterborough had, with support from the Meeting and the City Council, been adapted to house "difficult-to-billet children". These examples were just a part of what was for the Society of Friends generally, and for Spiceland in particular, a large undertaking; but only a small part of what had to be done overall by others. The skills of construction, adaptation, cooking, housekeeping and hygiene, which had been part of the basic Spiceland tuition, quickly came into serious use. The skills of dealing with frightened, homeless, incompatible and, often belligerent, mothers and children, or of reassuring frightened and querulous older evacuees, had to be learned, and came more slowly.

The situation in London had eased but that in Birmingham and Coventry had worsened. Roger Warner and Dorrie Street spent some time organising the evacuation of people who were reluctant to leave the torn fabric of what had been home. They described the flattened city centre of Coventry as worse than anything they had seen in London. They watched unsafe buildings being blown up or pulled down; all water had to be boiled and meals were served from mobile canteens in the streets. But despite this, homeless people had to be persuaded to leave.

Using buses supplied by Cadbury's they collected about fifty people of all ages and took them to a centre in Selly Oak; but the air raids became so intense that they were forced to leave what was a mainly wooden structure to find safer shelter under the Bournville factory. Bournville staff fed and housed them magnificently — turning out of their beds to cope with the emergency. After breakfast in the canteen the buses were re-loaded to set off on a tour of country billets in Shropshire. Just before departure Roger returned to the canteen for a quick look round and retrieved three coats, two gas masks, one hat and, snug in a bundle on top of a double decker bunk, one fifteen month old baby!

Returning from Shropshire to spend the night with a Friend in Birmingham, Roger spent a restless night until, at about two o'clock a huge bomb fell outside and destroyed the houses of two women Friends who lived in the same road. Two rescue parties working for three hours, with bombs and flying wreckage stabbing the dark night, eventually moved Winifred Sturge who had been buried under the rubble. The following day Roger and Dorrie worked to salvage furniture and effects. They agreed that Bert's Spiceland lecture on the relative strength of different parts of a building had enabled them to move through the rickety building structure, with its cracked and leaning walls, and work in comparative safety as they kept to the sides of floors and stairs.

They left a largely waterless and gasless city on Sunday. Sunday night was spent on the floor of Coalbrookdale meeting house which had been prepared for evacuees. Monday was spent in securing services for the school room, so that that too could be converted; and Tuesday night was spent in comparing the relative comfort of a meeting house floor with that of the Congregational Church as they mounted a joint effort to provide accommodation there. The letter ended not with "and so to bed", but with "...and so to Birmingham to organise transport of bedding."

In the summer of 1941, John and Margaret visited London and the Highway Clubs to see for themselves some of the work that had been done. In a rare conversation John led off on how few openings there had been for C.Os in the 1914 war and how many, like himself, would have leaped at the chance to do some humanitarian work, no matter how dull, humdrum or menial. He said that there was sometimes an attraction about emergency work which was not all that healthy, and that there was need for C.Os generally to prove to the outside world that they could carry through jobs where they were kept "up to the collar" all the time, month in month out, and not just at spasmodic intervals. Bill Sessions, who was present at this conversation, wrote to Max Melling and said how stimulating it was when John did "open up", and that it had shocked him "quite a bit" because London had not been an unpleasant place during the summer of 1941, thanks to the lull in air raids; moreover, some of those working at Friends House at that time had been rather standing on their rights about fire-watching duties — standing on the letter rather than working in the spirit of the law.

An aspect of the age old problem posed by Martha and Mary is brought into focus here in words which I did not read until more than forty years after they were said and written. I often heard John commend, in all its variety, the work done by Spicelanders, but I never heard him select any service as being of the "better part".

The C.O's chief fear is of being thought to be a coward, and there is often the desire, or temptation, to prove to himself that this may not be so. Some Spicelanders, men and women, did work in dangerous conditions — making sandwiches and cocoa before serving them under the arches during an air raid could sometimes be Martha in dramatic style. Fire fighting and rescue work during and after air raids were the experience of some who shared the terrors of the East End and Coventry. Others worked in hostels for the aged or the young in safe areas of the country which suddenly became dangerous as did Exeter during the so-called Baedeker raids. Some worked in hospitals with long-term exposure to disease, and some served prison sentences for reasons which were very real and valid for them.

The needs and opportunities changed many times during the long years of the war and some people moved from one form of work to another as the needs were perceived while others did long stints in work which called for long term application. Farm work fell into that category and working with animals and farm machinery has its own element of risk.

John always looked for actions based on a caring regard for humanity. He may have known, but would not have identified, some who responded to the "glamour of emergency"; but he also knew, and felt, the temptation to make that response himself. He wanted Spicelanders to look at their opportunities, motives and principles with real perception. Part of the growth of the community in the autumn and winter of 1940 was due to a shared perception which emerged from the shared life of an extended family. It was contact with John and Margaret and the home which they made at Spiceland for themselves, and extended to everybody who went there which preserved the contacts for all.

Potato picking: see page 40

CHAPTER 8

Digression in Time

In 1929, at the age of sixteen, I was confirmed in the Church of England. It was a happy formality — the logical sequence of events through Sunday School to the top class followed by confirmation classes with the Vicar. At State grammar school my history teacher was the daughter of a Scottish non-conformist minister, and she taught history with a firm devotion to the protestant faith. When the Vicar said that, at the time of the English Reformation and the break with Rome in the reign of Henry the Eighth, the Apostolic succession passed to the Anglican Church, I asked how he knew this to be so, and was told in reply that it was part of "received truth". In 1929 sixteen year old school boys from working class backgrounds did not argue with teachers or clergymen, but the words "received truth" remained as a niggling doubt in my sub-conscious.

Our Vicar had been a missionary in Southern Africa and he was suddenly offered and accepted the appointment as Bishop of Swaziland. St. Mark's had been a low church — no incense, no statue of the Virgin, no confession — but a very good choir, good congregational singing and plenty of social activity.

Whether by policy or administrative accident the Bishop of London appointed a very High Churchman to the vacant living, and the heavens fell. The new man was authoritarian, dogmatic and tactless; everything had to be changed at once. To ease the changes for the new Vicar our beloved and liberal curate was moved to a new parish on the outskirts of Salisbury, and new curates were brought in. One of these was short, had little experience and insisted on being called Father Henry. He stood on a box in the pulpit and a merciless choir formed a rota to remove the box just before the service began. A senior choir man told him that he was prepared to call him cousin but not Father. The congregation divided, petitioned the Bishop, and debated articles of faith and observance with passion and vigour — although they had scarcely been matters of concern before. The new man stayed.

After confirmation I had joined the young men's bible class which was the special concern of the curate. There were about forty of us with an age range from sixteen to the early twenties, and our minds had been opened to a wide range of thought in the context of a very simply presented religion. The Reverend Mauleverer — Mav to all of us — invited people from many walks of life to speak to us about their work and the part that religion played in it. I remember well, Frank Woolley the England and Kent cricketer, Lady Scott, Dr. Cove-Smith paediatrician and rugby football international, and many local men and women engaged in public and political life. By this time I had left school, and my daily journey to work in the City, and work itself, had widened my horizons. We are educated in large measure by association, and my education had taken new directions.

Father Henry could not compete with what we had come to know, moreover his was the task of instructing us in matters of the new doctrine. Received truth was very important to him and it was presented forcefully. After one arid Sunday afternoon we called on the Vicar and asked that something like our former programme should be restored. His study was crowded with young men; the room grew very warm, and the Vicar grew very angry before he turned us out into the street. We thought that that was the end of the class, but it was not.

Some of the class members met with a senior choirman who was also a local Councillor. He introduced them to an Estate Agent who had an "upper room" in his office building. Word was passed round and on October 5th, 1930 forty members attended a meeting at which the Old Markonian Bible Class was formally launched and a committee elected.

The Class remained active until May 29th, 1938 and something of its history is worth recording. It remained Anglican, and every year a copy of its annual report was sent to the Bishop of Willesden. The list of invited speakers grew long and the range of interests wide. With one or two notable exceptions the Anglican clergy declined invitations to speak rather than be seen to be involved in controversy. But active laymen came, and so did the non-conformist clergy who included a very lively Unitarian, whose total congregation was very much smaller than our class, and who opened our ears to some aspects of theology completely new to us. On one occasion the Bishop, acknowledging our report, expressed concern about the growing non-conformist influence.

To maintain and strengthen the fellowship, social events were arranged at which there was always an atmosphere of enjoyment and fun.

more serious activities of worship and study brought about a lively interest and involvement in social affairs. Some members were active in Youth Club work, some in the League of Nations Association, some joined scout and rover groups attached to other churches; but the more significant social work was the befriending of a few local families whose fathers were unemployed.

The money raised by dances and whist drives supplemented by appeal was used to provide a Sunday lunch cooked on gas rings and primus stoves, and served in our "upper room" before the afternoon session of the Bible Class. The Estate Agent was generous about the rent and use of gas, and was repaid by attention to maintaining and cleaning the room. In the summer months the Class went into recess and some of the children were taken for camping weekends at a farm on the edge of the Greenbelt near Enfield.

These were exciting times. The reluctant farmer had to be persuaded, and he exacted promises that there would be no interference with livestock or hedges under pain of instant cancellation of facilities. The first camp was nearly the last. The farm help — a young expatriate Scot — told us quietly that two boys had chased the cows being brought across the field at milking time, and if he found out........ At evening camp fire we talked to the boys. There was a long uncomfortable silence before two boys owned up, but said "mister they weren't cows they were bulls, and we didn't chase them, they chased us. They had horns."

The farmer never became friendly but we camped there for several years and the Scots lass helped out in her few off-duty hours, and became a great favourite with the boys — and with us. We were group parents and introduced the boys to many things, including soap and water above the wrists and below the neck line. Soap and hot water were expensive items for out-of-work families.

Another incident is worth telling. Two brothers failed to turn up at the meeting place for the second camp and the others just said "they couldn't come." It transpired that they were Catholics and, because they had missed mass the weekend before, had been in trouble with their priest, who had caned them! Three of us called on the priest and eventually secured what I suppose was a dispensation which allowed them to camp again. We had difficulty in convincing the priest that our simple prayer after cocoa was far removed from any attempt to convert the boys to Anglicanism.

The strongest links with our former liberal church values were with Mav. and his new parish in Salisbury. We made group visits — especially at Easter time when some of us camped on the floor of the surplus army hut which did duty as church, church hall and many other things. Others were given hospitality by parishioners in their homes, and many friendships were made. This association with St. Francis' Salisbury lasted far beyond the life of the Class.

There are vivid memories of Easter cycle rides. A group would meet at Muswell Hill Broadway at midnight on Maunday Thursday, and ride through the night — sometimes cold and frosty, cloudless, and with a full moon — along what is now the North Circular Road, but was then a series of linking single carriage way suburban roads. We joined the A 30 at Staines and cycled on through Basingstoke, then a small market town, Stockbridge and on to Salisbury — a distance not far short of a hundred miles. The coldest part of the night always seemed to be near Basingstoke where we opened flasks of Camp coffee, and restored our circulations with draymen's exercises. Somewhere near Stockbridge we stopped to to look back and watch the sun rise, and once or twice this provided scenes of incredible beauty. There was very little traffic; occasionally the headlights of a car would stab the darkness, and we could watch its progress, but for the most part it was as social a ride as our energies would permit. We were tired on arrival, but much more tired at the end of a late Good Friday evening.

Saturday was a holiday which always ended with a visit to Salisbury's provincial theatre where the start of the evening performance was delayed until the last shops closed and shop keepers and customers, loyal theatre-goers, could join the audience. I cannot remember anything that we saw on stage; but I do remember the sense of occasion as the auditorium slowly filled amid a buzz of conversation and of greetings waved and shouted across the tiered space completely drowning the efforts of a small orchestra; and the sudden expectant hush which followed the lowered lights and the rising curtain.

Sunday was devoted to the church and its services, and on Bank Holiday Monday the cyclists set off in daylight for home — an altogether different journey from the night ride. Thrill and satisfaction gave way to careful response to heavy traffic as London got nearer and nearer.

The reverse link was an annual service arranged in London, near enough for former parishioners to join the Class and meet again their curate in the atmosphere and style of worship they had known, but outside St. Mark's parish boundary. Our hosts were a church at Manor House devoted to work with the deaf and dumb and many friendships developed with the clergy and their remarkable congregation.

It could not go on for ever. Members grew older, changed jobs, got married and moved away. Some lost interest altogether and many found homes in other churches. Although a few, attracted by what we were doing, joined with us there was no consistent source of new members, and we did not proselytize. In 1938 the Class was wound up while it was still active but much reduced in numbers. It had been a marvellous experience.

The link with St. Francis' Salisbury had bound most of us to the Anglican Church, and we had made our regular communions on the first Sunday of each month; but we had also travelled widely in search of spiritual nourishment and our church attendances were not made without question. I have to admit that had the Old Markonian Bible Class not come into existence my interest in organised religion could have waned. I was active in outdoor sports and was passionately fond of the countryside. I cycled thousands of miles and walked many hundreds more. I could easily have persuaded myself that I was nearer to God outside the church and under the arch of heaven. But the Class was formed at the height of the industrial and agricultural depression and at a time of social and political ferment. There was mass unemployment, appalling slums, malnutrition and a host of other social ills.

I had cycled through Blaenau Ffestiniog on a hot summer day and seen the whole population sitting on their doorsteps with nothing to do. I had shipped on a cargo boat and steamed from Wapping to Newcastle to witness the listless ranks of idle men watching the river in dejected degradation of unemployment, before cycling over the Pennines to enjoy a Lakeland holiday. I had seen the hard struggle against poverty and tuberculosis of some of the children in the families we had befriended.

I had started work, at fifteen shillings a week, in an Import/Export business which traded with India and the East. I worked at the India desk where the trade was mostly in cotton goods and corrugated iron sheeting. The work was interesting, and I gained some vicarious knowledge of life in India and the Civil Disobedience campaign; but when I found out that my senior by three years was still only earning seventeen shillings and sixpence, I thought that it was time to look for another job. Two hundred letters and some interviews later I became a junior clerk in a Life Assurance Company at a salary of twenty-five shillings. The Company encouraged study and I attended evening classes at an L.C.C. institute and passed the examinations of the Chartered Institute of Secretaries. The study stimulated an interest in economics which has remained with me.

Our Newspaper at home was the News Chronicle, and at the office I had a half share in the Manchester Guardian which we bought at a special students' rate of 1¼d a copy — paid quarterly! I was appalled by the government's policies at home and even more so — if that were possible — by the Foreign policies pursued at the League of Nations after 1931. I read widely in an undisciplined sort of way, and argued and talked a great deal. If it was to hold me, the Church had to say and do something positive about the issues which troubled me or it would become irrelevant: the churchmen who moved me were Dick Sheppard, Canon Raven, Donald Soper and George McLeod. I became a Christian pacifist.

In 1935 my parents moved a short distance from Wood Green to Southgate, and another Class member also moved in the same direction. We explored a new range of churches together but found little joy. Our most conveniently placed church was St. Paul's Winchmore Hill which was about mid-way between our homes. The music was splendid, but the sermons were tedious and irrelevant. A short distance away on the other side of the road was a Quaker Meeting House. We knew very little about the Society of Friends beyond the fact that they had no priests nor ministers. I had stayed at the Jordans Youth Hostel without ever going to see the nearby meeting house. The Class had never had a Quaker speaker, but we knew that one or two members of our local P.P.U. group were Quakers.

On one Sunday morning in 1937 we entered the meeting house. The plain benches were placed in the form of a rectangle facing inwards towards a small table on which there was a small flower arrangement and one or two books including a bible. We took our seats in a back row, and waited for the service to begin.

There was no service. A few late comers came in and took their seats, and then we were caught up in a deep enfolding silence. There came a point at which we knew, without explanation, that we had become part of what Friends call a "gathered" meeting. Three or four Friends spoke briefly at intervals bridged by the same deep silence. The ministry made a coherent whole, but it was the quality of the silence from which the ministry came which made the experience memorable. There was an atmosphere of tranquility, but it was tempered with a feeling of warmth and expectancy, and when, finally, two Friends shook hands to signal the close of the meeting, of fulfilment.

What followed was something completely different — we became part of what I have come to describe as the "not so silent assemblies of Friends" — no pious whispering here, but a warmth of greeting and conversation, not outside the church building, but in the actual place where we had gathered to worship. It was our first introduction to a Society which holds that the sacred cannot be separated from the secular — that there is a wholeness which is life.

There was no dramatic break with the Anglican Church. The ritualised communion service seemed less and less to represent a shared meal with Jesus, and the creeds became more and more difficult to say. As we explored the Quaker understanding, and appreciated the underlying belief that there is something of God in everyone which calls for a response, we were drawn closer to them. The experience of organising the Bible Class was preparation for a recognition that a separated priesthood was a throwback to pre-Christian practice which had no warrant in early Christian practice. Equality for men and women was easily accepted by boys who had been educated in two of the earliest of state co-educational schools — we knew from experience that it was so. Later when we had experience of Quaker business meetings and the search for the sense of the meeting it all seemed to fall into place. When we both joined the Society it was not because of the Peace Testimony — important though that is — but out of firm theological conviction.

My love of the countryside had found expression in cycling and walking. Camping and Youth Hostelling had been the means of making the most of the precious time available. The West Country, Wales, The Lakes, the Cairngorms, Arran and Ireland had all played a part in satisfying a hunger for enjoying the natural world. I still ride the bicycle which I bought in 1930 and, until very recent years, I claimed that I had cycled more miles than I had driven a motor car.

The 1937 Easter visit to Salisbury had fallen through and at the last minute I accepted an invitation to join a youth hostelling group who had planned a walk in the Surrey hills. Someone had dropped out, the party had become uneven, hence the invitation. So, fortuitously, I met one who shared my love of the countryside and much else besides, who became my companion and my wife. One thing we do not share is a religious attitude to life. Marjorie has never experienced a "God element" : the teaching of Jesus and the New Testament are important to her, but the idea of divinity is not. Without becoming a member she has given time, energy and thought to the Religious Society of Friends and has sometimes said that she would welcome a secular one, but she has also said that in the meantime it is the best we have.

CHAPTER 9

Working and Waiting

When war broke out in September 1939 I expected that it would become immediately violent in Britain, and I thought that tolerance would prove an early casualty. I was wrong on both counts. Most of my friends and colleagues accepted the war as the inevitable consequence of what had gone before, and some of my pacifist friends thought that the war had changed things for them and they joined up. Although I hold minority views on a number of issues, I like to be part of the main stream. But my conviction about war was deep and publicly declared; I never seriously doubted what I should do. I registered as a Conscientious Objector.

Marjorie and I married on the 14th of October — the anniversary of the Battle of Hastings and the day on which the sinking of the Royal Oak was announced. We had decided that we would volunteer for any relief units which might be set up by the Society of Friends — if they would have us. In the meantime life went on more or less normally.

In May 1940 we took the first step in training for relief work. We had heard about the Spiceland Training Centre and volunteered to go there for a working holiday. It was the time when France fell and the British Forces were being evacuated from Dunkirk. There was an air of menace and foreboding at that time which was heightened by the intense and sultry heat of an early summer. A day or two before we left for Spiceland we went to the Old Vic — with some tickets given to us by some friends who understandably preferred to stay at home with their children — to see a John Gielgud performance of King Lear. The weather, with a threat of thunder, and the state of the war, provided an unparalleled setting for the play. The theatre was only half filled, but the cast were magnificent, and the high drama of the occasion stayed with us as we travelled homewards through a silent city.

The memories of that performance and the working holiday which followed have to be recalled against the background of the changing war situation. However different our views and understanding about dealing with the existence of evil, we were part of the human situation, and we shared with everyone else the emotions, the fears, the hopes and, yes, the pride as the no doubt heavily censored story unfolded.

We were welcomed by the Spiceland community and its first batch of trainees and, because the most pressing need was for work on the farm and garden, that is where we worked. Marjorie worked with Rudi Weiss in the vegetable gardens while most of my fortnight was spent in breaking up clods of heavy Keuper Marl which had baked hard in the hot relentless sunshine. The intention was to make a late planting of potatoes in a large area of this intractable soil, and for days on end I used a spade with sharp downward jabs to break up the lumps into smaller and smaller pieces. It was hard, jarring and monotonous work.

I had one fully compensating day. My mother was a country girl, and I had spent school holidays with an old village school girl friend of hers whose husband was the herdsman on a large dairy farm near Reading. I had played and worked with the farmer's sons and had acquired some, now dormant, skills. I loved the work and had wanted to be a farmer, and surely the farmer would have been glad to give me employment when I left school; but my parents were convinced that it would be a waste of my secondary education, and pointed out that the farmer's six sons must always come before me, and that they themselves had no money with which to help me. My mother knew well the hard life of an agricultural worker's family, and her father and brothers were living reminders of it.

One morning towards the end of our stay, when we reported in the farmyard for allocation of duties for the day, I admitted to this rusty experience, and was handed a halter with instructions to go and catch the horse. I left for the field followed by smiles of amusement which were difficult to interpret. In the field was a beautiful chestnut mare with a white blaze on her face and four white socks. She was grazing, but as I approached she lifted her head, pricked her ears and moved a few paces. Beautifully muscled and quite broad in the beam she yet had slender legs and eager movement. I spoke to her softly, walked quietly to her left shoulder, fondled her muzzle with my left hand and slipped the halter over her ears with the right. I stroked her ears gently. It was more than ten years since I had caught the very similar cobs which had pulled the milk floats round the streets of Reading, but the technique I had been taught then still worked. Together we walked happily back to the farmyard where I found I had established a reputation — no one, apart from Hugh Flatt, had caught June single handed for many a day, and some hopes that I had been led a merry and frustrating dance were dashed. My reward was to spend the rest of the day using June as a timber horse to haul stacks of felled ash saplings from the thirteen acre copse. Marjorie and I spent little time together. We worked hard and joined in whatever was toward in the evenings. Already we were caught up in something infinitely compelling but satisfying.

We did have the middle Saturday afternoon free, and together we walked along the beautiful Devon lanes with their high banks clothed in summer greenery and flowers — foxgloves, campion and honeysuckle. It was the weekend when all the signposts were removed as an anti-invasion precaution, and the speed and efficiency with which it was done gave rise to some problems, and to one lovely local story which was told and retold over the succeeding years. A traveller to Exeter from Taunton took to the lanes and, in the absence of the signposts, missed his way and arrived in late afternoon in Kentisbeare with no idea of his whereabouts. The local man from whom he asked directions had heard a broadcast warning not to help strangers asking for directions, and refused to tell him where he was or where to go. The frustrated traveller eventually exploded with "But my good man, don't you realise that I'm lost?" and received the reply "You bain't lost maister — not so long as I know where you be."

On that Sunday we all walked along lanes and footpaths to the old Spiceland Meeting House. This was our first sight of this lovely old building with its large south facing windows — on hot sunny days as inducive to sleep as to worship, but who is to say that on such days, to sleep is not to worship? — and the old burial ground with simple headstones overgrown with grass and wild flowers.

We broke our journey home at Salisbury to stay a night with Mav. His church, replacing the old army hut we had known, was nearly finished when war broke out and permission had been given to complete the structure. We climbed on ladders high into the roof and walked across planks to inspect the painted beams which were to be a feature of a distinctive building designed with a flat roof to accommodate open air services. It seemed like a prophetic gesture.

The later summer was filled with the Battle of Britain, and the autumn and winter with the London Blitz. Charles and Harriet Howarth who were wardens at the Quaker Centre at Barnet Grove, provided a base for volunteers who spent the evenings working in East End air raid shelters underneath the railway arches in Watney Street, Shadwell, and in the basement of the Free Trade Wharf, Wapping, returning to spend the nights sleeping on floors at Barnet Grove. Early in the Blitz we both did a stint at this work, but the number of volunteers increased to the point when Marjorie's long journey from North London seemed to be unecessary, and I went direct from the office to Barnet Grove on several nights a week. This stage of the war was unsettling. My employers were reluctant to release me until after my appearance before a tribunal, and to be dealing with life assurance matters during the day — including the training of school leavers to learn tasks which had previously been the preserves of older staff, and serving food in the shelters at night, had more than a touch of incongruity. One of my colleagues, concerned for my safety while walking the streets of London, insisted on lending me a tin hat which had been issued to him as a member of the office fire brigade.

The walk from Barnet Grove to Mile End and Wapping seemed to be much longer than it actually was as we picked our way through the blacked out streets of London. On dark cloudy nights Vallance Road was made particularly hazardous by the buckets of sand left on the pavements by shopkeepers and residents for use against incendiary bombs. Most doorways were flush to the pavement and the buckets were traps for the unwary and shortsighted. On clear quiet nights the London silhouette — gaunt and scarred — could look remarkably beautiful. When shrapnel made sparks fly off the road surface it was spectacular but frightening, and on one occasion two of us dived into an open doorway for shelter — we had the one tin hat between us, and could not agree which of us should wear it. As we flattened ourselves against the wall a brief, vivid flash of light revealed that we were standing in the glass store of a builder's yard, and we were just as quickly out in the road again. On another occasion one of our party walked into a lamp-post and gave himself a black eye and a cut head. A nearby ARP unit gave prompt and efficient first aid, but then came a problem of recording the incident. The post officer said that they were only allowed to deal with air raid casualties, but our man refused to be described as such, and also rejected "injured while hurrying to take shelter". This good pedantic fun was enjoyed by both parties on what was a grim night, and the eventual compromise was "injured on the way to shelter work".

The railway arches in Watney Street had been bricked up apart from a narrow entrance protected by a heavy tarpaulin curtain. The cocoa was brewed on gas rings in a small kitchen on the third floor of a building on the other side of the road. It was no mean feat to carry the large field dixies full of piping hot cocoa down a narrow stairway, across the road and negotiate them through the heavy tarpaulin. There were some anxious moments. The glimpse of a partially blacked out torchlight was enough to provoke a cry of "put that light out", but, seemingly unknown to the shelter dwellers, the railway track loading lights, also partially screened, were giving more light than our poor torch.

The Quaker cocoa was followed by prayers led by Father Groser. We never met because we had always moved on to the wharf before his arrival. His visits were a tremendous comfort to the people spread uncomfortably on hard ground tempered with makeshift bedding, and with little to cheer them. He was a much revered person.

The Wharf was more spacious than the arches and for some reason there was more variety of refreshment — rolls and buns to supplement the cocoa. The arrangements here were well organised by Douglas Millard, a Quaker publisher and bookseller, who lived in a flat nearby from where he also organised youth club work, and was the main support of the small Ratcliff Quaker Meeting. He was well known to all the shelterers who greeted him warmly and cheerfully as he walked amongst them while the refreshments were served.

In both shelters the sense of togetherness was very strong and this helped to create, from small resources, a sense of shared safety and comfort. One day we were told that a Home Office Official had inspected the wharf and had declared that it was very vunerable should a bomb fall on the river side. But there was no better place. In fact the Wharf and the Arches had always looked vulnerable, but they were no doubt better than many of the poor buildings in which the shelterers lived or had lived, and an illusion of safety may enable us to think about the probability of tomorrow.

After registering as an objector I had prepared a statement for presentation to a Tribunal, and the appointed day for my appearance proved to be wet, foggy and miserable. There had been an all night air raid alert, but only sporadic activity — a nuisance raid. Transport between the East End and Fulham Town Hall was pretty sketchy and I had a job to get there in time for the hearing which took place while the alert was still on. The case before mine was dismissed. The young man was appealing in part on political grounds, and he was given a very rough ride — particularly, I thought, by the Trade Union representative member of the tribunal. It was, and still is, a sad comment on politics, which is after all the art and science of people living together, that there was scant room for the admission of conscience.

Judge Hargreaves read my statement aloud in an even voice with no expression and no punctuation. It came over to me as a monotonous string of platitudes with little meaning. My nervous system was jolted into anxious turmoil. I had brought with me three letters of support and, because none of the handwriting was easily read, I had typed copies which were attached. Hargreaves studied them and, when he had worked this out, he leaned towards me and said "These are typed copies — very considerate of you." He read them aloud to the tribunal with much more expression in his voice than he had used for the statement, and asked whether there were any questions. At that moment a court official stepped forward and announced that hostile aircraft were approaching and that the court was to adjourn and take shelter. The court room emptied and, as people moved away, Hargreaves and I were left facing one another. "I think that we can settle this before we go" he said and read out a list, which included agriculture and civilian ambulance work, of alternatives to military service before gathering up his papers and leaving. No questions, no discussion (although the transcript which I received later indicated that there had been); I had not been asked to speak. Bemused, I walked to the door where a commissionaire said that I was free to leave or to shelter as I wished. I was glad to walk out into the misty drizzle. By the time I reached the nearest Underground station the local threat had passed and the station was open.

It was a curiously unsatisfactory experience which matched the "something and nothing" character of the day, an anti-climax, but I have to confess that my feeling at the time was one of relief.

With two other members of the Friends Meeting at Winchmore Hill — Sidney Harrison, who had been my Old Markonian companion, and Alan Green — we applied for training at Spiceland and were accepted for a course starting in mid-January 1941. My employers, who knew of my intentions, gave me leave of absence for "the duration" but they paid me a full month salary for January and this was about enough to pay the very modest training course fees.

The three men decided to save money by cycling down to Devon, but Marjorie, who was no cyclist and had no machine, planned to travel by train. However, pacifist friends of ours offered to lend her a cycle, and we decided to make the final fling of a winter holiday, and to spend a week cycling and youth hostelling our way to Spiceland. Our friends lived at Warlingham, and we spent a hectic and noisy weekend with them. Hectic because we were all intent on making the most of the time we had together — we did not meet again for many years — and noisy because the nearby Keston aerodrome was attacked heavily on both nights.

We set out on a sunny, but very cold, Monday morning and cycled to Ewhurst Green Hostel, where we had first met. It was a relatively short journey so that Marjorie could get used to the cycle and to an unaccustomed form of exercise. The second day was gruelling. A south west wind strengthened against us. The Hampshire Hills were formidable obstacles for a novice; the wind gave no respite on the downhill stretches which offered little in the way of free wheeling — only strenuous pedalling. Four Marks Hill, beyond Alston, was so demanding that strength ebbed away and, by the time we reached New Alresford, our progress was slow indeed. Our goal was the old Water Mill Hostel at Winchester where we had arranged to meet our other two companions; but the weather worsened. Rain turned to sleet, then to snow and it was very dark.

Without much discussion we made our way to the railway station where we were glad to rest and recover in front of a coal fire in the deserted waiting room, until a steam train chuffed in and took us and our bicycles the last seven or so miles to Winchester.

Not surprisingly we were the only hostellers and were allowed to use the women's dormitory — a vast dark chamber with a high roof dimly perceived. Snowflakes were driving through gaps in the roof and settling in calmer air on to the two-tiered bunks. We grabbed extra blankets to make ourselves warm and snug on a bottom bunk where we drifted into deep and undisturbed sleep. We woke the next morning to find the top bunks and the timber floor covered with snow, and there were snowflakes still drifting about in the vault of the timbered roof. We visited the mill again in 1984 and found it still in use as a hostel. We spent some time watching the mill stream as it creamed and bubbled away just as it had done in 1941 when it had provided our washing water.

We met Alan and Sidney at the hostel as arranged, but one of their bikes was giving trouble with a succession of punctures. We spent the third day making frequent soup meals and exploring the refractory tyre until we found the tiny splinter of flint that was causing the trouble.

On Thursday the snow ceased and the sun shone, but the roads were treacherous and reduced in width by piled roadside snow. We were aiming for Sutton Veny Hostel which was listed as still open. Winchester,

Stockbridge, Salisbury — we resisted the temptation to stop at St. Francis — and pressed on to Great Wishford where we chose the unclassed roads on the south bank of the River Wylye. While the sun shone we made good progress and enjoyed the day and the winter landscape; but as the evening closed and the cold strengthened cycling became more difficult. At last we reached the village of Sutton Veny and in pitch dark ran into a stationary unlit military convoy. We all slid into a ditched hedgerow, cushioned by snow, but not soft enough to save Marjorie from a wrenched foot.

We found the hostel after a weary search but found it to be closed. The wardens lived close by and were marvellously helpful. They re-opened the cold building and found straw filled palliases and blankets which made a sort of nest into which all four of us poured fully clothed; but not, I think, before our hosts had contrived a meal because I have no memory of hunger.

Friday provided a hard slog to Taunton — tiring enough for experienced cyclists after the conditions of the previous days, but a more than severe introduction to distance cycling for Marjorie whose total experience was less than a week. Fortunately the wrenched foot gave no trouble after the initial stiffness, and there were many happy and enjoyable moments. We remember riding through Huish Episcopi, partly because of its name and partly because of its Norman arched doorway, but we remember much more a scratch meal eaten outside a shop in Langport. The hastily buttered Marmite rolls are recalled by Marjorie as the most satisfying meal of her life! Our spirits were restored and we found new energy for the remaining miles to Taunton. There we were glad to find a small hotel near the railway station with the promise of a bath, food and a real bed. Marjorie had the bath. Taunton suffered very little bombing during the war, but that night a lone raider dropped a clutch or skein of bombs diagonally across the railway line without doing very much damage. He chose to do it just as Marjorie was stepping into the hot water.

On Saturday morning we took our time over the remaining sixteen miles to Spiceland. There was a slush of melted snow on the roads and it was uphill nearly all the way — gradual at first, but with that steep climb up the Blackdowns at the end. Our "winter holiday" was over.

CHAPTER 10

The First Weekend — Wallpaper

We needed the rest of that weekend to recover. Our main luggage — spare clothing, working clothes, wellington and walking boots — had been despatched by rail in a large wooden chest that I had made for storing camping gear. It was heavy in its own right and, with four people's effects crammed in, it was very heavy. The railway staff decided that the contents were "non-essentials" and could not be delivered, despite the fact that we had paid an extra charge for "carriage home". When John saw the chest at the station he immediately christened it The Sarcophagus — a name which stuck for the rest of its long life. Too heavy for the Austin Ten, the Sarcophagus remained at the station until a farm cart had occasion to go to town, but the railway staff did allow us to open the chest and remove some essential clothing. For a week or two our gear was very limited, and it did not take long to settle our few belongings into our new surroundings.

Marjorie and I had been given a room in the old servants' quarters. It was at the top of a steep narrow stairway leading to the second floor. Generous in size, it had but one small window which faced north, overlooked the backyard, and by a strain on the imagination and of one's neck, offered a view of Exmoor. It was airy, never very light, but it became home and was known affectionately to everyone as The Smithy. Some weeks after we had settled in, a painted name board embracing a genuine horse-shoe came miraculously out of the Construction room and was fastened to our door; like the village smithy it became a place where people met and talked.

It was good to meet again the Semi-perms whom we had got to know the previous May, to meet our fellow trainees — one or two of them we had met in other Quaker surroundings, but most we were meeting for the first time. Saturday afternoon was quiet. Most of those not on rotas for preparing meals or for feeding farm stock walked or cycled to nearby towns; a few retired to the Quiet Room to read or write; others sat in the Common Room before a blazing log fire and listened to the radio, but a small ever-changing group clustered round the long Common Room notice board to read and talk about Wallpaper.

Our arrival coincided with the first issue of Wallpaper — a weekly magazine of one copy only which graced a specially prepared notice board spanning most of one wall of the Common Room. It was the brain child of Tony Hyndman, a former secretary to the poet Stephen Spender, and a one-time member of the International Brigade which had fought in the Spanish Civil War. During the campaign he had seen wall magazines of this type used effectively to give information, to provide a vehicle for self-expression and for the exploration of ideas and ideals. His war experience brought him to a realisation of the futility of it all, and he became a pacifist. A moving and vivid description of how this change of heart and mind came to a head in the heat of battle, and of the actions which followed appeared, unsigned, in a later edition of Wallpaper.

The Editorial Board was composed of all those interested residents who cared to meet on Friday evenings for the purpose of discussing policy. An editor was appointed who was given carte blanche for one edition. The current Wallpaper was displayed for all to see, read and talk about for one week only, after which it was unpinned, gathered together, put in a folder and placed in the library. Dressed in motley it was presented on assorted size and quality of paper, hand-written or typed, with original drawings in pen and ink or crayon. Sometimes when the skills were available the presentation was elaborate and artistic, at other times it was plain. The content ranged from the very serious to the outrageously comic, from the reverent to the irreverent; much of it centred round the strange new life into which we had plunged, but always there were attempts to relate what was going on at Spiceland to what was going on in the world outside and to establish a relevance to what we were doing.

The group who produced the early editions were literary birds. In addition to Tony Hyndman there were Clive Sansom, a poet, a lecturer in English Studies and a speech therapist, his wife Ruth who was also a writer, Tim Evens, Jonathan Field and many others with writing skills and imagination. They set a standard to which all later editions were compared.

One early contributor was Reginald Reynolds, author, friend of Gandhi and in every way an original. Towards the end of his time as a trainee he fell from his bicycle in the dark hours of a winter morning while trying to avoid running down a farm worker. He broke his thigh and wrote to Wallpaper from a hospital bed. Reg had had something of a feud with the village Special Constable Schwind, who had earlier reported him for riding a bicycle without lights. From that incident he had elected to serve a prison sentence of one week in lieu of paying a fine — for the "experience". In this later episode, Reg had mistaken the farm worker for Schwind, and had called out to him by name. This case of mistaken identity led to a police enquiry to establish whether the attempt to avoid had in reality been an attempt to run down the Special. Reg recounts these and other incidents of his time at Spiceland, with a wealth of interesting detail, in his book "My Life And Crimes" published in 1956.

Reg Reynold's wife, Ethel Mannin, was staying at a nearby farm where she kept open house for Spicelanders with literary interests. She also sent contributions to help the infant magazine on its way, and inspired Tim Evens to write the first of many Spiceland Clerihews:

"Ethel has no man in
He's gone with a van in —
To Exeter
To see a legsetter."

Reading the magazines nearly fifty years on is an experience in itself and the interests and character of an ever-changing Spiceland population are recorded in their pages. Here are the early writings of some who were to become university professors, lecturers, engineers, nurses, probation officers, teachers, doctors, clerks, bookkeepers, carpenters .... For some, writing was their joy or their trade, others found writing an unaccustomed chore. They all responded nobly to the appeals, demands and threats of a succession of editors. At times the muse weakened and Editors were haunted by that first editorial with its hypnotic suggestion that the success or failure of Spiceland itself was somehow bound up with the success or failure of Wallpaper.

It was not and could not be so. For the first nine months of Spiceland history there was no Wallpaper, but the extraordinary fellowship which developed was rooted in those months. Wallpaper was one of the fruits of corporate life but not its life blood. Wallpaper, all one hundred and five of its uninterrupted editions, is a preserved commentary, like the files of other newspapers. Browsing through its pages has quickened and corrected my own imperfect memory, and has provided entertainment and enlightenment.

Perhaps the mixing of the intellectual and artistic aspirations with the physical and practical skills which we shared freely with one another, prevented intellectual snobbery and its counterpart from ever becoming serious factors. We were so dependent on one another for nearly everything, and recognition of this brought us together in a way which was never an end in itself.

At one evening discussion an Oxford Classics scholar asserted that no one had really lived unless he or she had read Agamemnon in the original Greek. He meant it. Neither reason nor laughter moved him. For others it might be "The way of an eagle in the air" (or on the Blackdown Hills more likely the way of a buzzard!) We were able to acknowledge the values of others without conceding the values which held good for ourselves. This was true for members of many Christian denominations, for agnostics and atheists who all gathered together under a Quaker umbrella.

Occasionally the status of Wallpaper was challenged in letters to the Editor. Sometimes the fun and the parody were challenged by serious philosophical and religious articles. Verse was offset by worse. Letters came from Spicelanders away from home. There were articles about Spiceland "happenings", pre-war occupations and post-war aspirations. And, of course, there were over one hundred editorials written by over one hundred editors — Fleet Street could never have achieved such quality with such mobility in the Editorial Chair.

I have compiled a specimen Wallpaper selected from hundreds of pages as an appendix to this book. Choice is nearly always invidious, but will not, in this case, excite envy nor ill will. The best is almost certainly buried in the carefully preserved, often tattered and pin-holed, sheets of paper which were once spread across the Common Room wall.

'The Sarcophagus': Railway platform, Cullompton, Devon

CHAPTER 11

A Month on the Farm

The names of those forming the work groups for each week, together with the names of the evening and weekend work rotas, were posted on the main notice board on Sunday evenings. As our first Sunday drew to a close we made our way with others to learn our fate, but were waylaid by farmer Hugh Flatt who, with his shoulders hunched against the cold of the unheated hall, asked us whether we were prepared to reverse the usual order of training and start our three months with a month on the farm. The Semi-perms had argued, he said, that as we had cycled all that way in all that weather we must be tougher than some and better able to weather the bleak winter weather than most. We could only make one answer and reported for farm duties at 8 o'clock on the following morning.

Since our working holiday in May 1940 the farm had been extended in area by the addition of the forty acres rented from Mr. Hillier who was the owner of a secondhand goods and antique shop in Cullompton. The War Agricultural Committee were anxious to see the land improved, and had ordered that one field should be ploughed up and planted with potatoes, another should be improved by draining, another ploughed for market garden crops, that thistles and ragwort should be controlled and that the hedges and banks should be put in better order. In addition one of the steeper parts of Spiceland's own land — too steep for machine or horse cultivation — should be dug by hand and planted with market garden crops. There was a thinly veiled threat that this exercise would do the conchies good.

The whole eighty-odd acres formed an interesting geological study. The fields sloped steeply down from the Blackdown spur towards the River Culm valley. The soil at the top was Upper Greensand. Black in colour, belying its name, it was easy to work despite being full of stones — some of them quite large — and proved to be very fertile. The black soil presumably gave Blackborough village its name, and in times past good quality whetstone had been quarried from the steep side of Blackborough Beacon. The stones in the field had similar properties, and steadily sharpened the plough shares as they cut through the ground, so that they quickly wore out and had to be replaced.

As the fields fell away towards the valley the colour and the character of the soil changed through varying shades of brown and red, and to belts of marl and clay. The result was a patchwork of small fields, irregular in shape, and with a wide variety of plant life. The marls and clays were also fertile but were difficult to cultivate, partly because of the multi-sloped steepness of the fields, and partly because the soils had to be caught at just the right time if they were to be broken into manageable condition before the furrow slices set into lumps as intractable as fired bricks.

The field to be dug by hand was one such heavy marl, but it presented problems beyond just digging. Ordinary spades and forks broke quickly in the appallingly wet and heavy conditions of that winter, but Charles Bubb, a trainee with experience of how market gardeners dealt with the heavy land of his native Worcestershire, remembered a tool local to his home county which was used specially to dig heavy pasture land before use as market garden ground. Known as the two-tine fork, it was a very strong tool with two steel prongs much thicker, flatter and tougher than those of the best quality garden fork, and set about eight inches apart. With one of these forks, great clods of turf could be prised loose, and in wet conditions, con-

siderable strength was called for to lift and turn the sod over. Hugh's idea, a good one, was to dig the field in the depth of winter and to hope that frost and wind would do the rest.

The field was quickly named the Two-tine Field and two-tining was an occupation to be remembered for the rest of one's life. My first days were spent two-tining. The day's work started in dismal darkness; snow and slush had turned the field into a quagmire, and we slipped ever further into the mud as we shifted weight from one leg to the other. Those digging in wellington boots quite often found themselves balancing, or failing to balance, on one leg while trying to retrieve a boot which had parted from them by suction. We dug in a cheerful sort of misery which eased with the coming of light — a light which revealed a curious mix of digging styles.

One man dug in a circle round the little island on which he stood only to be confronted with what to do with the undug island before he floundered to a new pitch. The purists tried to dig in straight lines, but found that the uneven size of clod produced by the two-tine system gave little help and small satisfaction. Most dug pragmatically and got some satisfaction from looking at a choppy sea of clods stretching up hill before them. The decision to dig by turning the clods up hill was made to frustrate the law of gravity which tends to move the top soil from the top of the field to the bottom. The field was dug thoroughly, and the hard winter did its job and shattered the clods into a reasonable tilth. In the fulness of time there were good cabbages, cauliflowers, peas and beans. Sadly by that time most of the two-tiners had moved to fresh woods and pastures new, and they did not see nor taste the fruits of their labours.

During our second week I was introduced to the "working out" scheme — an arrangement made with local farmers which gave trainees opportunities for a wider experience of farm work under commercial conditions than could be provided at Spiceland. It also promoted working relations as well as social contact with our neighbours. Although some farmers maintained a hostility to conchie labour, others, despite their doubts about the usefulness of townee labour, were glad of extra help. They often drove hard bargains about rates of pay — the County rate of pay for a skilled adult farm worker was only twenty-eight shillings a week — but then they had to take the rough with the smooth. Payment was not made to an individual but to Spiceland, and the money was paid into the Spiceland Pool administered by John for the benefit of C.Os with small or no resources.

No trainee was pressured to take part in this scheme, but when Hugh told me how it worked I was more than willing to see how Devon farming compared with my boyhood experience of farming in Berkshire, and to find out whether the boy who had worked for fun had learned enough and grown strong enough to survive.

At 7.30 am on a late January morning I collected a packed lunch from the kitchen and walked the mile and a half to Bodmiscombe Wood Farm to meet Roland Wood. It was still pitch dark when I arrived at the farmyard and found the half opened door of the cow shed — ill lit by a partially blacked out hurricane lamp. Roland was tucked into the flank of a cow, and I could hear the steady streams of milk hissing into the pail. I entered the shed and said that I was from Spiceland. "You 'm better wait till I be finished y'ere." I waited. When he had finished milking that cow he emptied the milk through a straining cloth into a churn and made towards another cow. With some nervousness I said that I could milk, and he looked up at me with unbelieving eyes. I am only five foot six inches in height, but he was shorter than me and his back was bent. Slowly he straightened and reached for a bucket from a rack on the shed wall. He pointed down the byre to a shadowy animal and handed me the bucket. "Do 'ee try that'n one." I found another bucket containing water and a cloth and washed the cow's udder before taking a three legged stool from a rack. I settled the milking pail at an angle between my legs, eased my head into the cow's flank and applied myself to a job which I had only attempted once since my last school holiday in 1929.

She was not a heavy milker — no farmer would have risked one of his better cows on an untried stranger — but, slowly at first, the rhythm came back to me with about a gallon of milk which I showed questioningly to Roland. He gave me a surprised nod and pointed towards another cow — a better yield from that one. No conversation — grunts and nods and a smile or two, a shifting of positions, milk frothing into pails and filtering into churns, and the job was done. There were about fifteen milking cows and I had milked about four of them. It was getting light when we rolled the churns out into the yard and dumped them into a trough with water running in from a tap and the overflow disappearing into the farm drain. It was the only cooling system.

Roland beckoned me to follow him into the house — still dark with drawn blackout curtains and dimly lit by an oil lamp. Mrs. Wood, Cicely, was cooking breakfast, and the smell of frying bacon mingled with the aroma from the wood fire. Mrs. Wood remarked that we were early, and Roland said "We 've gotten a bit o' help." Roland asked me whether I had brought some food. I produced my packet and unwrapped three enormous doorstep sandwiches — two were filled with sardine and the other with jam.

I was a little taken aback by the sight of them, but Roland was staggered. "You cain't do what I want for you to do on that." He turned to his wife and said "Mother do you put suthing more in ther." He pointed to the pan, and soon we were sitting down to a meal of home cured bacon, fatter than anything I had eaten previously, eggs and fried sliced potato.

Towards the end of the meal something stirred in a corner of the room and Roland left the table and hurried across to a well curtained cot which contained their young son who was gurgling into wakefulness. "Michael, Michael," he said softly and pushed his fingers into the stirring bundle as he looked down at him. He turned to me and said "Six months thereabouts" and added "if he were a heifer he'd be nearly fully growed." Which told me more about Roland than it did about young Michael.

Mrs Wood had said nothing, but now she gathered up her young son and cradled him in her arms and made gentle murmurings as she did so. Roland returned to the table and his meal, but was quickly on his feet again and ready for work. I followed him out into the yard and an unusually dry winter day.

We first harnessed a horse to a tumbril, and took the full churns of milk along a farm track to an adjoining farm where we lifted them on to a shared wooden platform to await collection by the dairy company's lorry. A family group from this farm watched the operation and looked at me curiously. They shouted a greeting to Roland, but he hardly paused before loading some empty churns on to the cart to take back to his farm.

On the way back Roland commented that I had handled churns before. The churns in use in 1941 were dumpy in shape and held ten gallons. A nearly full churn weighed about a hundredweight. The churns of my boyhood were tapered from a broad base and held thirteen gallons, while the special brass finished churns with domed lids which stood imposingly in the chariot-like two wheeled floats which were used to deliver the milk in Reading, held seventeen gallons. There is a method, which becomes a knack, of balancing, rolling and lifting churns which I had watched, and with the farmer's sons, had tried to emulate years ago. Men who had the knack made the job look easy, but without it there could be a price to pay in spilled milk to say nothing of physical damage. Ten gallon churns were easier than I had remembered.

The main job of the day — and the one which paid for my breakfast — was to spread basic slag on pasture land. Basic slag is a by-product of steel manufacture, and contains potassium and calcium carbonate. The potassium is dissolved by acids in the soil and made slowly available to plants. It encourages the growth of clover and some say that it is as good, or better, than sowing clover seeds. The properties of basic slag were less important to me than its texture. It is ground to a very fine powder and is so dense that a relatively small sack weighs a hundredweight. We spread it from a horse drawn drill and I cannot now remember how many tons we spread nor how many acres we covered. We loaded the tumbril with the stuff and carted it to the field, switched the horse from cart to spreader and filled the hopper. Roland led the horse while I walked behind in a cloud of fine purple dust and made sure that the hopper did not clog nor run out half way across the field. Then back to the barn for another load, and on with the spreading.

At mid-day, every working day, a stone quarry at Burlescombe about five miles away, fired its blasting shots and the noise of the explosions was used by farmers in the fields as a time signal. It was known as hearing "the rocks." We had just started spreading one load when "the rocks" went off. "We didn't hear they rocks did us?" said Roland, and on we went. When we eventually returned to the farm for lunch I was covered from head to foot in a fine purple grey dust. It was in my hair, it rimmed my eyes, my boots were full of it and my watch — shock and dust proof according to the maker — had stopped. We washed in a bucket in the open yard. Roland was nothing like as covered as I was — leading the horse was an altogether cleaner operation than looking after the spreader.

It was well into the afternoon. Mrs. Wood was cross but gentle. She knew her husband, and knew that it was no good quarrelling with his priorities. In fact over many years I never saw her show anger, although more than once I saw her near to tears. She clearly did not believe that we had not heard "the rocks", but she quietly produced a meal from her range oven. My sandwiches were banished to the pig bucket, and I shared the farm table.

Then it was back to the slag until the job was finished and dark had descended upon us. I walked back through the shadows to Spiceland, and to a hot shower which few farmers, and no farm workers could have enjoyed at that time. Someone once said that farming is a series of unpleasant jobs that taken together make a satisfying life. There must be something in it because I was strangely and unaccountably happy at the end of that day.

I never worked for Roland again, but we had become friends. His progress from a cottager with one pig to successful farmer would provide the basis for a book in its own right. He had little formal education and reckoned his worth in terms of his animals rather than money. We remained friends, and kept in touch until both he and Cicely died in the 1970s.

My next assignment was a total failure. It was at the farm where

Roland shared a milk stand. Farmer Kelland was not much over forty but he had the appearance of an old man and, though I did not know it then, both he and his wife were slowly dying of tuberculosis. A fourteen year old son was ill equipped to take control, and there were younger children including very young twins who belied the general situation and looked pictures of health. When I arrived the whole family was huddled round a fire in a dark miserable kitchen and eating breakfast off plates balanced on their knees. Two high backed settles flanked the large open hearth — they were not comfortable, but they provided shelter from the wind when the farmhouse door was open. I was sent out with the teenage son to "do the hedge" and "nostle the binds". I had no idea what this meant and the boy could not really explain it to me.

There are many different methods and styles of making and maintaining hedges. Local customs become local traditions. Devon hedges, mostly of hazel and hawthorn, but sometimes of beech, with other species like oak, hedge maple, even willow muscling in to make an interesting botanical mix, are grown on the tops of banks. Periodically the top and side wood is cut back and cleared, leaving a residue of selected saplings to form the basis of a renewed hedge. The saplings are pleached — that is the trunks are partly sliced along the line of growth with a billhook or an axe — and bent over, layered, to form a living fence. New growth from the stools of the old hedge eventually makes a vigorous new hedge. The layered sapling stems are weighted down and held in place by turves cut from a strip of field at the base of the bank, and cast to the top of the bank with the aid of a three cornered spade mounted on a long curved handle and known as a sho'el — sometimes a Cornish Sho'el. Holes and gaps in the bank are made good by shovelling in soil held in place by more turves rammed in like bricks. The bank is trimmed by using the sharp edges of the sho'el as a cutting tool so that it slopes from a broad base to a narrower top on which the hedge grows.

The surplus wood from this operation is cut into even- sized bundles, called faggots, and each one is bound tightly with a twisted, pliable, first year growth sapling, thong. The thong dries out and tightens its grip and the whole faggot lightens in weight. Faggots were used for a variety of jobs such as making a base for a hay or corn stack, for plugging a gap in a hedge or making a temporary fence, as well as for firing. Making the twisted thong was called "noseling the bind". I knew nothing of all this, and young Kelland was not strong enough nor skilful enough to demonstrate the twisting process. Neither was he articulate enough to explain it. We spent a miserable and unprofitable day with little to show for it but my blistered palms, and a large quantity of unbound faggots which blew apart in a blustery wind.

After this hedging fiasco I returned to work on the Spiceland farm for the remainder of the training month. There was a lot of two-tining, and a spell of more orthodox digging in the garden grounds. A couple of days carting hay from a Craddock farm, some dung carting and spreading, a day spent sowing broad bean seed in the market garden, and another in digging a passage through a hedge bank to make a pig paddock in a small copse, added some variety; to which the weather added its own share with heavy rain and deep falls of snow separated by days of frost and sunshine.

On walks round the lanes I looked at the hedges with new respect. The local rabbit trapper and two sons lived in a cottage near the church, and I noticed that they had a large stack of faggots in their yard. It took some weeks to pluck up enough courage, or cheek, to ask one of them if he would teach me how to "nostle the bind." He roared with laughter and let me know in a broad aside that he, and probably most of the village, knew about my discomforture at Kelland's. But he did promise to show me how it was done, and one day turned aside from checking his traps to teach me.

Cutting the wood symmetrically to make the even bundles is easily mastered once you have learned to use a sharp billhook, and learned the essential safety technique of always cutting directionally away from your body and from the hand grasping the branches which are to be faggotted. It is selecting, twisting and binding the thong which is difficult. Long slim shoots of new growth hazel about three quarters of an inch thick at the butt end are the best, but willow or even beech will serve. Holding the butt end in one hand you lay the slender end on the ground and trap it with your foot about a foot or eighteen inches from the tip. You then twist at the butt end until the fibres of the stem under your boot separate, spread, and become malleable. Release this, bend it back on itself to form a loop, and secure the loop by twisting the bent stem round itself. Pass the thong under and round the waist of the faggot, thrust the butt end through the loop and pull the thong as tight as you can — using your boot to steady and hold the bundle under control. Some finger and hand strength is now required to force the butt end under the circling thong before tucking it into the bundle to finish the job.

Success is partly a matter of hand and finger strength, partly judgement about how far to twist the fibres to make them malleable without twisting so hard that the fibres break altogether, but essentially it is a matter of application and practice. I broke a lot of thongs and made a few blisters on my hands before Trapper Wright was satisfied with his pupil, and I was willing to risk a public performance; but, once mastered, the job takes less time to do than to describe.

The working out scheme did much to help local people to understand Spiceland, and enabled Spicelanders to meet and get to know local people. Not all the farmers were friendly; some of them were mean exploiters, not just of trainees, but of workers generally. Most of the farms were small. The work was done mainly by the farmer and his family who worked very hard themselves, and expected as much from anyone who had to be paid.

They had known very hard times during the depression, when they were exploited by the large dairy companies who bought milk cheaply at the farm gate to retail in the cities or process at factories. Cheap rail and road transport opened up the west country farmers to this entrepreneurial activity which changed much of the farmers' traditional practice, but brought about a dependancy on the dairy companies which had been absent before. The monthly milk cheque was a godsend, but it was sometimes a mixed blessing. More than one farmer told me of the days when the price of milk at the farm gate was lowered without warning and they were placed in a take it or leave it situation. The Milk Marketing Board, set up in 1934, did much to halt the exploitation, and to regulate the production and distribution of milk. It was not altogether surprising that the friendly west country farmer was often a hard man to reckon with.

Towards the end of my farm training month Hugh introduced me to Tinkers Orchard where we tackled a wilderness of brambles and some old and fallen fruit trees. The work and the situation had a profound effect on me, because Tinkers Orchard became an almost symbolic representation of farming at Spiceland.

CHAPTER 12

Walking the Farm

I have already indicated that Tinkers Orchard was something special for me. It lay in a secluded hollow and was bounded on two sides by some fine trees in a neglected copse, and on the other two sides by a neglected overgrown hedge. It was sheltered and warm when most of Spiceland's fields were exposed and cold. Green woodpeckers lived in the copse and I have watched nuthatch, tree creeper and fly catcher feeding at one time or another. Part of its appeal lay in the fact that I had more than once walked down Mendham's Lane without being aware of its existence. When Hugh took me there in that last training week Tinkers came as a surprise.

The fruit trees were very old and in various states of fallen decay. The whole area was overgrown with thick and vigorous brambles which spilled out from the hedges and embraced the fallen trees with murderous tentacles. For years it had been an uncontrolled free range for poultry and was a reservoir of fertility which could only be tapped for a price to be paid in hard labour. The two of us started hacking at brambles with slashers and bill-hooks until enough clearance had been made to use a bigger team. Then the trees were attacked in earnest with crosscut saws, and we learned the truth of the old country saying that wood warms you three times — once when you cut it down, once when you cut it up and once again when you burn it. The Common and Quiet Room fires gave comforting aromatic warmth as the old apple logs burned long and brightly. Surprisingly large craters had to be dug round the tree stumps before the roots could be cut and the boles levered out with the help of mattocks, crowbars and sweat. The bramble roots were almost as difficult as the trees. There were more of them and they were murderously armed and tangled. Moreover, small pieces left in the ground waited for spring and then pushed into vigorous tenacious life once more.

Although our month on the farm had weatherwise been harsh we had enjoyed it in our different ways. Marjorie had discovered latent interest and ability to deal with livestock and had spent most of her month in the farmyard — cleaning, feeding and caring for cows and pigs, and tending the poultry runs out on the pastures. It had been an altogether new and exciting experience for her. Although it was still February, the prospect of spring gave a little edge to the thought that the next two months would be spent mainly indoors on household, cooking, and construction work with the first week in the laundry of which we had heard horrendous, but probably apocryphal tales. The posting of the next week's work list on Sunday evening would be of special interest, but in the meantime we were happily on the weekend farm rota.

On Sunday morning we fed the stock, cleaned the cowsheds and pigsties, and were surveying the scene when Hugh asked us if we would like to "walk the farm" with him and Rudi. The farm walk was, and probably is, a traditional occupation for farmers — especially those who keep the Sabbath and consider that no good can come of work performed on that day. It enables a calm and critical assessment to be made of what needs to be done and it can be dismissed as "not real work".

We had not yet seen the whole of the Forty Acres. The short winter days had been full of work with no daylight left for exploration. Saturday afternoons and Sundays, if not on rotas, were filled with personal chores — making mending and altering, letters home, looking after the Smithy and sharing time and experience with other trainees including one shopping visit to Honiton. We jumped at the invitation.

As we walked Hugh and Rudi talked about the future, and we realised that for Rudi this was a valedictory walk. The government had decided to extend the policy of internment and Rudi, Johnny and Karl — the last remaining Carclew refugees — were to leave us for a camp "Somewhere".

We walked to the highest part of the farm, Blackborough Beacon — Mardle Pen on old maps — from which we enjoyed the distant views from southeast to northwest. The south face of the Beacon is nearly sheer and had been the site of the whetstone quarry, but brambles and gorse bushes covered the scars. The Beacon itself was crowned with a group of undistinguished trees which crowded together and made a landmark which could be identified from miles away. The north slopes were poor pasture infested with thistles and ragwort which, when in flower with the gorse, provided a scene of wild beauty — appreciated by artists and naturalists but not by farmers.

At the foot of the Beacon was a pasture field, soggy and overgrown with rushes. This was the field to be drained and some of the herringbone of trenches which were to hold the tile drain pipes had already been dug. Of course it was named the Drainage Field. Charles Bubb, who had introduced the two-tine fork, had also designed the drainage pattern of pipes which would carry the surplus water down to an uncertain stream which which ran by the boundary hedge. At the gateway to the field was a copse which had grown over the foundations of an estate cottage which had been demolished many years ago. Even so clumps of stinging nettles, some persistent degenerate raspberry canes and a gooseberry bush were indications of long ago human habitation. As we inspected the still open trenches Hugh told us that Charles Bubb, who was shortly to marry another Spicelander, Mary Quick, and they had bought a smallholding at Dunkeswell. This drainage job would be his last for Spiceland.

To the right of the Drainage Field three more small fields, Top, Middle and Bottom Path Fields — so called because an ancient right of way passed through them — stretched down to Mendham's Lane. Burma Road, the old disused and overgrown coach road, bordered these fields and, as more and more of it was cleared and dried out, it was more often used than the path.

The War Agricultural Committee had ordered that the Middle Path Field be ploughed up and planted with potatoes. This field marked the end of the Greensand and the beginning of the heavy Keuper Marl. On the house side of the Burma Road were a Greensand Tillage Field, another rough pasture field of uneven terrain interspersed with clumps of brambles and gorse bushes which gave an appearance of open moorland, and Big Field — all eleven acres of it — stretching from the Drive down to Tinkers Orchard.

It was still February filldyke — cold and wet. The climb to the top of the Beacon had been exhilarating, and the spread out map of the farm studied from that vantage point full of interest. We listened to the discussion about future plans, but we only partially understood what it was all about. Our chief delight was in the wild beauty of the place with its views stretching far beyond the farm to Woodberry Down, the Exe Valley, Exmoor and the Quantock Hills — a panorama to rank with some that are much better known, more often photographed and painted. The progress home across the fields was altogether different — muddy and treacherous, especially in gateways, the downhill walk was in places a downhill slide and there was a fair bit of personal cleaning up to do when we reached the farmyard.

It was in the farmyard that we began to realise that the Sabbath Day Walk had greater significance for us than just a friendly gesture at the end of our farm month. Rudi and Charles were leaving, a new gardener had been engaged but would not be free to come for some weeks, spring cultivations and planting would hopefully soon be under way, trainees had to be instructed and supervised — they had to be given as wide a variety of jobs as possible and could not, must not, be treated as the cheap labour that many thought them to be. Hugh could not be everywhere on the farm and in the gardens at the same time. Animals, especially the cattle and the horses, needed careful tending and handling. We were cleaning the mud off the brushes when Hugh posed the question. Would we consider deferring the remaining two months of our training course and work on the farm until the spring rush was over?

I loved farm work; but I had said many times that I would not consider agriculture as an alternative to military service because I would feel unhappy and uncomfortable about doing something that I had always wanted to do as a direct consequence of my objection to war. To Marjorie farming had come as a completely new experience, but she had developed a keen interest in stock feeding and had discovered an absolute flair for understanding and handling animals.

Spiceland at that time was experiencing its strongest ever demand for workers in hospitals, for the care of young and old in the projects which were being developed by Friends Relief Service, and in many other worthwhile and necessary activities. But there was also a plentiful supply of trainees who were anxious to take up such work. It was only a postponement that we were asked to consider, and the farm walk had shown us just how much there was to do at Spiceland. We already knew that very few trainees actually relished doing farm work as an end in itself, although most of them welcomed their month training as an essential muscle building and hardening exercise. Edwin Smart, Marjorie and I were exceptions in that we actually liked farming, and found a deep satisfaction in the work. That evening we agreed to cover the spring work. I became the spare hand — relief milker, occasional carter, but mainly leader of teams of trainees in clearing and cleaning the hedges as an aid to cultivation. Marjorie became "Food and Pigs" — guardian of the farmyard and the rations, improviser, mucker out, animal carer and Hugh's eyes and ears in such matters.

I have already written about the Devon hedge and bank; but in those days I was woefully ignorant about how to set about them. Cutting back the spreading branches and fallen trees to the bank line was hard physical work and simple to plan. What to do with the decayed bank, which trees to cut out altogether and which to leave, which saplings to pleach and bind in for the future hedge — these things were an altogether different matter, outside even Hugh's experience. For some unknown reason we did not get the local advice which would have enabled us to do a better and more economical job, and have saved many future difficulties. The improvements were obvious enough, and the work with axes, billhooks, slashers and sickles was immensely satisfying to me and to the gangs of cheerful trainees who worked with a will at their unaccustomed trade. Welcome supplies of logs for the fires were carted home, large fires of brushwood carefully extinguished by blackout time, gave primitive enjoyment, and heaps of precious wood ash were taken to the garden.

The main effort was concentrated in the Middle Path Field which was to be tractor ploughed in preparation for a potato crop. The field was very steep, particularly so at one bottom corner, and more than one farmer turned down the job because turning a wheeled tractor on such slopes was deemed too risky. One farmer came to survey the job on a Sunday morning.

He shook his head as he eyed the sideling knap before stating quite emphatically that only a caterpillar tractor could work safely. He looked at our hedge work and made approving comments on the clearance, but also asked Hugh, who passed the question to me, why we had left some bushes growing out of the banks. When I replied that they would form the future hedge he just smiled. I am sure that if we had asked him what we should be at, he would have told us. Devon farmers rarely offer advice before it is requested. If he had said that the bank should be sloped and clean, and that the hedge should be growing on top of the bank, we would have learned something important. Years of agricultural neglect had ensured that there were very few well managed hedges in our part of the County at that time; it was long before observation and, eventually, demonstration, taught us what we ought to have done.

Quite apart from their inefficiency as boundaries and animal barriers, the neglected hedges presented another serious and costly problem — they were rabbit warrens alive with furry creatures which ate our crops. Repaired banks and filled rabbit burrows would have made life more difficult for these predators, but, even more helpful, would have revealed tell-tale new workings. The rabbit-catching Wrights held the rabbit catching rights. It was not in the family interest to reduce drastically the colonies which ensured their livelihood and supplied unrationed meat to wartime rationed Britain. With our untutored help they were able to husband the rabbit crop and, when one of them taught me how to "nostle the bind" and make faggots, he said nothing at all about hedges and banks. Why should he?

The rabbits also presented a continuing and never resolved moral problem. Rabbits were a serious threat to food production which was acknowledged by vegetarians and meat eaters alike. Trapping was carried on by the use of a very cruel trap — the gin — which had savage toothed, spring-operated, jaws which caught the animal, as often as not by a leg, but failed to kill it outright. One of the Spiceland cats — a magnificent ginger tom named Pentecost — who was himself a notable rabbit catcher, was twice rescued from gin traps; each time with a different broken leg. Devoted nursing saved him the first time, but on the second occasion he was severely mangled and was put to sleep. Whether it is a loved cat or a rabbit, the suffering is there. Spicelanders were never directly responsible for setting gin traps, but "he who does a thing by another, doeth it himself." We were never free from guilty feelings about rabbits, but the enormous damage they did to growing crops made an uneasy equation. I was sometimes ashamed of myself when I thought about the eagerness with which I pursued the beasts as they scuttled from a corn crop when the reaper and binder had remorselessly reduced the area of cover.

Hedging is a winter job which must stop when the sap rises and the spring work takes over. Our late start made a shorter season than we needed to make the impact we would have wished, but, almost without realising that the change from winter to spring had been made, we were caught up in broader issues. Days of hard physical toil were followed by hours of discussion with Hugh — often conducted in precarious comfort on one or other of our beds.

A feature of the farm training month was the evening series of farm lectures about basic farming theory and practice. To keep tired trainees from premature slumber Hugh enlivened his presentation with vivid word pictures of success or calamity, and many of the well used phrases became part of Spiceland vocabulary. Animals were always "my pretty horse, cow, chicken, pig.......... the sad putting down of a terminally sick animal was euphemistically described as being done to "save its life". In consequence many another unrelated but necessary action was carried out to "save its life". A "one-way-plough" was so called because "it could cast a furrow both ways". Attention was secured by a loud introductory "Hello" addressed to people, animals and inanimate objects alike. "Hello spade" would secure the surrender of that tool so that its proper use could be demonstrated; at meal times "Hello salt" or "Hello jug" would ensure that salt or jug passed along the table.

But the lectures had a serious content and, with greater involvement, Marjorie and I began to relate what we had heard to what was being done, or not being done, on the farm. We asked a lot of questions.

Spiceland farmyard

CHAPTER 13

Food and Pigs

Feeding stock in war time was not easy, especially for a farm starting from scratch with no stocks of home-grown feeding stuffs. In the beginning foodstuffs like oats, maize, cattle cake and the like were obtainable from hay and corn merchants — if one had the money. But gradually, as with rations for people, rations for animals were introduced, and they were based on past history. Farmers were rightly expected to grow their own basic requirements, and were then allowed to buy further supplies based on production performance.

We were permitted to buy oats for our working horses, a small quantity of cattle food for our small number of cows, some barley meal for the pigs, and some basic rations for our few ducks and hens. Hay and straw, which were unrationed, we bought on the open market from any neighbours who had a surplus.

Rationing began to bite hard in early 1941 just as we joined the farm staff, and under Hugh's tutelage, feeding the stock and husbanding the rations became Marjorie's special care. This collection of farm tasks had been known from the beginning as "Food and Pigs", and to the trainees Marjorie herself became known as "Food and Pigs".

Most trainees spent one week on Food and Pigs. On the first day they repaired to the farmyard with a mixture of apprehension and interest which, by the end of the week had changed to surprised satisfaction. Apprehension because few of them had any experience of dealing with the larger animals like cows and breeding sows. Surprised satisfaction because the collection of arduous jobs, many of them messy, and performed quite often in bad weather, proved to be so rewarding.

The first job of the day was to release and feed the chickens. This entailed lugging heavy buckets of water and feeding mash along the muddy farm lane to the Top Field, where the poultry were housed in moveable arks with wired runs attached. The bulky, but not heavy, run was detached from the ark and moved forward to cover a completely new area of ground, before the much heavier ark was lifted and manhandled to this fresh position. When the run had been re-attached to the ark the squawking hens were released.

When fresh water and the mash had been placed in the feeding troughs a few minutes were well spent in watching the birds as they moved eagerly around feeding and scratching the new area of pasture. It is by watching animals when they are well that one learns to detect the telltale differences in behaviour which point to something being wrong.

Moving the arks steadily across the field to a new position each day not only fertilised and improved the field, but also provided a fresh and healthy environment for the birds. The job was pleasant enough in fine weather, but

in the depth of a west country winter the farm road was deep in mud, and the entrance to the field was a quagmire; an old fashioned wooden shoulder-yoke eased the burden of the buckets, but could not prevent, and even exaggerated, their unwieldiness when one slipped in the mud. The occasional inelegant stagger on one leg following the loss of a Wellington boot was slapstick comedy to the beholder but not to the bucket carrier.

A second visit was made in the afternoon to check the water supply, scatter a feed of tail corn, suspend bunches of fresh green cabbage and broccoli leaves for the birds to peck, add variety to their diet and, pleasing reward, to collect any eggs from the nesting boxes. Yet another visit was made at dusk to check that all was well, and to shut the birds in the arks where they could roost safe from any marauding fox.

The small number of ducks, an egg laying strain of the breed Khaki Campbell, had a quite different regime. They laid their eggs in the morning, but when allowed free range they chose such secret places to do so, that to find them was a puzzling and time-consuming operation; moreover, no-one could be sure about the age of the eggs which were found. The ducks were kept in their ark until about nine, or sometimes later, in the morning. Despite the fact that the ark had no window, the ducks were well aware of the morning light, and their restless murmuring activity intrigued and puzzled passers by. When the hatch was at last opened, they tumbled out in a forward rush, dribbling like rugby footballers, some of their eggs with them.

The ducks were economical foragers; spending their days endlessly searching for slugs and other unconsidered trifles. Their sometimes noisy, always ungainly, comical progress round the farm and the approaches to the house, together with their manifest friendliness, made them more than welcome members of the community. Because they had no access to open water, and spent their days on dry land, they were prone to develop small but painful cysts on their webbed feet. Marjorie, distressed by watching the effect of a limp added to a waddle, experimentally and successfully removed one of these cysts with a scalpel, and duck manicure was added to the Food and Pigs job.

One of the quiet "spare time" jobs was to clean all the eggs and pack the surplus into boxes ready for the weekly visit of Lloyd Maunders' van which took them away for retail.

The cows were milked at half past five each morning, and were fed at that time with a concentrate, based on current milk yield, which had been measured and put in readiness the day before by Food and Pigs. After breakfast they were fed again, this time with hay and any turnips, swedes, mangolds or green crop that was available, before being driven to the field for a few hours — even in winter time. Unchaining a large cow, eager to turn quickly on its move to freedom, was an unnerving experience for most trainees. To stand close to the cow's shoulder to release the chain, to experience the frustration by the fumbling brought about by inexperience, to be physically aware of the cow's impatience and the proximity of its twisting horned head, could, until the knack was mastered and the pulse steadied, end in defeat and undignified retreat.

Once clear of the cowshed the cows, especially those with spirited wayward characters, would play up and contrive to snatch a mouthful of forbidden hay, or some other delicacy, stored in the open barn, or would threaten with lowered heads the farm cats — anything to delay being herded down the farm road to a bare pasture. To keep them steadily on the move — milking cows should be sedate and peaceable — shooing them past beckoning gaps, and steering them past unexpected obstacles, is an art form calling for a quiet commanding voice, and the use of raised arms to guide but not to threaten. Excited gesticulation, panic rushes and wild shouts can produce mayhem in no time.

In winter when there was little grass, and after any hay, roots or green fodder which had been scattered around the field had been cleared up, the cows would stand disconsolate at the gate until they were herded back to the shed for the afternoon milking. Fetching them back was usually combined with the afternoon poultry visit to avoid double journeys along the farm road.

Cows establish their own "pecking" order when entering the milking shed and find their own accustomed stalls. It is unprofitable to interfere with the ritual, and unwise to place food in the mangers before all are safely chained — opportunist theft is a considered perk of the pecking order!

Between milkings the cow shed was thoroughly cleaned and disinfected. The dung and soiled bedding straw was cleared from the stalls and gutter, the horse manure from the stables and the soiled straw and pig manure from the sties was added and then heavy barrow-loads of the stuff were pushed to the midden. This was a tax on arm and leg muscles and a severe test of strength and balance as the heavy, awkward, one- wheeled vehicle was steered across the uneven farmyard. The final forward surge to propel the barrow up a wobbly plank and to empty its contents on top of the large steaming bulk of the midden was, all too often, the last disastrous straw.

On bitterly cold winter days to stand on the steaming dung heap and "square" it so that, instead of becoming an inefficient untidy mess, it fulfilled its proper function of converting raw dung and straw into very useful farmyard manure, was a sure and certain means of warming cold feet, and restoring a feeling of wellbeing.

Preparing food for the stock was probably the most important, and mentally demanding, task of the day. Marjorie became very interested in the nutritional requirements of animals and the desired balance of carbohydrates, proteins, vitamins, roughage and the like. Until Spiceland harvested its first crops of oats and dredge corn in the Autumn of 1942, there was never enough of anything to do more than get by. Hugh and Marjorie between them worked out many ingenious ways for overcoming the shortage.

Protecting the precious food store against the ravages of rats and mice was distasteful but necessary. One day Marjorie saw a rat's tail dangling from the beam above her head and instinctively reached up and pulled. The surprised rat came tumbling down on to the floor where Jack Sogan, that week's trainee, quickly and instinctively killed it. There must have been something of great interest to rats above that beam for, shortly afterwards, another tail was dangled temptingly, and another rat despatched. A patient watchful hunt continued throughout the day and a gruesome collection of dead rats was displayed to convince the rest of us of the truth of an unlikely story.

One of the farmyard buildings, known as the boiler house, contained a large copper in which the kitchen waste and any other eatable commodities were cooked and converted into pig pudding. The copper fire had a voracious appetite for fuel, and Food and Pigs trainees chopped up large quantities of small bore wood to keep the fire going while load after load of swill and potatoes were cooked. Marjorie developed unsuspected strength in lifting half hundredweight sacks of raw food on to the copper top before tipping the contents into the cauldron, but suspects that the exercise did her no longterm good.

There were compensations. The accumulation of hot wood ash was used to roast many a tasty potato to relieve the boredom of thickly sliced bread which formed the usual tack ofthe "voore-noons" break.

Once Hugh bought a quantity of substandard potatoes which had been dyed with a purple dye to prevent their sale for human consumption. Some of these were fed raw to the cows as recommended in a leaflet issued by the Ministry of Agriculture. A series of numbered leaflets dealing with a whole range of farming practices was advertised in the farming press and could be obtained free from the Ministry's office at Lytham St. Anne's. We acquired most of them and very interesting and helpful they were: but I do remember chuckling over an Emmett cartoon depicting a gaitered farmer surveying a small haystack standing beside a huge stack of paper with the caption "We got this one from Fiveacre and the other from the Ministry."

The main use for substandard potatoes was as the foundation for a nutritious chicken mash. A large oval cooking pot was filled with spuds and, by arrangement with Jo, was placed overnight in the slow oven of the Esse stove. By morning these were beautifully cooked, and by a protracted hand mixing process, during which some of the precious basic rations and some bran were added, a pleasant crumbly, nearly dry, mash was made and eagerly devoured by the chickens. This tedious operation was welcomed by trainees as handwarming on cold days and because it provided a skin treatment which was cleansing and beneficial.

When a large surplus of broad beans, grown originally for house use, were made sodden by a heavy storm, Food and Pigs spread the rather smelly wet haulms and pods over the corrugated iron rooves of the cow shed and pig sties, turned them as time, opportunity, and sunshine offered, until, after many days, they were dry enough to shell and use as a good high protein animal feed.

Spiceland nearly always had at least one breeding sow, some piglets and some fattening pigs, but seldom was a profit made out of pigs. The pig cycle was the classic Economic example of boom and slump. When pig prices were high, farmers rushed into pig breeding and, because the breeding period is relatively short and sows are prolific breeders, there was soon a surplus of pigs and the prices dropped. Spiceland was not the victim of boom and slump; it was a simple matter of available food. When there were weaned piglets there was rarely enough food to fatten them, and they could not be sold because no one else had surplus food. There were rarely weaners to sell when the demand was good.

However pigs were good training and an excellent means of introducing trainees to the care and management of livestock. Our breeding sows, Martha and Matilda, were Wessex saddlebacks, black in colour, but with a white "saddle" on the shoulders which continued down the forelegs. Wessex are dual-purpose animals and produce good pork or good bacon piglets — dependent on the chosen sire. Ours were mated with a Large White boar belonging to a neighbour and the piglets were white and good baconers. The farmer was a large bluff man of few words, and conservative nature. When Marjorie took Matilda down to Bodmiscombe Farm for a mating, he was very embarrassed and muttered that he did not think it was "a prapper job for a young maid." However, he pocketed the half-crown fee, and Matilda was happily accommodated.

Pigs provide plenty of interest and plenty to do. They are naturally clean, and use a special area of the sty for dung. When they are well, which ours were, they feed eagerly and happily and give pleasure to the pig keeper. Martha and Matilda were large, weighing in at about three-hundred-and-sixty pounds apiece. Many a trainee was knocked sideways while carrying a heavy bucket of food into the sty by a sudden rush from one of these hungry matrons. When they were suckling eight or more piglets the sight of their huge frames stretched across the sty with the eager little suckers frequently changing station at the teats as they pushed and shoved, was a never-failing source of interest to the mainly city-based trainees who, hearing the happy grunts, would call "Milk Bar Open!"

Thirteen acres of our land was coppiced hazel with some oak and a lot of ash trees. Hugh would have liked to let our pigs forage in the wood, and this would have undoubtedly eased some of our feeding problems; but our boundary fences were so bad that the probable damage to neighbours' and our own crops was too great a risk to take. He did make a paddock in the copse but this was not proof against their powerful snouts and could not contain them so we were denied the satisfaction of keeping pigs in a natural forest habitat.

Although kitchen waste and potatoes were the main diet, barley meal, which was more easily prepared and on which they thrived best, was sometimes available and eagerly devoured. On one occasion our baker supplied some condemned wholemeal flour which, on its own, was quite unsuitable. After a number of experimental mixtures ended in failure, bowls of this stuff were added to huge boilings of young stinging nettles and made a very palatable pig pudding.

Financial instability apart, there were other aspects of pig keeping which we found disturbing. Their lives are relatively short, but friendly attachments to them can make parting something more than sweet sorrow. I never liked depriving four week old male piglets of their masculinity — but they speedily recovered from this indignity and the unkind cuts healed quickly after a generous splash of permanganate of potash solution.

Matilda had an unhappy end. She became an increasingly clumsy mother and, despite a protecting farrowing rail in her sty, she crushed eight of her last litter of nine. The survivor grew up and waxed large as befitted a spoiled only child. He heaved himself up on to the half-door of his sty and, with his jowl framed in his fore trotters, surveyed the farmyard in search of food and attention. From this angle there was a perceived likeness, and he was promptly named Winston.

Eventually we were given a license to add Winston to the Spiceland larder and the Kitchen learned a great deal about the use and preservation of pig meat. Our local butcher performed the last rites, and the educational value of his demonstration could not be minimised. However, not only vegetarians were put out by the demise of a familiar animal friend. During the ensuing discussions Hugh, quite rightly, said that we must face up to the consequences of living. While it was one thing for our local butcher to slaughter two or three animals a week; we had so far come into intimate contact with the slaughter of just one; but people who work in abattoirs are asked to spend their working lives in an atmosphere of continuous killing and butchery. With what effect?

Matilda went to market, but her protest was protracted. She maintained her dignity to the last and, by the carefully timed use of her prodigious strength, she broke the side of a wagon, shook herself free from a strong net, leaped out of a moving cart, and returned empress-like to her sty on three occasions before her final submission to the inevitable.

The spring of 1941 was slow in coming and, despite spreading nitrochalk on one of the pasture fields, there was no early bite on our hill side. Our hay was all but exhausted when Hugh was offered a stack of barley straw. The feeding value was not high but it was fresh and clean and smelt sweet. Hungry cows and even the horses ate with avidity and a real crisis was avoided. Cecil Snell, who farmed at the bottom of our hill, had folded sheep on a large field of swedish turnips and there were many partly eaten roots remaining in the ground. He offered them to us; Edwin and Marjorie went down with a horse and cart and, armed with mattocks, dug about in the mud to salvage several acceptable loads of feed which in other circumstances would have been despised and ploughed in. It was late April before the grass on the top pasture was good enough to receive the cows and horses. With what eagerness they scampered through the gateway and with what frenzied joy they kicked up their heels and gambolled when the field was at last opened to them!

Another joy of that spring was Marjorie's introduction to the art of rearing chicks and ducklings by the age-old method of setting fertile eggs under broody hens. Nowadays the lovely old breed names seem to have vanished to be replaced by numbers. Then we talked about Rhode Island Reds, White Wyandottes, Light Sussex, Black Leghorns, Anconas — and each name conjured up some characteristic of importance according to the need to produce eggs in abundance, birds for the table, or a combination of both.

Most of Spiceland's resident birds were Anconas and Black Leghorns. The Black Leghorns were prolific egg layers, but carried little flesh. Their light weight seemed to find echoes in their character — they had difficulty in remaining broody long enough to hatch a clutch of eggs, and were poor featherbrained mothers. The Anconas were little better, but that little made a lot of difference. Hens are at their most prolific during their first season of egg laying and only the best birds are kept on to lay for a second season. In those circumstances it was important to choose breeds which laid well but were then acceptable table birds. Hugh had decided that the breeds to choose were crosses between Rhode Island Red and Light Sussex, and between Rhode Island Red and Silver Wyandotte.

This is not a treatise on poultry breeding but the importance of choosing these breeds was that all were good egg producers and were also meaty. There was another advantage. They were "sex linked" which enabled the male chicks to be distinguished from the female chicks as soon as they were hatched. The female chicks were the colour of the cock and the males the colour of the hen. Hen chicks were altogether more desirable.

Marjorie kept her eyes open for hens which remained in the nesting boxes and were reluctant to come out and feed — early signs that they were going broody. When this happened the hens were removed from the runs and placed in single coops with nests of warm straw to encourage their maternal inclinations. When broodiness was confirmed Hugh cycled off to poultry breeding farms to buy clutches of fertile eggs of the chosen breeds. Rhode and Light Sussex he secured but had to be content with a less obvious sex linkage of Rhode and White Wyandotte for his second choice.

The copse at the bottom of the front kitchen garden was chosen as the quiet haven for the breeding pens and here, away from the general bustle which was Spiceland's life, the coops were placed in secluded clearings and the precious eggs were set under the chosen hens. More adventurously, Hugh had also purchased some clutches of fertile Khaki Campbell duck eggs — the breed of which we already had a small number. Adventurous because the incubation period for ducks is twenty-eight days in contrast to the twenty-one days for chickens, and this sorely tried the patience of our unpredictable mums.

The daily visits to feed and water the hens, and encourage them to spend only a short time off the nest, were fraught with an anxiety which was not allayed when reluctant Black Leghorns scurried off to perch on low bushes where they cackled protestingly, and was only eased when the hens were safely coaxed back to their nests and had tucked the eggs back under their feathered rumps. The presence of a curious trainee and the consequent muted whispered conversation, was both a delighted sharing and another source of anxiety. Successful hatchings rewarded the weeks of care; the chicks and ducklings were brought in due time with their mums to rearing pens erected on the piece of ground near the back door which was sheltered by the holm oak tree. Here they provided a happy rural spectacle of never-failing interest. To recall the tender care given to these small creatures, to remember the patient chopping of young clover leaves to blend with the chicks mash feed, and to compare these memories with pictures recently shown on our television screens of hundreds of day old chicks tumbling through a sorting machine.........

Hugh's father, Cecil Flatt, had been poultry advisor to the County of Devon, and was at that time an advisor to the Ministry of Agriculture. His rare visits to see Hugh were always translated into practical demonstrations of poultry care, and it was he who taught semi-perms, and some trainees, how to kill, quickly and humanely, the birds that were to be prepared for food. He also taught us to pluck, draw, and truss so that we were able to tackle such jobs with professional understanding if not professional skill.

If it be true that variety is the spice of life then Food and Pigs put some of the spice into Spiceland. Certainly it was an introduction to the peasant farming that was thought then might prove to be important at the end of a war. Certainly the principles and practice, once learned, could be used on larger scales and, for many of us it anticipated, with its intimate personal involvement in small scale enterprise, Schumacher's confident assertion that "Small is Beautiful."

Food and Pigs entailed a lot of hard work spread over a long day, but it also provided a very important and worthwhile learning situation which complemented the important catering and cooking parts of the main training course. Many who were never afterwards involved in farming acknowledged this to be so.

CHAPTER 14

Cows and a Bull

In March 1941 Hugh realised that our best milking cow, a black polled crossbreed named May was not in calf, and that her lactation period was coming to an end. There had been persistent rumours that our land was infected with the disease contagious abortion. Had May lost her calf or had she never conceived? Although we searched the fields and hedgerows thoroughly, we found no trace of a dead aborted calf. Spiceland had four cows. April, a pretty roan shorthorn, was the practice cow on which trainees learned to milk. She was patient and accommodating, but she was elderly and the telltale rings on her horns spoke of many calves. July was also elderly and was nearing the end of her lactation. She was not in calf and was likely to remain barren. November was already dry but was an obviously expectant mother. Their names represented the months in 1940 in which they had been purchased.

The loss of May's expected flush of spring and summer milk was serious enough. The cost of feeding a barren cow with a question mark over her future, and with only an outside chance of getting her into calf again, was an additional problem. Hugh decided, with reluctance, that he would have to sell May and buy in two elderly milking cows to provide Spiceland's summer requirements.

In early April both April and July surprised Hugh by coming into season although their advanced ages had prepared him for the probability that their breeding days were over. Because of the fear and threat of contagious abortion, local farmers who owned bulls were reluctant to let them serve our cows, and Hugh was reluctant to press them. Despite the smallness of the Spiceland herd he thought seriously about acquiring a bull — he was a qualified and able dairyman — but bulls are not pets and there were a lot of inexperienced people about. Raised eyebrows were a certainty and opposition probable.

The three of us spent many hours talking it through. Most evenings Hugh would knock on the Smithy door and his call "Hello Farm" was the prelude to another session — literally a bed-sit session because there were no chairs. Although we recognised the need for the summer milk which May was not going to supply, we were unhappy about buying two cheap cows just for the season. They could make no long term contribution to the farm. On the other hand we responded readily to the idea of breeding a herd, and were all too ready to be persuaded that trainees should be exposed to the larger difficult animals which might be encountered on any farm. May added some point to the discussion by herself coming on heat.

While we talked about large animals we talked about horses. With fields too steep and sideling to be safely cultivated by wheeled tractors, and with expensive caterpillar machines out of question, horses were the obvious answer. June was light, fast, spirited and wilful; Bonnie was a heavy Clydesdale, very powerful and eager. They were not a matching pair and could not be yoked side by side to produce an even pull, but a strong matching pair was needed to pull farm implements, especially a plough, across the heavy hilly ground.

I had recently done some more work under the working out scheme and had watched neighbouring farmers preparing their fields and sowing their crops. I thought we ought to be growing some corn and making some hay, and pressed this point strongly. The cost of buying hay, corn, and straw was high, and going higher. More cows would call for more food, and we were already feeding cows on half-eaten swedes. Always the way forward seemed blocked by lack of capital, and our endless permutations on how to use what was available produced no satisfactory solutions.

After Hugh had left one of these sessions we went on talking to one another. We had saved two hundred pounds towards setting up the home we had hoped for when we got married. We looked long and hard at this sum and decided that we must keep one hundred against possible future emergencies, but that we would offer the second hundred to Spiceland so that Hugh could buy a matching horse to partner Bonnie and buy one good cow as a long term prospect to replace May. This would leave Hugh free to buy his two cheaper cows and a bull from farm resources — that is, if John and Margaret agreed that the package was reasonable.

We were not at that time members of the Semi-perms' meeting, and do not know how long it took, or how persuasive Hugh had to be, before the proposals were agreed; but one day Hugh told us that our offer had been accepted and events moved quickly. The farm stock book, which every farm had to keep, showed that a new horse, a shire named Prince, arrived on April 19th, November's bull calf was born on April 21st, two "summer cows" Dainty and Maisie arrived on May 17th, a bull Benjie on May 24th, and that on May 31st May was sold back to Roland Wood, who had bred her, at a sadly low price. The pace of change was maintained in June with the purchase of a new in-calf cow Prunella.

On April 14th a local contractor ploughed the Middle Path Field with a caterpillar tractor, and clean slices of deep red earth shone brightly in the spring sunshine — a beautiful sight, but one that was fraught with danger as the slices quickly dried into brick-like ridges. Spring work had arrived with a vengeance.

The bull was a seven year old Dairy Shorthorn, roan in colour, and weighing about seventeen hundredweight. He was a magnificent animal; Hugh had inspected some of his progeny and was impressed by their appearance and encouraged by what he learned about their milk yields. The foundation stock of most of the local herds were the beautiful native Ruby Red Devons which produced rich creamy milk and fattened on to produce high quality beef. The war time demand for more milk had encouraged farmers to cross these natives with one of the heavier milking, if less creamy, breeds like Friesians or Dairy Shorthorns. The appearance of the herds grazing the Devon fields changed dramatically from the traditional ruby red as the "up country" dairy breed bulls stamped their colour characteristics on their children. The black and white patches of the Friesian bull are dominant, and whatever the colour of the mother, her calf will eventually prove to be black and white. Shorthorns produce various patterns of brown, red and white, with a sprinkling of roans and brindles — all of a distinctive shape.

Benjie was a subject of local interest and one or two neighbours were willing to risk the often stated, but unproven, connection between bulls and contagious abortion. Fear of the disease was real indeed, but hope may overcome reason, and where there were many uncertainties logic was very difficult to apply.

Very soon after his arrival Benjie provided his first "bull incident" and set a few pulses racing. One day, towards the end of lunch, Hugh came and sat down between us, and whispered in a low voice "Hello Farm, Benjie is loose in the yard and we must do something quickly before the beginning of the afternoon work session." We discreetly left the table and strolled unconcernedly down to the farmyard which was steeply down hill, and out of sight of the house. The yard was an irregular rectangle in shape, there was a shed for six cows, a food store, an empty laundry and boiler house, stabling for two horses and another boiler house where the pig swill was cooked — all ranged down one of the longer sides; at right angles to them were some pigsties, some calf pens, and a larger shed where Benjie had been tethered; opposite the cowshed and stable block was a large covered barn and cart shed. Closed gates guarded both ends of the fairly narrow open space of the yard itself.

Benjie was quietly eating hay snatched from the barn store, but round his neck was his tether chain with the stout post to which it was fastened swinging like some grotesque pendant. Just occasionally he tossed his head and swung the pendant in a dangerous, uncomfortable, arc which threatened to shatter his, so far, even temper. We surveyed this scene from the vantage point of a closed gate. We had not known Benjie long enough to have any idea of how he might react. He was sold as a "Quiet bull", but then he would be wouldn't he? Quiet he might be, but he was very powerful, and a bull is a bull.

Hugh had handled bulls before, but never I think one in these circumstances. He first distributed a number of pitchforks in strategic positions round the perimeter — defensive weapons for use in case of dire need. Even as he did so he expressed doubt about the wisdom of what he was doing and, fortunately, dire need did not arise. He next decided that the unused laundry was the safest temporary bull shed, and I was deputed to open and prop the door as securely as I could and to back away. Hugh advanced calmly, quietly, without hesitation, and with a "Hello, my pretty bull" waived an arm directionally towards the laundry. To our astonished relief Benjie turned away from the hay and, with his mooring post pendant swinging clumsily against his forelegs, he lumbered into his new home. Hugh quickly closed the door behind him.

It all happened nearly as quickly as it has taken to describe and, ourselves apart, there were no witnesses, so the story quickly became hearsay and in some danger of "embullishment". We were lucky and wiser.

The next pressing job was to remove the chain and post which were a potential cause of bull frustration. Nothing for it but to open the door again. Tribute in the form of a bowl of crushed oats was offered and accepted, and while Benjie explored the platter, Hugh ducked in, released the chain, and emerged intact from under that great head with the chain and post in his arms. No longer hungry, Benjie set about exploring his new home and quickly found a weak spot in the wall adjoining the cow shed which he worried with his horns until a sizable hole appeared. A member of the current Construction gang was detailed to brick up the hole from the cowshed side and after a time Benjie lost interest. He remained in the old laundry for a few days while Construction set a new solid oak post in strong concrete in his original shed, and when it was pronounced "set", Benjie returned home.

Benjie discharged his duties honourably and in a few weeks April, July and November were all in calf and Benjie was eating us out of hearth and home. Although he was no gourmet he had an enormous appetite, and we had no safe field where he could graze. Huge quantities of green stuff were cut from waste ground and road verges to keep him happy. One of Hugh's farmer contacts who had a farm at Stentwood, four miles away, offered to give Benjie board and lodging in return for his services, and guaranteed that he would be returned when we had need of him again. Moving a bull by lorry was a relatively costly business so we decided to walk him to Stentwood along the lanes.

Bert Baldwin made a "bull pole" from a strong ash pole to which was fixed a strong spring hook to go through Benjie's nose ring. One summer day I set out with Philip, a trainee, for company and assistance in case of need, to walk Benjie four miles. The hooves of a stalled bull grow too long and curl upwards at the toe. He needs exercise or chiropody, and Hugh's parting words of encouragement were that the walk on the hard road would be good for Benjie's feet! I remember the tension in my wrists and forearms as I tried to hold the pole firmly without putting over-much strain on Benjie's nose, and I wondered whether we could maintain friendly relations during the whole of a journey which must take all of two hours.

It was a peach of a day and the countryside presented a picture of summer beauty. Philip's leisure interest was in painting — in peace time he worked for an artists' supply merchant — and as we walked, the changing scene of hills and valleys, sheltered farmsteads, banks covered with wild flowers and prolific with wild strawberries, and with an idyllic babbling brook at the roadside, was an enchantment to him; but not to me. Philip quickly became oblivious to Benjie. Serenely confident that I could handle him, he tried to draw my attention to these unfolding delights as we made our slow but steady progress while I tried to concentrate on the bull, steeling myself against the possibility that we might meet the milk lorry or a tractor. We met nothing of the sort — the distractions were of a different order. As we passed beside fields containing grazing cows, the cows came hurrying to the hedgerows and gates to stare at us with bovine curiosity. Sometimes

Benjie stopped, raised his head high, and sniffed the air through dilated nostrils; at others he showed eagerness to break into a purposeful trot. Some firmness with the pole and some soothing conversation checked him, and allayed unbidden fears that Bert's contraption was not up to its job. It was, and thankfully, we encountered no lovelorn cows to tempt Benjie to a-wooing go — something I had not reckoned with.

Once a horse galloped along the side of a field bordering the lane where it lay deep between banks, and at intervals it stopped to look down with curious interest at our strange cortege. Sometimes the grasses on the verge were too tempting for Benjie who rarely enjoyed such rich fare, and I was torn between letting him graze and urging him on to shorten the journey in time if not in distance.

It proved to be well over the estimated two hours before we entered the approach lane to Stentwood Farm, but soon after that we were in the yard and handing over our charge with some relief — relief tinged with reluctance, because I had been emotionally as well as physically attached to my large lumbering companion for what seemed close to eternity.

The journey home was a picnic — literally. We ate our packed lunch seated by the roadside while Philip gave a dissertation on the art of landscape painting, to which I listened as if that were also my main interest in life.

CHAPTER 15

Carting and a Christening

The late ploughing of the Middle Path Field gave no time for the old turf to rot down, and the spell of warm sunny weather which followed gave more than enough time for the furrows of heavy marl to bake. There is an old gardeners' saying that you should never dig more on an April day than you can break down and rake on the same day. If we had heavy- harrowed this hard ground great clods of unrotted turf would have come to the surface. To press the furrows down and break the surface soil, would have called for a heavy roller which we did not possess.

Whilst hedging at the bottom of the Drainage Field I had uncovered an old roller which had been abandoned many years earlier. The wooden shaft pole and frame crumbled to the touch, but the stone roll and its axle were intact. Construction measured it where it lay, and made a new frame which they carried to the roll and fitted with some difficulty and considerable skill. Bert Baldwin pointed out that the roll was a block of enormously heavy granite.

One Sunday morning, after meeting for worship, all three horses were taken to the field with the construction team plus a small crowd of interested spectators. Bonnie and Prince were harnessed in tandem to the frame and with the help of levering poles, men and horses together heaved the giant cylinder out of its long-time resting place. The effort confirmed Bert's fears that the roller had been abandoned because it was a horse killer, but no one else was prepared to accept that without trying. The Drainage Field sloped but was not one of our steeper fields, nevertheless, the horses made only slow progress and that by "touring" along the field contours. The field exit was short and steep and Hugh decided to give the team a breather before hitching on the third horse for the final effort. Marjorie held Prince's head while June was backed into line. June's ears were laid back, her eyes rolled and her tail swished — after all Prince had only been a Spicelander for a day or two and was an unknown quantity to June — she let fly with her hind legs, missed Prince, but caught Marjorie a painful blow on the hip. Stoically she held on to Prince, who hardly batted an eyelid, and, such was everyone's concentration on the job, that no one realised that she had been kicked. A three-horse pull heaved the roller up the slope and brought it to rest at the top of the Burma Road.

Then we realised the damage. Alan Thomas, a trainee who owned a small sports car, ferried Marjorie back to the house where the painful blow revealed itself in in the shape of many multi-coloured bruises but, fortunately, no worse injury.

Hugh made a valiant effort to roll the Middle Path Field with the salvaged granite, but it was so heavy and so unwieldly that by a process of

slow gravitation it found itself another resting place in yet another hedge bottom. Perhaps we should have erected it there as a "standing stone" monument to human folly and horse sense.

A neighbour came to the rescue with the loan of an old steel roller which Bonnie and Prince hauled with little difficulty over our other tillage ground, but the problems of cultivating the Middle Path Field increased. The sun continued to shine and the soil to harden; no way was found by which ridge furrows could be split open to receive the potato seed, and the field was planted by hand. Teams of trainees used spades to chop out triangular holes about a foot apart, into which other trainees dropped seed potatoes and a third group filled the holes. The scene presented was of a peasant economy with lines of folk in motley garb stretched across the field and toiling under a hot sun. It was effective, if not cost-effective, and a relentless slog finished the job.

The field remained difficult all year. Thistles and other weeds competed vigorously with the potatoes and many Spicelanders spent many blistering days with hoes. The very steep bottom third of the field was planted with Kale for the cows, but the rabbits got there first; it was then sown with Kohl-rabi with the same intent, but germination coincided with a hot spell and flea-beetles ate the emerging seedlings before they could establish. Finally a sowing of turnips succeeded, persistence paid, and a sowing of mustard on the headland provided a good textbook finish.

Spring work stretched into summer, and the pressure was such that there was no talk of resuming our training. At what stage John invited us to attend the Semi-perms' weekly meeting we cannot remember. We do remember an expedition to Tiverton to buy two fireside chairs — which we still have and would not willingly part with — with the object of making the Smithy more comfortable.

The introduction of double summer time had ensured, by what can only be described as one of the greatest confidence tricks of all time, that the farm day extended into times on the clock which should have been night. Cows were milked by the clock and daily routines were planned by the clock, but the dew went late from the fields of hay and corn, the sun stayed high in the evening sky, chickens went to roost by the sun, and hay and corn were carted and stacked as long as there was light to see by and sometimes beyond.

It was part of the understanding that I should always be available to support trainees on the "working out" scheme, and to earn some money for the Spiceland Pool. I spent long hours turning, carting and stacking other farmers' hay, and helping them to gather their harvest crops. There is a skill and rhythm about pitching hay and sheaves which I found as enjoyable and satisfying as I had found playing games in peace time. The scents of summer are sweet, the sight of buzzards soaring and wheeling against the skyscape demand an appreciative pause, while the hard physical condition which came from toil in the fields was in itself some sort of reward.

But some of my happiest days were spent with horses. There was a day spent with June, harrowing a neighbour's field of winter-sown barley with light drags, to disturb and kill small annual weeds. There were days carting hay or straw purchased from other farms, and other days carting dung to spread on the market garden ground. One carting job proved something of an adventure. Building materials for restoring the house were hard to come by, but Bert had noticed that a small builder's yard was for sale at a village some ten miles away and was successful with a bid for bricks and timber. Professional motor transport was expensive and difficult to arrange — there were many lucrative defence transport jobs available on a cost plus basis — so I was sent off with the two big horses and a trainee to bring back this valuable purchase.

It was a generous ten miles to the builder's yard at Smeatharpe, nearer twelve, and it was midday before we found it. The bricks took time to handle and stack on the wagon and we quickly appreciated that, although they were less bulky than farm loads, they were very heavy. Smeatharpe is on the Blackdown plateau. The route we had chosen, across Luppit Common, avoided any up-hill of consequence but did entail two steep descents at journey's end — the long hill down into Blackborough village and the Spiceland driveway, both of which had "one-in-four" gradients. Despite some doubt about the weight, I did not want to make a double journey so we set off for home with the total purchase.

Bonnie and Prince knew that we were headed for home. Refreshed with a feed of oats and a rest, they threw themselves into their collars and hauled away steadily. I enjoyed myself. Walking beside two magnificent horses which were pulling well in tandem, listening to the sound of their hooves on the road and the ringing harness chains, speaking the occasional encouraging word, listening to the pleasant friendly noise they make when they clear nose and throat, was to experience a companionship which I like to think was shared with them.

With little more than the odd word to the trace horse to "keep up" and not leave too much work for the shaft horse, the miles slipped away behind us until, on the long straight stretch across Luppit Common we met a tractor towing a wide implement. We pulled over to let him squeeze past but the near side wagon wheels found soft earth and the load stuck. It was beyond our strength to get the wagon back on hard ground, and we faced a long delay if we had to off load, lighten the wagon and reload. The tractor driver was sympathetic, as well he might be, but said that he had no hooked chain and no strong tow rope.

I remembered that Bob Lake, our blacksmith, had shown me a method of looping chain links back on themselves and locking them by tying two parallel links together with a piece of string. No strain falls on the string but the links hold firm and take the strain. The tractor man was more than doubtful but agreed to try; we took the trace-horse chains, made the improvised loop-hook, secured it to the tractor bar and tied the piece of string. The links held in place, and with a slow steady pull, the tractor hauled the wagon back on to the road, with Bonnie steady between the shafts and steering it to safety. Weeks later Bob told me that "he'd heard tell" that I pulled a wagon "out o' the mud wi' a bit o' binder twine." Bob was as pleased with the story as I had been relieved when it all came right.

Although this had taken time, the horses had rested and were eager to be off again. Twenty-four miles is a long day for heavy horses on the road, and daylight was running out as we neared Blackborough — this happened in March before the advent of double summer time. The trainee and I discussed tactics for the steep downhill stretches. We had a "drag-shoe" and chain for locking one of the back wheels of the wagon, but the shaft horse would have to hold the load and the moment of truth was upon us. My anxiety eased when, out of the "dimpsie" — the local name for twilight — came Hugh riding on a bicycle. He thought that I had done enough and insisted that I should take his bicycle and the trace-horse home. I was reluctant, and stayed with the load until we reached the top of the hill. As we fastened the drag-shoe we knew that the day was not done. The wagon axle was hot and smoke was issuing from the hub of the wooden wheel. The heavy load had found a dry hub and friction had done the rest.

There was nothing for it except to do what I had been resisting all day — offload. Instead of retiring I set off with Prince to fetch the tumbril, and both horses had a share in holding back heavy loads on the "one-in-fours". It seemed to have been a long, long, day before we finally went down to the stables to run a rule over our fed and watered horses before turning them out to pasture and a well-earned rest.

There was a tail piece. "Wagon wheels, state size, £5. — cash only .... Hampshire." We sent the five pounds; but heard nothing until a policeman called to say that a well-known confidence man was then serving a prison sentence for selling many a non-existent wagon wheel for cash only.

Soon after this Spiceland experienced a minor blitz. At one o'clock in the night a lone bomber, probably lost and anxious to jettison his load, dropped a string of bombs along a curved line the mid-point of which was very close to the house. We woke to once familiar sounds of whine and crunch first coming towards us and then receding from us. With my head stuck out of the Smithy window I heard the sound of galloping horses and rushed downstairs to pull on Wellington boots before dashing out — still in my pyjamas. Hugh was already at the back door, similarly attired, and together we hurried down the farm track to the field where our horses had been turned out to graze. The simple wire gate had been trampled down. There was no sign of the horses and we walked into the field. There was no moon, it was cloudy and pitch dark. Hugh was carrying a stick and with this he prodded the ground in front of us as we walked; about a hundred yards in he found the edge of a crater, and we turned back to the farm. In the later light of the morning we could see that the crater was wide and shallow and smiled at our earlier timidity; but at the time we had felt that we were on the edge of an abyss.

Hugh went to check the farm buildings, and I went up the drive hoping to find the horses or to hear the clop of hooves which would lead me to them. The night was then still and quiet, but strain as I did I could hear nothing. There was little more we could do, and as I took off my boots I realised how cold was an early May night if one was more than a little anxious, and clad only in pyjamas.

It was a very short night. We were soon up and about again and, after milking the cows and eating a snatched breakfast, I set out on my bike to search the lanes. At the church I met one of the Wright brothers who told me that they had heard horses thunder passed their cottage "going like the clappers". That news determined which of three roads I should take, and I started a long free wheel with many stops to scan the fields for familiar shapes and colours. A mile down the road at Bodmiscombe Farm I was told that they had heard horses go by in the night. At a cross road I was faced with another choice of route, but, while I hesitated, a man approached from the Ashill direction who said that he had seen three horses grazing the bank. The number was reassuring, and I went hopefully on for another mile to Leigh Hill Farm, where I spotted them grazing in a field next to the road. As soon as I appeared in the farm road their heads went up with pricked ears and they turned to stand in a row facing me. The farmer appeared from nowhere and told me that he had seen them wandering in the road, and had put them into his field for safety. We exchanged news of the night's events — he had heard that some sheep had been killed at Reid's, but by then Bonnie was at the gate pushing his head into my back, whether in greeting or impatience who can tell?

Haltered and linked together the horses and I started for home. I tried riding my bike beside them, but they were altogether too boisterous and I was glad to change to a slower walk for comfort. Would they have found their own way home if they had not been turned into the field but had been left to themselves? I like to think so. They seemed to me to have got over their fright and to be making a circular tour which would have brought them back to Spiceland. We examined them thoroughly. June had a gash on her near side shoulder, but whether this was caused by a bomb splinter or by breaking through the field gate, we could not decide. Certainly June never went near the bomb crater willingly, even after it had been filled.

One of Spiceland's neighbours was Tom Finch — a retired army sergeant in his seventies. He lived in a small cottage and owned about eleven acres of pasture on which he grazed a few cows and kept some poultry. His wife was a retired nurse who found the loneliness of this life more than she could accept, so she left him for long spells and went a-visiting. For many years he had persuaded a neighbour to mow his hay meadows which he afterwards turned and raked by hand, built into haycocks, and eventually carried the haycocks on his back into the barn. "While you'm a doin' this you b' aint a doin' anythin' else," was his laconic comment. He had no great liking for pacifists, but he must at last have been feeling his age, because in that summer of 1941, he asked Hugh for help. The grass had been cut several days earlier and was laying in swathes ready for a final turn, when he came to the house and asked for the loan of a horse and wagon with some extra hands.

We arrived at his cottage to find that Mrs. Finch was away, and Tom was cleaning up in the kitchen. I had never before visited his home. It was spotless, almost clinical, and he was polishing the cutlery preparatory to putting it away. We were too early. The sun was shining out of a clear blue sky, but there was a heavy dew and the grass was not fit to turn. Tom was impatient, but in a slow methodical sort of way. He walked up and down the swathes fingering the grass lightly and holding wisps of it to his nose until, at last, he pronounced it "viddy". He produced some long heavy wooden rakes and demonstrated how he wished us to walk along the swathes turning them over with a deft pull and flick which left the grass standing tall to catch the sun and the light breeze. His own movements were very effective and it all looked deceptively easy as we soon found out when we tried to keep pace with him. When he was satisfied with our techniques, and our rate of progress, he left us with instructions to keep a-goin'.

It was hard work and we saw no sign of Tom until the whole four acres had been turned, when he appeared, as if by magic, and said that it was time for lunch. As usual we had brought our thick sandwiches, but Tom had other ideas. He motioned us to follow him to his cottage door and waved us to some straw bales arranged as seats round the entrance. He went into his kitchen and came out with a wicker basket from which he took two small cold roast chickens, neatly halved, and some thick slices of buttered bread. Then he went to a well head in the cottage yard, and wound up a bucket containing bottles of farm cider which had been cooling in the depths. On such a day and after such work it was a feast. Tom did not talk himself and discouraged conversation altogether — it was a curious situation in which he dealt with us fairly and generously, but resisted any approach to familiarity or friendship.

After lunch the hay was considered fit to cart. It had lain in the sun and breeze for four days and the single turning of the morning had ensured minimum handling and maximum curing. It was dry but still green — perfect meadow hay. There followed a long afternoon and evening of sustained effort. I was on the wagon making the loads from the sweet-smelling hay as it was pitched up to me by the two trainees. Tom fussed about with his rake to make sure that little was missed and kept horse and men on the move so that no time was wasted. I had a job to keep balance and make a good load at the same time. Once, when the load was high and the over-eager thrust of a pitchfork grazed my thigh, I called out to "have a care!" "Drive on," said Tom "men are being killed in Russia." Russia had been invaded on June 22nd. They were almost the only words he said all day — most of his directions were demonstrations without words, and the food and drink were produced and served with wordless courtesy. There was a break for bread and butter with more cider, followed by the last chore of the day — a return to the long rakes and a steady gleaning of the field. The evening and the gleaning was made memorably beautiful by the swallows swooping and wheeling as they feasted on the insects abounding in the disturbed grass arrish.

Our efforts must have saved the old man a great deal of hard graft as well as the anxiety attending a hay crop left out in the field for long days and weeks of changing weather, which was the usual pattern of his self-contained farming practice. A raised arm, a brief word of thanks, and a near smile, acknowledged all that when we climbed on to the empty wagon to begin our journey home.

There were other memorable days spent with trainees on neighbouring farms. Two days were spent sweeping hay to build a rick in the middle of what passed for a very large field in our part of the country. The sweeps were like the business part of a modern fork lift in shape, but were pulled by a horse coupled to the implement by long chains. Two strong curved handles enabled the horseman to steer the fork along the swathes of hay until he had collected a heaped mass of the stuff. This he drove to the side of the stack where, without stopping, he gave a quick heave to the underside of the handles and the whole contraption turned a somersault and left the mound of hay to be pitchforked to the stack builder. The horseman retrieved control of the handles and set off on another sweep. Our job was to pitch and clear the heap before the next sweep load arrived to embarrass us. As the stack mounted higher and higher the work got harder, but when we were stretched to the limit it suddenly became easier as the farmer brought into use an elevator driven by a small oil engine. Then we had only to pitch into the elevator bowl, and the hay smoothly ascended in a more or less continuous swathe.

The sight of this brightly-painted rig plus the phut, phut, phut of the oil engine and the ritual excitement of the somersaulting sweep had one of the horses, a big grey shire, rearing on to his hind legs and pawing the air with his forelegs. While the horseman strove to regain control of his handles one of the reins got trapped under the swishing tail of the horse and he lost control altogether. As the nearest man to the horse, I went for the trailing rein at his head accompanied by conflicting cries of "mind yersel" and "hold 'im" as the farmer tried to balance the rival claims of safety and necessity. The excitement was defused by a soothing voice and the steadying feel of a hand on the horse's neck, and the normally quiet horse became quiet again.

The more usual method of making hay was to load wagons in the field and cart the hay to barns in the farmyard. The earlier tasks of mowing, turning the swathes, and horse raking the swathes into rows had usually been carried out before the Spiceland team were called upon. It was the pitching from field to wagon, and from wagon to stack or barn, that fell to our lot. As each load built up beyond the height of the laides — the ladder like supports at each end of the wagon — there were ritual jokes about the skill, or lack of it, of the load maker with prophecies about the likelihood of the load falling off before the barn was reached. The load maker's boast that his load would ride steady without need of a rope was ridiculed and rarely heeded; the exchanges nearly always ended with a cart rope being cast diagonally across the load and secured to a shaft or a wagon ring. The risk, and probably the experience, of shedding a load in a narrow lane or in a rough gateway, made sure that such boasts remained boasts.

Corn harvest in the high rainfall west country was always an anxious time. Summer storms often beat down the growing crops to make the job of the reaper and binder difficult. Once cut, the sheaves were grouped in sixes or eights and stood in long lines called stooks or stitches across the open field where they dried and matured but remained prey to the weather. Oats, which were cut before they were fully ripe, should hear the church bells thrice, wheat should hear the bells but twice, but barley which was cut when fully ripe was cut and carried with little delay and, in the old rhyme, need never hear the bells at all. In war time the church bells were mute, but the Ministry of Agriculture, with a fine sense of tradition, quoted the rhyme in its advisory leaflet issued to farmers who, for many years, had had no occasion to grow cereal crops at all.

When the weather and the crop permitted we worked until the light had gone from the late August and September skies. One late evening with a threatening storm in the offing and a stack unfinished and unprotected, there was one of those debates about whether to let it take its chance or to cover it with a tarpaulin. The crux of the matter was that the tarpaulin was back at the farm in an uncertain resting place. Eventually the farmer took me with him in his car and we entered an unfamiliar barn where there was a long whippy ladder stretching upwards into Stygian gloom among the beams and rafters.

Calling on me to follow, he ascended and disappeared into the vaulted cavern, leaving me standing precariously about forty feet up. I could hear movements as he rummaged among piles of empty sacks and the hoarded junk of years. Suddenly there was a shout of triumph followed by heaving and dragging sounds followed by another shout — this time of warning! About two hundredweight of heavy sheeting rolled into an uneven bale descended from above on to my head, arms and chest. I do not know how I held on. The ladder jumped and swayed, my eyes watered, my head swam. Slowly everything cleared and balance of a sort returned; with the farmer steadying the load from above I somehow wriggled round and made a slow descent using my back as support for the bale, the ladder as a slide, and my hands groping behind to find holds on the sides of the ladder. From above came little help beyond "Do 'ee be careful now" but whether for myself, the ladder or what? As I got nearer to floor level the words changed to advice and encouragement and, when we arrived back at the stack, the triumph was in having found the thing — my contribution, mere porterage, was a forgotten and unconsidered trifle.

I spent many haymaking and harvesting days with many different trainees at that farm and we all got on well together. He had one regular farm worker, a small man who lived in a small thatched cottage with a large family. He was small because his frame had not properly developed in the harsh surroundings of his childhood, but his ability to cope with the physical demands of his job was remarkable. He had no book education, but the skills of his trade were well founded and largely unrecognised. They were certainly ill rewarded — not so much by the farmer as by the agricultural system. His hay and corn stacks were beautifully made, and built with a deftness which conserved his small stores of strength and energy. His pride was to take his family to admire the beauty and symmetry of those stacks when they took their Sunday afternoon walk. Yet there was no permanency about his achievements; the stacks were soon demolished by the appetites of farm animals or devoured by the threshing machine on its autumn and winter rounds.

At home the family lived in a squalor which was not of their making or choosing. The cottage was old, and in poor repair; it was too small for the large family of children born too close to one another for their mother ever to cope with their needs or the household chores. There were rats in the cob walls and smaller active vermin in the decaying fabric.

Another baby was on the way, and as her time drew near, the exhausting drudgery and the sheer inconvenience of cottage life brought the mother to a low ebb. Moreover she had quarrelled with the village woman who usually "came in" on these occasions. Help was not at hand when it was most needed.

It was the Vicar who came to Spiceland for help. He rightly perceived a neutrality in village affairs. A relay of helpers tackled the washing and other chores until young Anthony was born, and for some weeks afterwards. They took some Spiceland gaiety into the cottage but, inevitably, they brought back some unwelcome guests. Many and varied were the methods used to prevent them taking up permanent residence. Two girls jumped fully clothed into a Lysol bath as soon as they got back, and hopefully drowned the fleas in situ. Others undressed standing on a spread white sheet, and hunted the black hoppers with bars of moist soap. Laundering in an old outhouse, using a wood fired copper, preparing food with cook pots on an open hearth, and coming face to face with poverty, not in a city slum, but in the heart of a beautiful countryside, was an unexpected experience, but it generated some friendly understanding.

We were not, however, prepared for the request which came through the Vicar that we should become god-parents. How could a Quaker and an

Agnostic accept responsibility for watching over the spiritual growth of an Anglican baby, and promise to bring him, in due course, before the bishop for confirmation? For us it was impossible to make such promises and retain our self-respect. But the Vicar saw it differently; he explained that the theological aspects of baptism and confirmation were a closed book to this family. Christening was a social necessity and what greater tribute could they pay to us and to Spiceland than to ask that we stand by their sides when they brought their small son to church? They did not expect us to do anything.

What about the Vicar's own scruples? He had been a working railwayman for most of his life; a lay reader in the church he loved. He had come to ordination late in life with the intention of devoting his retirement to the people of the two villages which made his parish. He was a pastor rather than a priest. He could understand our position, but he could not accept it, and was happy to try and persuade us for the comfort of the family and in disregard of church dogma.

We did not give way and dogma — both of the church and of ourselves — came between the wishes of the family and the humanity of the vicar. The letter killeth .... Fortunately two of the helpers were Anglicans and were willing to become god-parents; We all went to the church together and stood by the family. The whole sorry business of doctrine is encapsulated in this story. The institutions which were thought up to be the vehicles for expressing the love of God in practical terms, become barriers. They become the focus of argument and dispute even when conducted on a level of friendly attempts to understand them. We did keep in touch with the family for many years. The father eventually got a job on a large farm in his native Somerset, and with a good cottage and the slow improvement in the rewards of farm workers, they hopefully moved to a better life.

Elevator and hay-sweep

CHAPTER 16

A Ploughing Lesson

Corn harvest over, there were fields of potatoes to lift and store, and stacks of corn to thresh. Kenneth McQuillen, who subsequently became a distinguished bio-chemist, and I were sent to Stentwood, the temporary home of Benjie the Bull, to thresh barley. We spent a hard day pitching sheaves from the stacks to the platform of the threshing machine. As the stacks got smaller as a result of our efforts, we worked in a perpetual storm of dust, straw, chaff and other bits and pieces which dropped from above as the sheaves, pitched above our heads, were mauled by the shakers and spindles of the relentless machine. During the "Voor noons" break we were asked to give a hand with the churns to be collected by the milk lorry, and found ourselves looking at a 1924 bull-nose Morris Cowley which was used to ferry the churns along the farm road to the milk stand. That was its sole employment but the engine started from cold with a half swing on the starting handle. In response to our gasps of appreciation Cecil Edmunds said that we could "have it for five quid."

After this interlude it was back to the cloud of dust, to toil and sweat. The next morning I awoke, after a restless night, to find that I had a pimply rash round my neck, on my shoulders, the front of my chest and round my waist. I thought that I had contracted some horrible disease and stayed in bed while Marjorie went to get advice. The irritation was intense and the urge to scratch almost irresistible. Marjorie returned to tell me that Kenneth was in a similar state and also in isolation. Close examination revealed that the rash was caused by the sharp awns of the barleycorns, which had broken off and lodged in our clothing. We had worked, as no farm worker would have worked, in short sleeved shirts and shorts — scant protection against Nature's armoury. Our strange condition had a mundane cause.

John and Margaret had a 1937 Austin Ten which had done yeoman service on Spiceland's behalf, but the need for another vehicle to share the taxing journeys to and from Cullompton had been discussed many times at Semi-perms meetings. At the next meeting I mentioned the old Morris and suggested that at five pounds it might provide an answer. I was woefully ignorant about motoring matters, and could only report how easily the engine had burst into life, and how smooth was the engine note while it was running. Following good Quaker practice, a small committee was appointed to inspect the vehicle and report back. It is one thing to try for a quick sale and extract five pounds from a cold potential buyer, and quite another to receive a triumvirate approaching with a declared interest. The price rose to thirteen pounds, and Cecil declared that he did not really wish to part with the car at all — the five pounds had been a joke. However, if .... The upshot was that Spiceland became the owner of the 13.9 horse-power, Hotchkiss-engined, open tourer Morris, with registration number TT 1185 and, inevitably, it became known as the Spiceland Special.

The spring work for which we had left the training course unfinished had long ended, the summer work had come and gone, and a vista of more and more work stretched out before us. No one suggested that we should return to training. We were so caught up in the Spiceland farm — Marjorie in particular — in Spiceland community life — both of us — and in the life of a number of farms round about — me in particular — that we stopped talking about it. I also stopped worrying about whether farming really was an easy option for me, and one which I ought not to enjoy.

Hugh had not had a holiday since he had joined the Carclew Community. John and Margaret, reinforced by encouragement from the Semi-perms, pressured him to have a break and he agreed to consider an autumn holiday. There is never a time on a farm when nothing is happening, but the nearest foreseeable major event was the birth of a calf to Prunella, and according to the date given when she had been purchased in the spring, that was weeks away. Marjorie and I had joined in the general encouragement for Hugh to take a break, and we were not going to admit to any apprehension about the alarms of a "normal" farming day. In early October, Hugh packed his bag and went.

Towards the end of the first holiday week, on the Friday, Marjorie noticed the bloom on Prunella's udder, and we realised that calving was going to be earlier than anyone had thought. In fact the birth was imminent. We kept her in a loose byre with plenty of clean straw, and watched her anxiously at frequent intervals during the evening. Most calves are born naturally without complications — we reasoned to ourselves. As a boy I had held the lantern for my uncle at assisted calvings, and had witnessed birth, but I had never been the midwife. At about ten o'clock a heifer calf — October of course — was born. We were excited and happy. We watched Prunella clean the ungainly baby, and watched its struggles to find its feet and suckle. We cleaned up, spread fresh clean straw and milked out some of the surplus first milk to relieve pressure on the mother's udder. We went late to bed and that reluctantly. I was up earlier than usual and hurried to make sure that Prunella and October were well.

I was shattered to find October well, but Prunella swaying on her feet, and rolling her head in distress. Even as I watched she crumpled and lay on her side. Although I had never before seen milk fever in its early stages, Hugh had described it clearly enough in his farm lectures, and I guessed this to be the trouble. Again, as a boy, I had stayed up all night with my uncle as he tended a cow with milk fever. In those days the milk bag was kept inflated with air — how this was set up I did not know. My job was always to hold the hurricane lamp and to run errands; I could not even remember whether the cow recovered. My job now was to prop Prunella with bales of straw, to get her off her side, and to phone for the Vet.

The first milk from the calf's mother is rich in calcium and other minerals, and is very laxative. It is very necessary and important for the calf in its first hours, but the modern dairy cow produces far more than the calf needs or could suckle. The previous night's surplus I had taken to the kitchen. Known as beest, this first milk after parturition is sometimes made into a custard — called beestings custard — and I had thought that the kitchen would wish to try its hand. Milk fever is caused by a deficiency of calcium. I do not think that this fact was known when I was a boy. Had I

drained too much from Prunella, or was what had happened inevitable?

I phoned the Vet, described the symptoms and my fears, and told him what I had done. There followed a period of anxious waiting, but it was mercifully short. No inflated milk bag, no all night vigil; the Vet made an injection of calcium salts into Prunella's neck and was away again, only pausing to pay a bedside manner compliment on the speed of the action.

Prunella soon recovered and, happily, we did not have to recall Hugh from his holiday. October, a lovely deep red Devon calf, became not only Spiceland's first heifer calf, she also became a symbol of hope and, perhaps not such a good thing, something of a pet. She became a nuisance, and more attached to Marjorie, who had bucket fed her in the early days, than to her own kind. She would escape from all sorts of situations, and worry her way through hedges to make her way back to the farmyard and to her foster mother. At one stage we had to make her a triangular wooden collar to deter such escapades.

On Hugh's return from holiday we turned to the vexed problem of how to plough our hilly fields. Most of Spiceland's horse work had so far been done by Edwin Smart who was one of the very first group of trainees. At the end of training he had worked as an orderly in a Ham Green Hospital team, but during his Spiceland training he had developed a real love of the country and of farm work. He decided to return to Spiceland and work full time on the land. He identified himself with local farm life, adopted west country speech without much difficulty because he was a gifted linguist, and became a self-made rural character. His abilities were soon recognised and his services sought after, so much so that he acquired a cottage at Dunkeswell, where his parents joined him, and he became a freelance farm worker. His contacts with Spiceland, where he was a frequent visitor, remained strong, but almost without notice the horse work fell more and more to me.

Hugh had acquired a plough, and some only partially successful efforts had been made to plough out the potatoes in the Middle Path Field. It was a "one way" plough, so called because, as Hugh was wont to say in his farm lecture, it could plough two ways — it could turn a furrow to the left or to the right. The standard single furrow plough can only turn a furrow one way — usually to the right hand side of the implement. It is therefore used to plough the land in strips, called lands, with furrows gathered round an opening ridged furrow, and with an open furrow left between the lands; hence "ridge and furrow" ploughing. It cannot be used to lay a second furrow directly against the first one, and it is not possible to commence ploughing by opening a furrow parallel to a boundary hedge and then lay succeeding furrows against it until the opposite boundary hedge is reached. But a "one-way" plough can do just that.

It is still a single furrow plough — i.e. it ploughs one furrow at a time — but it consists of two single furrow plough bodies wrought as a single unit mounted on a single axle and fashioned so that the two bodies are diametrically opposed to one another. One plough body casts a furrow to the ploughman's right hand and the other to his left hand. At the end of each furrow the release of a strong spring-clip allows the whole contraption to revolve round its axle to engage the second plough body, which lays its furrow slice right alongside the previous one — and so on.

It is, of course, considerably heavier than a standard plough; ours was made by a local agricultural engineer and weighed in excess of two hundredweight. It was unwieldly to manhandle, and the skills of horsemanship which make manhandling unnecessary do not come easily. To start with there is a little matter of balance; the fact that the "spare" plough body is travelling above the centre of gravity means that it must be held in equilibrium. This is effected in part by the setting of the plough wheels and of the adjustable hook to which the horses are hitched, in part by pressure exerted by the ploughman on the plough handles, and in part by control of the horses. Plough horses move slowly, but speed is relative; the first time one gathers up the reins, takes a grip on the plough handles, and calls on the horses to "hold up", they seem to move at a terrific pace, and the plough itself seems to have life and will of its own. My boyhood acquaintance with horses was mainly with the lively cobs which pulled the milk floats round Reading. My only experience of heavy horses at that time was of leading in the hay and harvest wagons, stroking noses, patting necks and fondling ears. Ploughing was outside my experience.

Hugh made contact with a farmer who used a plough similar in design to ours, and asked him to give me a lesson. One December day I cycled over to Foxhill Farm and reported at the stables where the farmer's son was preparing for a day at the plough. His team was a pair of magnificent matching black shires. He let me brush and comb one of them, but the finishing — he plaited their tails and dressed rather than harnessed them — was his own pride. We set off for the field on a fine, dry, cold morning with the harness chains ringing, and the breath vapour puffing from the horses' nostrils as they stepped eagerly along.

The field to be broken was an old pasture, nearly a perfect rectangle in shape and with a very gentle slope. I choked back rising feelings of envy. First we marked out the headland by placing marker sticks, cut from the hedge, at the four corners of the field, but about six paces in from the boundary. The horses were hitched to the plough, already in the field, and the wheels were adjusted to produce a shallow furrow about three inches deep and nine inches wide. The plough lines — reins — were carefully adjusted so that they were just the correct length when the horses were up in their chains ready to pull and the ploughman's hands were on the plough handles. Driving in a straight line from sighting post to sighting post produced a furrow running parallel to the boundary of the field and marked out an area — the headland — on which horses and plough could be turned round at the completion of each furrow. My teacher said that as the slope of the field was negligible he would plough along the longest boundary and so reduce the turning to a minimum. Because the field was not a perfect rectangle this would leave a triangle of what he called the "short work". This he would normally leave until the end, but would do now to demonstrate how it should be done.

The plough wheels were re-set to produce a furrow about seven or eight inches deep, and the importance of the hitching hook — described as the hake in agricultural catalogues but known locally as the whang — was explained. On a perfectly level field the whang should be set dead centre to produce a straight pull, but on a sloping field, the whang must be offset, so that the directional pull of the horses is altered to make the plough coulter — the knife that makes the vertical cut — and the plough share — which makes the underside horizontal cut — bite harder into the unploughed land. The adjustment is made by positioning the hook in a horizontal slide in the draw bar, and fastening it with a locking nut. This was the most important part of the lesson for me, because finding the correct directional pull for our peculiar slopes was the key to successful ploughing. The whang became my talisman.

I watched the deft way in which the short furrows were laid. It involved frequent turning of horses and plough on the headland, good timing of the operation of the mechanism which released the plough body, and patient command of the horses, who plainly disliked the fussy nature of this part of the work. At the end of each furrow downward pressure applied to the landward plough handle, freed the plough from work so that it slid out, and came to rest on the headland balanced on an hexagonal wheel attached to the plough beam by a short bar. The horses wheeled slowly together. When they reached half turn, the ploughman pressed a foot pedal and released the spring-grip which held the body in position on the axle. As the horses completed their turn, the plough body revolved through one hundred and eighty degrees on its axle, with the hexagonal wheel acting as the fulcrum. The spring-grip re-engaged and the reverse plough body was then in position for the return journey. The horses pulled ahead into their work, one walking into the open furrow and the other on the unploughed strip. The ploughman slid the plough back into action.

Soon the frustration of the short work was over, and long straight work was the order of the day. I watched. There were a few minor adjustments to secure the right width and depth of furrow, a small adjustment to the whang, and in the early stages some scraping of earth from the plough breasts until they shone brightly in the winter sunshine. This encouraged the furrow slices to glide smoothly along the polished surface and to fall in ordered place. At midday we stopped for a sandwich lunch and shared a bottle of cold sweet tea – a new beverage for me, but one which I found to be refreshing and palatable. We ate standing with the horses in the shelter of a hedge and their body heat was welcome comfort. They enjoyed a feed of crushed oats and sacking was thrown over their backs to keep the chill from their sweating bodies.

A short break and then back to the plough. I walked discreetly behind, watching every little move, but the only conversation was between man and his team, and there was very little of that. They, all three, knew exactly what had to be done and they got on with it. For me it was a new and exciting experience. We had company in a mixed flock of gulls, rooks and jackdaws who settled on the newly turned earth to feed on the rich mixture of worms and grubs. They rose with protesting cries and caws when the passage of plough and horses disturbed them, but quickly settled again as the cavalcade drew away. The strip of brown sweet-smelling earth grew wider and wider as the afternoon progressed, and, at last, the unasked, but hoped for moment arrived when I was offered a chance to try my hand. There was a brief repetition of some of the things I had been told at the start of the day with emphasis on the importance of tying the reins so that they were of correct and even length; then, because all good horsemen have a voice relationship with their horses, a warning that he would command. I gathered the reins and grasped the handles.

The plough was already well and truly set and the furrow straight, and I turned in a flattering performance. I mastered the trick of turning the plough over on the headland, but had difficulty in guiding the heavy implement back into the furrow while keeping the horses moving together. When they threw themselves into their collars to take up the expected strain, the plough plunged and lifted alarmingly. Gradually the feel of the thing came to me, and I stopped over compensating for movements which were strange to me. My tutor was generous, but he took over for the last furrows of the day and straightened out the few kinks which my unpractised hand had introduced into his near perfect work.

Back at the stables I helped to unharness, rub down and feed the horses, offered my words of thanks and cycled home along the now winter-dark lanes.

The following morning Hugh and I repaired to the seclusion of Tinkers Orchard which, in addition to privacy, had the advantage of providing our only near level acre of land. We marked out the headland with sighting sticks, set the plough wheels and the whang, measured and carefully tied the plough lines. Hugh stood by the first sighting stick. I gathered the reins, grasped the handles just as I had done the previous day, called to Bonnie and Prince who set off as if that was what they had always done. The shallow headland furrow was finished in no time.

The next stage was not so easy, and I soon realised how much of the day before had belonged to another man and other horses. Manoeuvering on the headland proved to be more difficult than I had remembered; the plough got out of position, the horses stepped out of their chains, I grasped the carefully measured reins in the wrong place. After a time Hugh left me to sort myself out; gradually confidence came and the work took some shape. I stopped blaming the horses, and cohesion and rhythm returned to their movements. I began to enjoy it. The orchard took three days and was not a work of art, but it was ploughed. Then other work intervened, and it was nearly Christmas before we took the plough up to the Middle Path Field to meet the real challenge of heavy soil and sideling knaps.

Hugh's objective was to horse plough the field as deeply as we could, and prepare for a second crop of potatoes. The 1941 crop had been planted after a very late ploughing which had given little time for the turf to rot down and release the latent fertility in the soil. The field had baked in the early spring and summer, and lain sodden in the late autumn. It had not been a good crop. On the last day of October the whole of Spiceland — trainees, semi perms, visitors — had turned out in force in a final onslaught to hand dig and slither in mud to rescue what was there. The effort had universal support but not universal approval, and it did not provide universal enjoyment.

With earlier and better cultivation and with well rotted turf contributing to soil fertility the prospects for a good harvest were hopeful — even encouraging.

I had asked my tutor how he would tackle our fields, and he had advised me to choose a diagonal line across the slope and as steep as I thought the horses could manage. This would increase the short work but reduce the tendency for the topsoil to roll down hill which would certainly happen if we ploughed an easier line across the slope. We marked out the headland and chose our diagonal line. For the sake of symmetry and appearance I disregarded part of my lesson by deciding to do the short work first. It was a mistake. The horses did not like the frequent turns, and to turn them downhill on the steepest part of the field proved a clumsy exercise; but I would not give in, and persevered until I reached the line of the long furrow. The triumph and satisfaction of at last being able to plough long furrows was short lived. The weather took a hand and we experienced six weeks of very hard frost; so hard that ploughing was out of the question. That such frosts were very rare in Devon was no consolation. It was March before we had the satisfaction of seeing the Middle Path Field ploughed by our own efforts.

CHAPTER 17

Integration — Making a Hole

I once heard the Rev. George McLeod describe how, in the early years of creating the modern Community at Iona, they had entertained a German professor of philosophy, who having read an article about the integration achieved by widely differing groups who worked together in a common project, asked to come and study the process in action. At the time the groups were wrestling with the preparation of new foundations for restoring part of the Abbey building. So complex were the building problems that the talk was of little else, and the professor, who had come to join in deep philosophical discussion, complained that all they talked about was a deep hole. McLeod replied that one meaning of the word integrate was to make a whole.

I was told more than once by my combatant friends that the battle is always fiercest where you are. The major impact of work on the farm was tiredness, brought about by long hours and the physical demands made by the mainly manual operations which made up the Spiceland day. The broader aspects of Spiceland life could easily have washed over us if we had given way to this tiredness and to our growing interest in farming for its own sake.

This did not happen. Trainees and Semi-perms shared a common life without distinction. Meals were a joyous sacrament with no doctrinal significance, where everyone shared food, conversation, laughter and, sometimes, sorrow. The dining room was simply beautiful — light, south-facing, with windows opening on to glorious panoramic views. We sat on plain benches, dined off bare wooden tables, ate from thick plain white plates and drank from thick plain white cups without saucers. The meals, despite war-time shortages, were good and plentiful, planned and prepared by knowledgable and skilful caterers and cooked by trainees as part of the training course. We were, most of us, always hungry, and there were second, third, and .... helpings for those who thought they had need. There was an informal unplanned rotation of seating which ensured a mix, and there were conventions of speech to secure attention and the passage of condiments, gravies and drinks up and down the long tables.

In the early part of 1941 numbers in residence fell because the Construction team went to Newnham Bridge in Worcestershire to work on the conversion of a large hop- pickers' barracks into a hostel for evacuees. It provided on-the-job training with scarce materials and saved the Friends Relief Service an appreciable sum of money. There was a great deal of coming and going because there were more calls for help than people to answer them.

By Easter the Construction team had returned and a steady influx of trainees raised the tally of residents to more than sixty, so that accommodation and resources were severely taxed by numbers and by the wintry conditions which persisted up on our hill.

Spiceland's first birthday had been celebrated by an outbreak of impromptu happenings beginning with a tasteful (?) birthday cake made of primroses, mosses, leaves and surmounted by a single candle — lit at supper time. The farm celebrated by producing thirty eggs from thirty hens and nine duck eggs from eight ducks! A frivolous evening followed — it was Saturday — and a full account of this happy day was written for Wallpaper and appears, unabridged, in the Wallpaper appendix.

Among the trainees in 1941 were a small number of men who had refused registration for military service, or who had been given unacceptable conditions by Tribunals. They had decided to spend the waiting time before arrest in useful training. John pondered, and expressed in a News Letter, the sense of worthwhileness they experienced at Spiceland which, despite its obvious limitations and shortcomings in terms of resources, strove to give help to pacifists in need of help — not in a place of retreat, but in an environment which would strengthen their spiritual and intellectual life and, at the same time, provide effective and practical training which would enable them to work with the F.R.S., the International Commission, in hospitals and elswhere.

Those of us in residence continued to uphold, and be upheld by, the growing number of Spicelanders who were active outside. Extracts from their letters made interesting, and sometimes hilariously funny, contributions to John's post-meal news review, and others were eagerly read in the News Letters or in contributions to Wallpaper. They reflected the practical achievement and the varied conditions in which we all lived and worked, and the following extracts give some idea of the kaleidoscope presented to us and, hopefully, complement earlier extracts in Chapter seven.

Ted Amos, writing from Liverpool "..... perhaps I ought to mention at least my experience in the gigantic London Blitz a fortnight or so ago. I was at a rest-centre in Bethnal Green. Soon after the raid started someone came rushing in to tell us that the large plywood factory across the road had caught an incendiary. I went to have a look at it and returned to reassure the others that there was only just a little smoke coming from two windows and that "they" would soon have the fire out. At the time I really thought that, and I was amazed to find ten minutes afterwards that an enormous fire was fast developing, and that any hope of putting it out was gone. All night long, above the continuous bedlam of guns, planes and bombs we had to endure the indescribable roar made by stacks of plywood going up in flames.

As big fires are known to receive continual showers of bombs, you can imagine what we expected. All that night I walked restlessly up and down, counting the minutes to dawn and the relief dawn usually brings. The number of bombs I heard whining down, and the number of times the building — a solid four storey school — trembled, seemed to run into hundreds. Finally I felt as if I were suffering from acute sea-sickness, and did not care whether the ship sank or not. The trouble was that we were not busy enough for our minds to be taken off the turmoil outside — only two or three people sought refuge in our centre, and amazingly enough, the next day only two homeless people turned up. Our little area, already so badly knocked about, had escaped lightly. Other rest-centres nearby were crowded out. Just before dawn, I ventured up on to the roof, and was met by the horribly fascinating spectacle of fires; enormous, flaming, smoking fires everywhere ..... In the light of day we found one incendiary on our concrete roof and two more in the playground — all three had burned themselves out on non-flammable material and we had not even known they were there."

In stark contrast was a letter from the Walthamstow Gang — a group of six friends who came to Spiceland from that district of London, and went as a team to Ham Green Sanatorium:

"The Gang officially took up residence last Sunday evening at Avonview Hall. We strode along the half mile drive with our shoulders back and our noses in the air ignoring the curious glances of the locals, mainly nurses in uniform. Our new home is truly luxurious in modern style, but as conveniently situated as any of the traditional homes of Old England. The Estates are vast. Several farms surround the grounds and we have our own fishing waters and riverside walks.

We are sleeping in a spacious dormitory — bigger than our beloved Sidcot. There are four bathrooms for six of us and unlimited supplies of hot water. We cook on a modern electric stove and eat and drink the results in our common room — that is during the evening. In the day time there are maids to see to such things. Seriously, it is super! But we are being ragged and truly so. Our beds become apple-pie, phone calls at 12.30 or at 1 am from night nurses who give no names, and ask for the small-pox ward or ask whether we have mice. We are told awful stories of hospital life which are not true, and they wander in when we are away and read our books. We are in no position to rag back.

The grub is real quality ..... real butter, meat twice a day and fish is not scarce. We shall be unable to face milk puddings ever again. But ..... we need full stomachs and a daily bath. We work a fifty-four hour week and the work is not pleasant. Scrubbing floors, washing up, cleaning sluices and similar jobs. But there is also much of real interest — feeding patients, bed-sore cleansing, blanket baths, bed making, and some very unpleasant personal chores for patients especially T.B. ones.

At first we thought we could not avoid the disease for long anyway. Our lungs breathed harshly in sympathy, and our throats felt thick and horrible. But we are getting used to it now, and realise that if we are careful and keep fit with regular meals there is little danger. We believe that we are doing a worthwhile job and we are proud to be doing it."

Leslie Mather had refused to accept Non-combatant Service and wrote from a Detention Centre at Ilfracombe:

"The position is that I have finished my first sentence of 28 days, and having refused another (military) order am now once more under close arrest awaiting trial by court martial, and wish to strengthen my case by having proof of all the facts mentioned in my statement to the court. Despite the notorious record of courts martial in this district towards conscientious objectors, I have high hopes of obtaining the three months civil imprisonment (i.e. to enable him to appear before an Appellate Tribunal) for I have the best advisers and help that one could wish for.

The treatment received was quite good .... I am now a competent 'char' ...... much of the time in detention is wasted ..... nevertheless it has given me first-hand experience of matters about which I only had theories. It is stimulating to find that the theories were not far out and that up to now my convictions have been strengthened by my experience. I should like to write more but the blue pencil would be applied so .... I should like to receive a News Letter and read about the work that co-Spicelanders are doing."

The political climate which returned the Attlee government in 1945 was formed in part by the more general awareness of how incompatible and divided both physically and culturally were the many groups which made up the nation. The evacuation of large numbers of city-centre dwellers into environments far different from their own, in which they were ill at ease, and to which they brought life styles which their hosts could neither understand nor accept, opened a great many eyes to a great many unpleasant truths.

John Benjamin — Benjy — who was working for Friends Relief Service in Bournemouth, but was himself an East Ender, gave prescient warning in a letter to John:

"We are considering an alternative scheme of taking an hotel, to house some of the London people who have been dumped in Wellington Road. Poor old Bournemouth — or rather rich Bournemouth — woke up one morning and found that it had a slum problem! The Council are, and feel, helpless and are only too willing to do what we suggest (but not if it costs too much money). The Wellington Road colony of about three hundred people consists of thirteen houses — large ones. Families are living and sleeping in one room, sharing the same gas oven downstairs; they don't trust one another. Mrs. A buys coal to heat the boiler, Mrs. B. upstairs pinches the hot water before Mrs. A. can bath, so Mrs. A. don't bath nor do Mrs. X. Y or Z!

We rather feel that the whole scheme should be scrapped and something new tried. If we have clubs, communal feeding, laundry and baths their homes will still be in the same state. It is our grand old Social Problem of Shadwell, don't you think? How much palliative, how much curative work to be done? The people have been here nine months — transferred from an Oxford cinema. The Mayor of Bournemouth lives between two of the roughest houses. They smashed his windows, burned his fence, pinched his apples and cabbages. He is the first ever Labour Mayor of Bournemouth and they called him the 'Old Bloke' then the 'Old Man' and now he is known as the 'Old Gent'. He says that he is going up in their estimation. Children with the inevitable chalk decorate the inside and the outside of the houses. There are now two hundred and seventy people — men and women and children — one hundred and fifty six children, with extras being born monthly. Relations and friends come and go when they like, and some stay to make the overcrowding more of a problem still. Come to Bournemouth for a cheap holiday!

One family did a moonlight flit with all the Council's furniture, blankets and all that goes to make a home. The welfare lady happened to call at the moment with the furniture van outside and all the stuff packed up; she came in the front door, they disappeared through the side door and have not been seen since. Washing hangs on the bannisters of the stairs where their rooms are, — even on a lovely sunny day; if they use the lines in the gardens — the clothes are pinched. 'Mum has knocked the handle off the tea-pot and wants another' 'The bath is blocked up' — (Water did not block up the bath!). They have more floor space, but miss their own homes and really need somebody who can get them to work together.

We have now taken up residence in the road. We are only here to see what can be done and to make a Report. It is intensely interesting."

Later on, when conscription of women was introduced, at least two women Spicelanders decided that their protest should be a refusal to register, and they served prison sentences in Exeter gaol. They were allowed to take with them a book of their choice and my copy of the Oxford Book of Mystical Verse was inscribed by the prison governor on the fly leaf in pencil "To be taken out on discharge — J.Mc.R." — a treasured memento of faithfulness in action.

A Spiceland "Who's Who and Who's Where" which listed over two hundred and forty men and women who had trained or were training at Spiceland was compiled and issued to all of us in August 1941. It was one of the ingredients in a mix which was helping to make the digging of many Spiceland holes into an integrated Spiceland Whole.

Ham Green Hospital

CHAPTER 18

Farewell June — A Winter's Work

The year 1941 did not end with my ploughing lesson, the practice session in Tinkers Orchard and the early efforts in the Middle Path Field.

It was a bleak period for everyone. Pearl Harbour was attacked on the day of my lesson, and the loss of the battleships Repulse and Prince of Wales followed soon afterwards. The war had extended with the entry of Japan, and the prospect looked ever more grim.

Spicelanders never sought isolation. Concern about the news and the general situation was reflected in all sorts of ways — serious and slight. There was always a desire to identify with our neighbours as much as we could. The fact that we were abnormal in some respects made us determined to establish our normality in others. The village was invited to a special Christmas social, and because it was a cause that everyone present knew about and could sympathise with, the collection of £5.10/-. had been given to the Lord Mayor's National Fund for the relief of air raid distress rather than to Friends Relief Service. Ninety visitors, most of them children, packed into the Common Room for a varied programme which gave full rein to Spicelanders' gifts for innovation and entertainment.

At about this time I had a mishap the outcome of which was received with relief by most, but with devastating sadness by me. Construction had agreed to install a semi-rotary hand pump at the Bubbs' farmhouse at Dunkeswell. The job would give valuable plumbing experience to a trainee, and improve the rather primitive water supply to the house. Francis Maw, a very able trainee who was nearing the end of his course, was selected for the job. He and I stacked the pump, lengths of piping, tools, and a number of other items not connected with the job on to the tumbril, and altogether they made a pretty full load. We led the horse, June, up the steep driveway to ease the pull, but sat on the cart while I drove through the village, and dismounted again to negotiate the steep hill out of the village. When we reached the near-level stretch at the top of the hill Francis asked whether he could drive and I readily agreed.

Before we could climb on to the cart, and while Francis was taking the reins from my hand, a tractor preceded by a large bouncing dog came out of a field gate just ahead of us. June, remember, had blood. She either pretended to be frightened or she was frightened. She reared and turned to go back the way we had come. Francis was swept aside, and the reins fell from his hands. I was just behind him and able to jump on the shaft of the cart, and make a grab for the trailing reins. Earlier in the day it had been raining hard, and I was wearing Wellington boots instead of my more usual hobnails. The smooth rubber soles slid along the shaft, and I fell between June's rump and the cart — still clutching the reins which dragged me across her back. June was beginning a gallop, her hind hooves caught me on the chest as I fell, and left me breathless on the ground as the cart passed over me without actually touching me! June set off for home.

Although breathless I was conscious; but to Francis I presented a dreadful sight. Drained of colour and motionless he thought the worst, covered me with his heavy coat, and went for help. The tractor driver dismounted and hurried towards me, but by the time he reached me, which could only have been a minute or two, I was beginning to move. He helped me to my feet, draped the coat round my shoulders, and asked if I was alright. I said I was stiff but could move, and thought that I could walk home. He watched me as I set off down the hill.

Halfway through the village I met the search party coming to meet me in the Spiceland Special — the bull-nosed Morris — and saw the anxious faces of Bert Baldwin who was driving, Brother Os who was clutching his first aid kit, and Hugh, change first to expressions of relief and then to smiles. By this time I really was stiff and felt bruised and shaken. I was glad to be lifted into the back seat and taken home.

Os felt me tenderly and decided that no bones were broken. He suggested a hot mustard bath, and I was half carried upstairs to John and Margarets' flat and lowered into their bath. The rescue party stood solemnly round as the steaming water engulfed me. My chest gradually took on new colours of blue, green and yellow as the bruising became apparent, and when the unmistakable shapes of four horse shoes were revealed in the colours, their concern, and mine too, changed to something near laughter. Brother Os was convinced that now the bruising had "come out" there was nothing to fear. After a good soak he gently rubbed me down, and bandaged me for cracked or broken ribs "as in the handbook". I spent two uncomfortable days in bed, but after the enforced rest I quickly recovered, and was none the worse for the experience.

Surprisingly, nobody thought to tell Marjorie what had happened, and she went on working in the farmyard until lunch time. Believing me to be well on the way to Dunkeswell, she did not even look for me in the dining room, and knew nothing of what had happened until Hugh brought her to my bedside. She says that the full story remained unknown to her until I came to write this book.

There had long been a school of thought that June, of the flaming chestnut colour, part bloodstock parentage, and wayward behaviour, was not the most suitable horse for a training centre. Although I had come to no serious harm, the Semi-perms asked themselves how they would have felt had the accident happened to a trainee. Hugh was put under some pressure to sell June. His first move was to buy an elderly cob with a proven reputation for easy handling. She was no beauty, and her appearance was not improved by the fact that she was blind in one eye. It seemed somehow appropriate that her name was Fanny. Her habit of dropping off to sleep between the shafts earned her some affectionate understanding. She was certainly never under severe working pressure.

Eventually June was sold to a farmer who lived several miles away. Hugh hated parting with her, and I lost an exciting unpredictable friend who had always responded well to me, and who left me with many happy memories of days spent in her company. I only saw her once more — it was on a Sunday walk to Spiceland meeting house that a small group who talked as we walked, were surprised by a chestnut head projected over a field gate. It was June's, and I like to think that she had heard my voice and had hurried to greet me. I caressed her ears for the last time, and pondered sorrowfully that she had gone from Spiceland because I had somehow failed her.

The hard winter with its severe frosts reduced the field horse work to almost nothing. There were a few necessary carting jobs. Hugh had bought a stack of hay from a Commander Metter's bailiff at Craddock, four miles away, and I made several journeys with the wagon and two horses to fetch loads for our stock. Cutting out swathes of hay with a hayknife is one of those jobs which looks easy when it is done by a skilled farm worker, but which is far from easy for the un-practised.

To start with, the knife is heavy, with an angled handle offset at the point where pressure or strength is applied. Secondly, the blade is broad at the top and curves to a point at its toe, so that, if the point is directed out of line, the cut is made out of line; the more the cut is out of line the harder the thrust that is required to complete it, and the more difficult it is to bring a fresh cut back into line. Thirdly, the knife blade has to be kept sharp by frequently stroking both sides of the edge with a carborundium stone, and it is easier to take the edge off, than to put it on!

I made heavy weather of learning where to direct the thrust of the cut, and my swathes were too often uneven in shape and size. I used a lot more brute strength than ought to have been necessary. Fortunately I have always used cutthroat razors so I quickly learned to keep the knife sharp, and this saved me from much drudgery. Trainees who made just one journey for experience were impressed by my efforts, but Commander Metter's man, William, who watched us with a critical eye, was pretty scornful in a kindly way.

Driving back a full load of more than a ton, with two horses pulling in tandem, was always a pleasure — especially over the last two and a half miles of the long hill up the Blackdowns when, with the scent of home in their nostrils, they powered along with taut chains.

Much of the hard weather period was spent in hedging and ditching. Our hedges had received no skilled attention for many, many, years. They overshadowed the lanes, restricting passage, and encroached into the fields. Although we had admired the symmetry of the hedges which some of our neighbours had reclaimed, we had not yet learned the proper way to tackle our own. We had done a great amount of grubbing out the small trees and bushes which had established themselves in the fields, and had cut back the overhanging hedge trees — mostly hazel and hawthorn with some beech — which were often twenty or thirty feet high, but we had done little or nothing to the distinctive Devon banks. Most of the articles on hedging which appeared in the farming journals related to hedges in the shires where hedges are rarely grown on banks. They described how to trim the trees which were to be retained, how to "pleach" the stems by splitting them part way through with an axe or billhook, and how to layer and secure the split stems one against another at an angle to form a barrier. They described how new wood would burgeon from the tree boles to provide the material for future years. No doubt these articles were necessary because the neglect of farming in the twenties and thirties had led to a loss of knowhow — ignorance was not confined to people like ourselves.

We had at least one hedge which was not on a bank. It ran from the point where the old coach road joined Mendham's Lane and along the boundary of the Bottom Path Field. It was all hawthorn, and the trees were nearer forty than thirty feet high. Some of them were so thick and old that doubts were expressed as to whether they could be pleached at all. The lane was used regularly by Spicelanders — it was a short cut to Kentisbeare and Cullompton for horses and pedestrians, but quite unsuitable for cars. The hedge was a nuisance in its then state and shut out sunlight to field and lane alike.

Hugh agreed to let us "have a go", and with a small team of trainees who liked using billhooks and axes, I went to survey the job and decide which trees would have to go and which we could save for layering. The trees at the junction of the coach road and the lane would have blocked the road had we layered them, and despite the fact that the coach road was unusable at that point, we all nurtured hopes that one day we would open and use the whole of the Burma Road once more. We felled them, cut off and burned the top wood — not forgetting the "blackout" — and logged the trunks. Few would have bothered to handle the murderous thornwood as we did; but hawthorn does burn well, and the Common and Quiet Room fires had seemingly insatiable Spiceland appetites!

It was when we came to layer the pleached trunks that the full impact of the unyielding thorns bore down on us. Very few of the stems were slim and pliable. Such as were there gave little trouble, and a quick well directed blow with an axe would slice slantingly downwards towards the heart of the tree which could then be bent over, placed into position and trimmed of unwanted top wood and side branches, but we badly needed to retain some of the older trees which had grown thick and brittle near the base. If, when we had cut the pleach — an operation which took not one but several axe blows, we allowed a tree to come down by gravity under the pressure of its not inconsiderable top weight, there was a good chance that the pleach would break altogether and present us with just another felled tree. The other probability was that an unrestrained fall would crash into the work we had already done and spoil it.

So, as each tree heeled over, we got underneath to support and guide it into position, trimmed some of it as it came slowly down and, despite leather gloves and our clothing, accumulated assorted sizes of thorns imbedded in hands, arms, shoulders and heads. With deft tweaks we removed most of them, but some remained to be winkled out in the evenings with the aid of monkey-like searches of the parts we could not reach for ourselves. All the team had lacerations but none turned septic and all healed quickly. When completed the job gave us a good strong hedge and much visual satisfaction — enhanced when spring brought new green growth, and an unsuspected bonus in the shape of a sheet of sweet-smelling white violets flowering at its base.

With the departure of the frost a rush of spring work engulfed us. I finished the deep ploughing of the Middle Path Field, and harrowed it at once so that the heavy Keuper marl could not bake hard as it had done the previous year. I also ploughed the Tillage Field at the top of the drive. Earlier in the winter Hugh had hired a contractor to plough the Drainage Field. We now had a considerably increased acreage of arable land to deal with.

The cropping programme had been agreed with the representatives of the War Agricultural Committee who had walked the farm with Hugh on one of their periodical visits. They had been more helpful than before, and were appreciative of what had been done. There were no more instructions to dig steep fields by hand. In addition to four acres of potatoes we were to grow for hay or silage a mixture of oats and rye grass on the Tillage Field, and, on the Drainage Field, two acres of oats and another two acres of mixed oats, barley and maple peas. This was to provide food for our horses and other stock and, hopefully, some surplus to sell.

Hugh's "social contacts" with neighbouring farmers were of enormous help at this stage. Our under-capitalised farm had few implements of its own. Neighbours lent us a one-horse flat roller, a two-horse Cambridge roller, some spring harrows and a corn drill. With these we cultivated and sowed the Drainage and Tillage fields. Bonnie and Prince were now working well together and they really earned their corn. Spiceland looked and felt like a "proper" farm. Hugh's cry "Hold up, my pretty horses! Let's roll the field, so that we can grow some oats, so that we can roll the field again next year, so that we can grow some more oats!" expressed enthusiasm and satisfaction which we all shared.

The borrowed implements were not new. They had come into use again after years of lying idle in sheds and corners of fields. The Tillage and Drainage fields were the greensand — black in colour with a content of flinty stones which inflicted harsh wear and tear on metal parts. We broke two or three sections of the Cambridge roller, and two coulters of the drill. Our blacksmith supplied new sections for the roller, and we wrestled with unyielding rusted nuts and bolts to remove the old broken parts before replacing the new; this while we balanced the heavy roller on improvised and unsteady jacks. It was even more difficult to get the heavy axle back into position in the roller frame once it was burdened with its full complement of sections.

There were no available new parts for the drill. I watched with fascination as Bob Lake heated a metal rod in the forge furnace, and hammered away on his anvil using skills of hand and eye which brought shape and usefulness to the iron. The painstaking operation involved re-heating the iron several times and, between each heating and each hammering, plunging the part, white hot and hissing, into the water trough to cool. In due time Bob gave me the hand-fashioned coulters. There was a satisfaction, and a kind of dignity, in such "make do and mend" operations which is sadly lacking in much of our present-day living.

We finished drilling the oats and rye grass on a hectic Thursday in March which started with ploughing the last furrows in the morning, harrowing and drilling into the late afternoon, and breaking off to take a load of market broccoli to Turner's before returning to complete a final harrowing in the light of a rising moon. The horses were tired and I was tired. Hugh sensed that I was prepared to un-harness, and call it a day. He took over, and with a fresh vigorous voice encouraged a new liveliness in the horses' tread and completed the job.

Rubbing down and feeding the horses after such a day is an experience in itself. There is a mixture of stable activity and scents which seem to complement one another; the eagerness of horses' appetites and the companionable way they lift their heads over the stable partition to nuzzle one another when the first pangs of hunger are over; the distinctive snort which seems to be conversational and which certainly has a simple practical purpose. It is part of the pattern of small incidents which make a horseman's life.

After a feed of oats, horses must be restrained for an hour before they are allowed to drink water. Time for the horsemen to rest and eat before turning his team out to graze and rest. This last chore was another which I always found strangely satisfying — especially those last watching minutes when, with their halters removed, they frisked away to lie down and roll in an ecstasy of freedom and to ease the sweaty irritations of the day.

Between drilling the Tillage and Drainage Fields, Marjorie and I made a quick dash to London to be present at the wedding of one of her school friends. It was our first break for a long time, and there was pleasure in the panoramic views of the English countryside seen through the windows of railway trains, and in meeting family and friends.

We made a journey across London to the Highway Clubs to see for ourselves where John and Margaret had worked, but there was little pleasure in passing through the havoc of the Blitz. Our own experience had been in the darkened winter nights of 1940, and our memories were more of sound and fury, and huddles of people, than of this bleak daylight scene of destruction.

The Clubs were in use as a day time creche, and the helpers were trying to induce post-lunch sleep in unresponsive under-fives. When we left the Clubs we walked into a cobbled square occupied by a large London brewery. There, dozens of draymen and their magnificent horses were also enjoying a post-lunch rest. We wondered how they had come through the experience of bombing, and what the future held for them. How little we knew about the complex character of London life, and with what its animals as well as its people, had had to cope.

Soon after the Drainage Field had been drilled Hugh received the result of a soil analysis carried out by staff from the Seale Hayne Agricultural College. They had taken samples from different parts of the field, using a tool which might have been used for making the hole on a putting green, and had taken the collection of soil cores back to college for examination. By far the most important detail in the listed information was that there was an estimated population of eight hundred thousand leatherjackets (the grubs which emerge as Daddy Longlegs!) in each acre with the added information that these would eat the oat seedlings in devastating fashion.

The suggested remedy was to spread over the whole area, as evenly as possible, a mixture of bran and Paris Green which was described as a vivid light green pigment composed of aceto-arsenite of copper, and a deadly poison. We were advised to choose a warm, moist, still evening, and were more than lucky to have the right conditions just as the oats were germinating. Hugh and Marjorie carefully mixed the ingredients — mindful of the dangerous nature of the bright green pigment. Marjorie broadcast the impregnated bran by hand, walking steadily to and fro across the marked out field, then washed the utensils and herself thoroughly. In dealing with substances like that one is left wondering how safe is safe?

The following morning the three of us walked slowly and watchfully over the field and found enough dead leatherjackets on the surface to encourage thought that the operation had been successful. The crop survived to prove this correct.

It is always exciting to see visual evidence that the seeds you have sown are growing; the even spread across a field of young green shoots of oats and barley delights the eye and warms the heart.

The sight which slowly emerged in the Middle Path Field was not a delight. There were no even rows of potato plants. It looked as if someone had broadcast the seed potatoes with careless abandon and, in a sense, that is exactly what had happened. The mud-covered potatoes that we had failed to see and harvest in the wet October of 1941 — the "groundkeepers and leftinnians" had, despite the hard frosts of winter, remained to sprout again and embarrass us with a higgledy-piggledy spread. Hugh decided that the best thing to do was to "take a line" and drive a ridging plough across the field to remove some of the unwanted plants, and push others into the semblance of rows. Once the rows had been defined, repeated operations of the same kind brought some sort of order out of chaos and, as the plants grew stronger and large enough to cover the bare earth, our embarrassment remained but was effectively hidden.

William, Commander Metter's man, who had always been ready to stop whatever he was doing so that he could watch us in action and offer improbable advice, had once stayed so long that I was prompted to ask him what he should be about. He had replied that he was off to drag the "tatie ground." He added "I doant like taties. Taties is all work. Fust you ploughs the gr'n and lets 'un bide all winter. Then you dungs'n and ploughs'n agen. Then y' cultivates and arrers 'n a time or two. You ridges 'n oop and plants taties. Then you ridges'n back and arrers 'n a couple a times more. When taties shows thru' you 'orse 'oes 'em and then you 'and 'oes 'em. You ridges 'n oop agen and later you 'orse 'oes 'em agen. Then you ridges 'em agen and lets 'em bide a bit. Coom September you ploughs 'em out and picks 'em oop. Then, no matter what you puts in nex' yer, oop cooms taties agen."

On another occasion I met William at the forge. He arrived with a load of iron sheep railings for repair. I was waiting for a horse to be shod, so I helped William unload the heavy and awkward sections. He said nothing until the job was finished and then said: "Oi reckoned that 'd tak me all mornin'. Now, dang it, Oi shall have to find summat else to do."

CHAPTER 19

Hay and Silage

Hugh and I were in friendly disagreement about whether to make our oats and ryegrass mixture into hay or silage. I favoured hay because it was a commodity with which I was familiar. It used routines at which I had worked while helping some of our neighbours, and which I understood and enjoyed. Silage I had never seen, and none of our neighbours made it. Hugh said that it was more nutritious than hay, was less dependent on good weather, and was a better use of a specially grown mixture like ours than was traditional haymaking. He sent me off to a demonstration of silage making at Knightshayes, the Home Farm of Sir John Amory, near Tiverton.

It was a very wet day in early May 1942, and as I cycled the ten or twelve uncomfortable miles, I thought that there must be something in the weather idea, but I also recalled the old saying "Rain in May, long hay". It had stopped raining when I joined the hundred or so farmers and farm workers who had gathered round the demonstration area. It was difficult not to envy the splendid farm buildings, the collection of brightly-painted wagons and carts, and the efficient-looking implements.

The Ministry of Agriculture lecturer had a good strong voice, good command of his subject, and a very good sense of humour. He started off by saying that it really was too wet for ideal silage making, and he was not intending to spoil too much of a splendid crop of clover and ryegrass by hauling in many loads — just enough to show how it should be done.

We were grouped in front of a number of newly-erected octagonal-shaped silos made of prefabricated timber panels bolted together. Each container was about twelve feet high, perhaps more, and about eight feet across. There were in addition one or two partially-erected silos which we could inspect, and one of these was to be used for the demonstration; no doubt other panels could be added as the work proceeded until the full height was attained. We were told that when the succulent green crop was thrown into the silo the breathing plants and micro-organisms would remove the oxygen and make carbon dioxide, and the temperature would rise. In these conditions bacteria of a kind that needed no oxygen, would convert the plant sugars into organic acids which would make unfavourable conditions for putrefaction or for further decomposition. A high protein food would result — just so long as air was excluded.

This statement — or something like it — was received in silence, and a rather uneasy shifting of feet as we looked doubtfully at one another. The demonstrator smiled and went on:

"You don't have to remember that. In a few minutes a trailer load of wet grass and clover will arrive here. Some men will fork it into this half made silo, and some other men will spread it evenly around and tread on it firmly to press it down and keep the air out. Because young grass and clover does not contain a large amount of natural sugar another man will, from time to time, spray the crop with a solution of molasses and water to help speed up the acid-making process. You do have to remember that, and please watch very carefully."

Almost as he spoke the trailer arrived and we moved to make room for a very efficient, almost stage performance, of what had just been described. The tractor and trailer went off to fetch another load, and we gathered round again. The demonstrator talked about the different crops that could be used to make silage, and said that thick-stemmed crops, like maize, would need to be shredded or chopped up in some way so that they could be compacted enough to exclude air. He went on to say that mature crops generally contained sufficient carbohydrates to make their own sugar, and did not require added molasses.

Another trailer load arrived and the stage play was re-enacted. The tractor set off again and the demonstrator asked for questions. A well-dressed gent with a plummy voice said that he had made hundreds of tons of maize silage, but had never used a shredder. Pressed for details about how the crop had been prepared, he said that he had used elephants to tread the maize at a farm in Kenya. A more typical Devon farmer asked what happened to thistles and ragwort, and was told that if thistles were nutritious we would grow them, but as they weren't we didn't, and that ragwort was a scheduled weed poisonous to stock, and should be pulled up anyway. The answer was pleasantly given and produced a lot of laughter, but the questions dried up — no one likes to be put down however pleasantly — and no one else was willing to take the risk.

After some talk about different types of silos, the conversion of old buildings into silos, and how to make silage in pits and heaps, the Min. of Ag. man said that he would hang around to answer personal questions, and there was a slow drift away. I cycled back to Spiceland in a very thoughtful frame of mind.

Cecil Edmunds, the farmer at Stentwood who shared Benjie the Bull, and who had sold us the bull-nosed Morris, rang up to say that he had found an old grass mower in need of repair; were we interested? Hugh arranged for a local agricultural engineer to recondition the mower at a cost of about twenty pounds, and it proved to be a splendid machine. Unfortunately we never bargained for its purchase, and later on we found that we were only part owners, and came under some friendly duress.

In mid-June Hugh mowed the Top Path Field, which was to be used for a childrens' camp, and we made some hay — poor thin stuff it was too — but it was our own. Soon afterwards we loaded the mower on to our wagon, and I set off with the horses to spend a few days with the Bubbs at Dunkeswell to mow their water meadows, and help them make hay. It was a very pleasant interlude of hard work in very pleasant company. It was my first experience of mowing but Bonnie, Prince and I were now well used to working together. I quickly learned to use the baffle board of the mower to control the mown grass as it fell in swathes behind the knife. The secret of good mowing is to use sharp knives, and Charles Bubb with his carpenter's background not only saw to it that the triangular sections on the eccentrically-driven knives were kept sharp, but showed me how to use a file to do the job myself.

There were two fields and we cut, and partially made, one field before mowing the second, so that we did not tempt the west country weather to spoil the whole crop. We had no horse swathe turner and no horse rake, so all the crop was turned by hand — shades of Tom Finch. So well did sun and wind behave, and so well did the hand operations dovetail with the loading and carting that, for once, there were no alarms and excursions, and all was safely gathered in.

While I had been away, Hugh had purchased a silo. Not one of the expensive substantial wooden structures I had seen at Knightshayes, but a circular structure made from sheets of cement asbestos held in place by metal clips. The principle was the same. The ground level circle of sheets was erected, and when this had been filled with succulent grass and oats, a second tier was added — and so on.

This was where the fun began. The crop had to be very evenly trod to preserve the symmetry of the pliable but brittle asbestos sheets; only a small departure from the vertical made it very difficult to fit and secure the metal clips in which the second tier sheets, which slightly overlapped the first tier, were slotted. The crop did not spread evenly, and treading the edges without actually touching the asbestos proved well nigh impossible. All too soon it became apparent that we were building a modern version of the leaning tower of Pisa. Wooden props had to be placed on the leaning side — much to the amusement of our sceptical neighbours, and the rabbit-trapping Wrights, who remarked that it was "leaning middling loike," "middling" being an all purpose adjective used to define the extent of success and disaster alike.

In the middle of all this activity Cecil Edmunds 'phoned to say that he wanted to use the mower to cut his hay, and we learned of our joint ownership. Moreover, he had only one horse, and needed to borrow another to make a team. His one horse was a partly broken filly, and he wanted to borrow the steadier of our two horses — Prince. Hugh was rightly unwilling to part with a horse unless either he or I went with it, and as Hugh could hardly leave Spiceland and the trainees for several days at such an important stage, we loaded the mower on to the tumbril and off I went to Stentwood.

I arrived just before noon on a lovely, hot, sunny haymaker of a day; we unloaded and refixed the horse pole to the mower. After a quick snack we introduced the horses to one another, harnessed them to the mower, and set off for the field. The part broken filly was a magnificent animal lighter boned, but slightly taller than Prince. She was a good mover and they proved a good match. The field was pretty well flat, and the crop thick with the grasses in flower — perfect. I suppressed, not for the first time, the feeling of regret that we had nothing like it, and cut the first swathe with Cecil watching anxiously, but the filly was not bothered by the noise and movement of the mower and we made good steady progress.

Came the time when the knife ran less smoothly, and I called for a change. I was well pleased with the way things were going. A mower knife consists of a series of equilateral triangular blades with sides about two inches long, sharpened on two of them, with the third rivetted to a steel bar which slides into a channel on the cutter bar. The knife is fixed by a bolt and hole mechanism to a hubwheel which is driven by a cog and ratchet mechanism fixed to one of the land wheels of the mower; power which is literally horse power. A crank on the hubwheel transforms the circular movement of the wheel into a forwards and backwards movement of the knife to produce the effect of a powerful scissor action on the cutter bar.

I put the machine out of gear, dismounted, looped the reins round the mower seat and secured them with a half hitch. The horses took advantage of the halt to snatch mouthfuls of grass, and were munching happily. Down on one knee, I released the catch which secured the knife and disconnected the bolt and hole arrangement to slide the worn knife out; this I did with no difficulty. The mower being out of gear, I was not worried about the horses who were standing comfortably still, and eating from the plenty within easy reach.

No doubt, with hindsight, I should have unyoked. Cecil handed me the fresh knife which I placed in position by balancing the blade on the tip of my index finger. Cecil was keeping more than half an eye on the horses, and was mindful of the possibility that his inexperienced mare could get restless and make a sudden move. More anxious than I was to get started again, he suddenly pushed the knife forward into its slide. I turned to him crossly, and said that it was a one man job and that he might have had my finger off. I had felt nothing; but he was looking at my hand and said "It seems I have."

The top of my index finger had gone and the finger was bleeding freely. I made a bandage with my handkerchief. We unhitched the horses and went back to the farm. I was in no pain, but mindful of tetanus and other possible infections, I wanted to bathe the finger in antiseptic. There was no antiseptic in the house, and I suggested salt which I had never used to such purpose before. I took a spoonful and plonked it straight on to the wound and passed out. I do not know for how long.

When I came round a concerned Cecil took me in his car to Dr. Lysaght Griffin in Hemyock, who gave me an injection of horse serum as an anti-tetanus precaution, and warned me not to let anyone give me a similar injection in future. He bathed the wound and dressed it with something called Chilean Balm, which he described as something new with claims to great healing properties. He also said that we should have searched for the tip which might have knit on again. The doctor became a friend and our family doctor.

With my arm in a sling I walked the four miles back to Spiceland, but I was in no shape to work. The index finger is in constant use without one realising it, and I could not do anything practical without touching it or knocking it. It throbbed, and was very tender and painful. I tried picking raspberries in the wall garden as a gesture towards doing something useful, and it may be, that there I learned by a very painful process to substitute my middle finger for the index. Although long years have passed, and the finger is only slightly distorted, it has little or no feeling in the tip, and it is my middle finger which unties knots and performs the small sensitive tasks.

There is a double postscript to this incident. First Cecil finished the mowing without me, — using the horse we had jealously protected, second, Roland Wood showed me his own right hand with two mis-shaped fingers and told me he had acquired them in very similar circumstances several years earlier. I asked him what he had done about it, and he said that he had wrapped his hand up in some rag and gone on mowing! He had never been to a doctor. Was my fear of tetanus a help or a hindrance, or is ignorance really bliss? I was in no distress until I applied the salt!

Half the oats and ryegrass were never made into silage, but grew too mature for good hay. August rains beat the crop to the ground. Eventually Hugh scythed what could be salvaged and the hand-made, biblical-style, sheaves were added to the stack of dredge corn from the drainage field.

Before long I was making yet another journey to Stentwood to collect the mower; then on to the Bubbs again where we took a second crop from the water meadows. This time we made silage in a disused piggery which Charles converted for the purpose.

Charles was not sure whether this late crop had enough natural sugars for silage so we added a solution of molasses poured from a watering can. To the spout of this can Charles tied a dessert spoon, and as one poured, the jet of liquid fell on the bowl of the spoon and produced a broad spread of spray which served our purpose well. Several gallons of the stuff were mixed in a large tin bath. Bonnie had a sweet tooth, rarely indulged in war time, and the treacley smell was too strong a temptation. He slipped his halter when no one was looking, and drank a gallon or more before he could be stopped. His soft white nose came out in a pimply rash; whether from over indulgence or allergy who knows?

CHAPTER 20

Harvest and a Sowing

We waited eagerly but apprehensively for our first corn harvest. The Drainage Field with its two acres of oats and two acres of mixed oats, barley, and maple peas was ripening fast but, like most small farmers dependent on a contractor for reaping and binding, we could only wait and fret as we watched the uncertain glory of a west country summer play havoc with the crop, and then look down, with some envy, at the farms in the Culm Valley as they were cleared of a bounteous harvest.

The Paris Green and Bran mixture had accounted for most of the leather-jackets, and those which escaped had not made serious inroads on the oats. Years of neglect had established a strong thistle population which resisted repeated attacks with hoes and thistle spuds. Cheek by jowl with the ears of corn were flowering and seeding thistle heads. When the contractor eventually came and we were able to stook — the local name was stitch — the sheaves in patterned lines across the field, the prickles seared our arms and chests as we hugged the sheaves in pairs to set one against another.

Oats are best cut before they are ripe so that the straw, which is good fodder, can dry out and cure like hay in the open field. The delayed reaping had ensured that our oats were very ripe and we could not afford to leave the sheaves long in the field before carting them to a flat spot outside the Tillage Field where we made our first corn stack. While working for other farmers I had learned to make reasonable wagon loads of hay and corn, and had watched others make stacks of enviable symmetry. I knew jolly well that my first effort would bear no resemblance to what locals called a "prapper job." I should be lucky if it looked anything like a stack, but I was determined that it should not fall down.

The secret is to lay the sheaves, butts outwards, in regular sequence along the outer edges of the stack and to overlap them at the corners so that they lock together to make a right angle. As the stack rises higher it can be allowed to spread a little so that the upper sheaves protect the lower from rain, but if this spread is allowed to get out of hand the whole structure becomes unstable. When the stack is dismantled at threshing time it is important to lift and pitch the sheaves in reverse order to avoid the strain of trying to lift sheaves that are "locked in".

I had watched experts quickly lay the sheaves in order using long-handled two-pronged forks, almost casually, as the pitchers fed them. But lesser men kneeled at the perimeter of the stack and laid the sheaves in position by hand, using their knees and body weight to keep the building process tidy and tight. I decided to be a lesser man, and we spent the evening hours needling out the thistle prickles imbedded in my arms and legs. The finished stack was not a work of art, but it stood up, and as none of us aspired to thatching skills, a heavy tarpaulin was thrown over the asymmetric roof until such time as the threshing tackle could be hired.

The War Agricultural Committee men had "suggested" during one of their regular visits that the Middle Path Field should be put down to wheat, and our next job was to lift the potato crop quickly so that seed could be sown by mid-October.

Hugh had bought a two horse "finger plough" to lift the spuds, and this proved the best and cleanest method of doing the job that I have ever encountered. The plough could be set deep and still be well within the strength of Bonnie and Prince. The disturbed soil slipped through the open "fingers" but the potatoes, most of them, remained on the surface for relatively easy picking, and to effect a speedy job the Semi-Perms agreed to an augmented team of "tatie pickers." To make full use of this large group by keeping the plough team intact and operational throughout the day, we borrowed a horse to cart the gathered crop down to the farm.

The borrowed horse, a thank offering from Cecil Edmunds, was an elderly cob of a distinctive light grey colour, almost white. Stronger than Fanny, who could not have coped with pressure haulage, but not as big or as strong as the sadly remembered June, the animal looked very odd when harnessed to our tumbril — like a man in oversize ill-fitting trousers. The elder rabbit-trapping Wright brother watched its uneven progress down the steep part of our drive and remarked that "it was a middling sized 'orse for that yer cart." Half an hour later his younger brother watched a similar erratic journey and said "that's a middling sized cart for that yer 'orse." Father Wright, a huge man in every way, passed by some while after, and stood arms akimbo, looking at the horse who was resting with drooping head at the top of the hill. "You'm got a middling sized 'orse in yon cart."

he said and confirmed the opinion of his elder son.

With the potatoes cleared, the field was shallow ploughed on a counter diagonal line from the one we used in the spring. The field was too steep, and the autumn rains had rendered the Keuper marl too heavy, for the corn drill we had borrowed in the Spring. Our wheat was broadcast in biblical fashion over the rough furrows, and the seed covered by horse harrowing.

Marjorie was the sower. Just as we could look down on the valley farms and note what was going on, so all the farmers on the west of our hill could look up and see the Middle Path Field. By some accident of slope it was easily identified for miles around. Hand sowing was not all that uncommon in our part of Devon, and our neighbours watched with interest, knowing that in due time the sprouting corn would reveal what sort of a fist she had made of it.

It was not easy. Apart from the uneven furrows, there was the sideling knapp to contend with as she walked to and fro across the field; the heavy bucket containing the wheat grains had to be supported in the crook of her left arm leaving the right hand and arm free to scatter the good seed on the ground. The seed had been treated with a mercuric dressing as a precaution against pest and disease; as her hand released the grains of corn, air-borne particles of the mercuric dust blew into her eyes, mouth and nostrils. By the end of the day her nose had bled, and her nose and eyes were very sore, but there was also a quiet satisfaction in having done a job that had been basic to human life for centuries.

In those days nobody thought very much about the side effects of using chemicals to control pests and diseases. The general view was that science was a boon and a blessing to man, and that increased yields were the result of better farming. One Spicelander, Jack Bazeley, who was an engineer, worked for a time at a seed merchants near Cirencester. We visited him there at a time when he was working round the clock dressing seed corn and was exposed to chemically impregnated dusts for hours at a time without any protection. He snatched a few minutes to talk to us, and was enthusiastic about the worthwhile nature of work which was ensuring food supplies. His eyes were red rimmed and his face, hair, and overalls were caked in a pink and blue rime. He was tired and looked unwell, but he shrugged off our concern, saying that it was seasonal work and that he would soon get over it.

Three weeks after the sowing the green seedlings proclaimed that ours had been a "prapper job." Neighbours, always ready to smile at failure, were quick to praise. Cecil Snell, whose farm adjoined Spiceland, told me that he had watched my "little maid" at work and added, "now all can see 'tis sewent." That is the nearest I can get to spelling what he said was an old word for describing an even spread.

The arrival of the threshing tackle was a great occasion. We had been advised to have ready a supply of steam coal for the traction engine, and a supply of cider for the engine men. The clanking cavalcade could be heard long before it came in view, puffing its way up and down the hills, making heavy weather of the steep ups, and idling fussily along the downs.

The foreman would not risk his heavy tackle in the field where we had built our stack, and settled upon a level piece of hard ground near the house. We had to unbuild our carefully made stack — a job made harder by my determination to bind it all tightly together — and cart the sheaves in wagons to feed the Moloch of whirring wheels and flapping belts. Apart from breaks for forenoons and lunch, we were slaves to the ceaseless tasks of feeding the material in at the top and shifting the outpourings of corn, straw and chaff until, the sacrifice complete, the corn was in sacks, the straw in bales, and the chaff in an untidy unstable heap.

The foreman was a disciplined, but kindly, Somerset man who ministered lovingly to his aged machinery. Walking round with observant eye, primed oilcan, and a blackened handful of oily rag waste, he paused occasionally to make adjustments here and there, to sample the quality of the grain as it poured into the four bushel sacks, and to keep the whole operation running smoothly.

At the forenoons break he called for the cider. I removed the cork and handed the heavy stone jar to him. "Local?" he enquired. "Down the hill." I replied, pointing in the direction of the farm which had supplied us. He balanced the jar along his forearm, lifted the spout to his lips and took a long swig. He looked at me and smiled broadly. "They only make two sorts of cider in Devon — bad and indifferent. This is indifferent." He took another long swig, wiped the spout with the back of his hand and passed the jar back for circulation among the workers. Threshing is thirsty work. I took a long swig myself — it was strong, sharp and very welcome.

Later, at the lunch break, I asked him about cider quality. He said that cider making on the farms in Devonshire had degenerated. Fewer farms made it, and those that did collected, without discrimination, all the apples from the orchard to make one big "cheese" from which the juice was pressed. In Somerset, he assured me, they selected the apples from one variety, or blend of proven varieties, and made several different types of cider — some of which were as good as champagne! This bare description cannot do justice to his rich west country voice ringing with scorn, and a passion stirred by memory and county pride. The Wright brothers always referred to Somerset folk as foreigners, and to Taunton, where they had never been, as if it were some place far away. It was all of sixteen miles. The threshing man expressed his home thoughts from abroad in terms as lyrical as Browning.

Walter Percy farmed All Hallows which, at more than three hundred acres, was the largest farm in our parish. He had a big grass field which bordered on our woodland, and adjoined our farm buildings. It was separated from his house and the rest of his farm by a lane. Our relations were cool rather than cordial, because he had made it plain in the early days that he did not understand pacifists. Nevertheless greetings were always civilly exchanged, and it was he who had lent us the corn drill. He possessed a "fiddle" — a contraption for broadcasting seed which was not unlike a large violin with the "bow" already attached. The device was held against the body between the chest and the hip, seed was poured into the box of the fiddle and, as the sower walked across the field using the bow as if he were playing a stringed instrument, the seed was scattered evenly. Mr. Percy had complimented us on our broadcast field and had offered the loan of his fiddle for the future — adding that we had done pretty well without it.

In mid-December he called to tell us that the Agricultural Committee had asked him to plough the big pasture field for wheat. He drew attention to the deplorable state of the hedge and bank between our copse and his field, and said that, as he did not want our stock breaking into his field once it had been ploughed and sown, something would have to be done about it. He guessed that we "wouldn't rightly know how to set about putting it in order, but, if Hugh would put a few chaps on it, his man would show them the way of it."

His man was Albert Bird. Tall and dark with a long drooping moustache, he wore a broad leather belt fastened with a large brass buckle, and a battered felt hat with an outsize brim. He had fought in the first world war, and was believed to be scathing and violently picturesque in his comments about "those chaps at the House." I was asked to seek him out, and sort things out.

He was repairing one of the Percy hedges, and stopped work to rest his chin on folded arms supported by a long handled spade of convenient height. He looked down at me for a few minutes without speaking, and then said that he did not greatly care for the idea, but he supposed that we must get on with it. He'd want four or five men with billhooks, slashers, an axe, trenching tools, and "sho'els" like the one he was using. He passed it over for inspection. The blade was slightly dished and pointed like the spade on a pack of cards; it was shining with the polish of use, and the edges were very sharp. The long handle was curved at the blade end and about five feet long. We had nothing like it, but I had seen local folk digging their gardens with what looked to be a very clumsy tool for that job, and I had seen them displayed for sale in the Cullompton ironmongery store.

I handed it back and waited, hoping that he would start work again and that I could watch him in action. After all, I had waited nearly two years for this opportunity. Back in the summer, Cecil Snell had cursed me roundly when some of our pigs had broken through into a corn field. After I had driven them back, and we were standing in his field looking at the trampled corn, he had shaken his fist fiercely at the broken down bank and the ragged hedge growth, and shouted that it should have been put to rights in the winter. I had looked pointedly at his own hedge, which was little better, and he had let out a great guffaw and softened immediately. "Us know how, but us don't allus do it." Restored to his usual boisterous good humour he had put one arm on my shoulder and gestured sweepingly with the other — "Do you keep they pigs outer y'ere."

Albert Bird thrust his spade into the ground, and lifted a triangular piece of turf which he swung dexterously into a hole in the bank and rammed it home. In a few minutes several more turf "bricks" had been dug out and put in place. Then, raising the spade above shoulder height, and using it with short jabbing and cutting movements, he attacked the earth behind the turfs and battered it firmly and tightly into the gaps between the triangles to bind them together in a neat repair. He stood back and looked with justifiable pride at his handiwork before pointing in the direction of our wood. "It'll not be that easy over yon." With something near a smile he turned back to his work. I was dismissed.

We bought a three cornered spade — the ironmonger said they were known as Cornish Shovels or Sho'els — and I practised digging and swinging with some misgiving. It was heavy and awkward. The small group of us who reported for work with Albert Bird were less than confident, and prepared for a torrid time. We were very wrong.

The bank should have been about four feet high but had collapsed in many places to much less than that. It was full of rabbit holes, most of them old and abandoned, but many showing signs of recent occupation with small heaps of freshly excavated soil spilling out all over the place. The hedge growths — mostly hazel with some field maple, hawthorn, and sloe bushes mixed in, plus an occasional unwelcome elderberry, were heavily laced with brambles and were growing out of the bankside and into the field as well as where they should have been — on top of the bank.

Albert Bird swept his eye along thirty or fifty yards of the hedge, indicated the stretch with an embracing gesture, and said "Clear all the side wood and brambles out o' the way and do 'ee make un clean. I'll be back."

This was straightforward work with which we were familiar, and we set to with a will, cutting the wood cleanly and slashing the brambles to such good effect, that we soon had piles of brushwood and rubbish for burning as well as some decent sized trunks for logging later on. On his return Albert Bird was impressed enough to make no comment, and he seemed to enjoy speaking the few sentences with which he described the next stage of the job.

The bank should be made out of turves dug from a strip not more than a yard wide from the base of the bank, and earth should be cast up behind the turves and rammed home to make it all firm. The bank must be wider at its base than at the top so that it does not topple down, and the hedge trees should grow on top of the bank. He looked disparagingly at the tumbledown ragged bank. There was no pasture from which turves could be dug within several yards of the base because the shade from the overgrown hedge had killed off the grass.

He stood sideways on to the bank, grasped his three cornered spade and, using his height and strength to good purpose, employed its sharp edges to slice and cut his way into the sprawling mound. By pulling and levering the severed earth away from the bank he quickly established a "bottom" line and a tapered face to the bank which was, even so, still riddled with holes, ragged stumps, and stools of the bushes we had chopped and slashed. Discarding the spade, he grasped a trenching tool with a pickaxe point on one side of its heavy head and an adze-like cutting tool on the other.

It is difficult to describe adequately the succession and variety of forceful movements which he used, employing in turn pick, adze, and the whole tool head held horizontally as a broad hammer, to move soil, remove roots, fill holes, collapse rabbit runs, and generally batter the old bank solid once again. When he had dealt with about fifteen yards he pointed to the heaps of spoil at his feet and told us to cast it up on top of the bank, spread it and beat it and so build the bank up to something near its proper height. It was this operation which taught us the value of the long "shoel" with its curved handle. This seemingly clumsy tool came into its own as heavy spadefuls were levered above shoulder height, sometimes using the knee as a fulcrum, and deposited just where they were needed. We took turns to use the one we had purchased, and found that the effort required to do the same job when using the standard short handled digging spade was in marked and blistering contrast. Knowing what tools were right for the job and how to use them was as important as "rightly knowing how to set about it." Now we understood what our neighbours meant when they talked about casting banks.

For a few days on either side of Christmas we worked as a gang. First clearing the side wood in front, and then working behind our mentor to build on the remodelled foundation. From time to time Albert himself layered the hedge trees on the bank top, forcing them into new positions and pinning them down with stakes and soil. He said very little, and worked very hard in that seemingly leisured way that folk have who know their trade and are masters of their tools. He was determined to keep us working, and resisted questions which might have ended in breaks for conversation, but tersely put us to rights when necessary.

We worked steadily along the bank, and his pride of achievement showed in the ungrudging way in which he acknowledged the contribution of his pupils. Our last day together was new year's eve; from then on he would have no more time to spare for a job which was rightly our own responsibility. It was all but dark — dimpsey was the local word — when we knocked off. The wind had veered to the north, and there was a lowering sky as our still hesitant, but no longer grudging, association came to an end with tentative new year good wishes. In those last minutes several skeins of honking geese flew over our heads, travelling from south east to north west. Albert leaned on his spade, chin on folded arms, just as he had done on our first encounter, and watched them pensively until they were out of sight and hearing. "There'll be snow before morning." He raised his spade in a farewell gesture, shouldered it, and slowly followed the geese out of our sight. He was right about the snow.

CHAPTER 21

Children's Camps

In the summer of 1940 the Peace Committee of the Society of Friends had an idea for a children's camp to relieve the pressure on foster parents who were caring for children evacuated from London and who were billeted in Somerset. They offered to finance the camp helpers on a "pocket money" basis and passed on the suggestion to Spiceland, who found the helpers and rented from a neighbouring farmer, a flattish field adjoining the copse. The camp ran through August to mid-September, and provided holidays for groups of children selected by the Bristol Health Clinic who may also have provided some financial support. Brief Spiceland minutes record a successful venture but little is recorded of human interest — that is stored in the memories of the helpers and the campers and spills out in conversation.

The initiative for a second camp seems to have come from Spiceland itself. It ran from July 5th until mid-September of 1941. Twenty-two children came for the first week, but numbers rose to forty for the succeeding weeks. Negotiations to secure equipment and children were very protracted, and there was an air of "will they, wont they" until the last minute.

Because the early weeks were in term time, provision had to be made for schooling so that the children's education did not suffer overly. In Victorian times the Vicar had housed the village school in his part of the house so there was historical precedent for a Spiceland school.

The frustrations and eventual triumph of the camp organisers were the substance of a fairy story published in Wallpaper.

"Once upon a time there lived on a high hill in the land of Flavring, a company of pure people who came to live in a ruined monastery and train themselves in good works. These good people decided to take in, and do for, the children of the cities where houses were being destroyed, and life was very cheap. They held a camp and the children came and were happy and survived.

The following year, the good people decided to take in and do for more children. From their number they appointed six to do the menial work, and their names were Benji, which means Leader, What-oh the meek, and Little-un his wife, Willi and Dalli who were also married, and Big Elf. All this happened in early June.

In February of that same year the Wizard had prophesied that there would be a Demand for this thing, and suggested to the Odds and Ends (who were a company of Learned Ones) that arrangements, similar to those of the previous year, should be made — only better. Micki the wise, who was leader of the House, did cogitate and ruminate, and passed on the suggestion to the Right Quarters. Unfortunately it was shelved. Later on, certain persistent people revived the idea, and War Vics (who were very good people indeed) sent money so that a beautiful field could be hired and other essential things bought.

Now it came to pass, on another day in June — a hot day when white clouds passed across a blue sky and the world was very lovely — that the chosen six called upon Micki the Wise and had a pow-wow. And it seemed that they must look slippy for the children were due on Saturday, and it was now even Wednesday. So they toiled in the field and built them a fire-place of bricks with a canopy of old tin, and they dug pits and carried wood which they used for a variety of purposes. When they had done all this they asked themselves, what more could they do, but had to confess that until the Equipment came they were snookered. So they called upon Micki the Wise again, but he could not help them because possession was nine points of The Law. But he did give them a line to go on.

So Benji, the Leader, went on it and it led him to the house of one Ren, an influential man and one who liked to do good works for the pleasure they gave to other people, and that reflected great credit on himself. Here Benji ran to earth the missing Equipment, and many times afterwards he buzzed along that line to keep his eye upon it. But it happened that Ren, and his wife Ji — who did good works for the satisfaction they gave herself, had need of the Equipment, and were loth to part with it. Also Ji was providing the children, so things were at a standstill.

The promised Saturday came and passed, and Big Elf, finding other good work, departed to it. Then Benji, the Leader, became unsettled and muttered vague threats of desertion — for the Equipment and the children were not forthcoming. What-oh put on his spectacles and looked at things through a glass darkly; the others were also glum.

But Benji buzzed along the line once more and returned with cheering news. Ji had promised the children for the following Saturday, and the Equipment would also be looked out. So there was great jubilation, and much wood was cut and stacked for a celebration (though the Blackout was borne in mind). Then Ji came along that same line, for there was only one, to say that the Authorities — who were even greater than the Odds and Ends — had raised a snag: but it seemed that there were more snags than one. So Ji and Benji buzzed at each other in turn, and the faces of the Five became glum again. They did not come up for "seconds" which was accounted a very bad sign in the land of Flavring. Once more Benji began to murmur discontentedly, for he was a very impatient man.

Before the mood became really serious there was more buzzing along the line, the Equipment was despatched and the children promised in a plain van for July 5th."

The snag raised by the Authorities was that the marquee and all the tents were to be camouflaged — an activity which produced a fine flowering of surrealist art.

A typical camp week was described, by John Trivett, in yet another Wallpaper article beginning:

".... on Monday afternoon when, having said and kissed very tearful 'goodbyes' to one camp party, we await another. They arrive, usually late, and the first half hour is spent in assigning sleeping quarters, collecting ration books, and learning names. This task is very difficult, because only when they leave have we succeeded in remembering all the names of the previous forty children, and now we must start all over again. We are usually 'Sir' or 'Mister' at first, but this soon gives way to Christian names or rapidly evolved nick-names — 'Lightning', 'Duck', 'Haircut', 'Big Bad Wolf' all to our faces.

The first meal is usually a moderately quiet affair, for which temporary relief we say 'much thanks', but once the children discover that we do not bite, the bubble rises to crescendo. Meals are really the events of the week. The children serve themselves — just reward after chores — and, although 'seconds' and its successors is an innovation, it is not long before the whole gang can show Spicelanders how to come up for more and leave them standing.

At mealtimes, too, the past, present and projected futures of the helpers is investigated by entreating enquiries and then embellished. Greta has been the wife of Benjy or Don more often than of John, and our ages range variously from sixteen to ninety, and from day to day. At present the life histories of Benjy and John are being pieced together, and it appears that they are — "honest injun" — twin step-brothers who have travelled extensively "up the Hudson" catching wolves and strangling bears with their bare hands (pun intended) or — in Panama where they built the canal by each digging from one end inwards or — in Spain where they were matador and toreador respectively. In less exciting periods of their lives they worked in a chocolate factory near Aldgate Pump, where Benjy put the bars in silver paper and Don wrapped them in their outside labels. Unfortunately when one does speak the truth one is seldom believed.

The week passes all too quickly, with the Podex match on Tuesday, where too many cooks usually spoil our broth, the Sports on Thursday, where everyone manages somehow to win a prize, the Concert on Friday, and the Picnic on Saturday.

Throughout these seven days the main characteristics of all children are very much in evidence — the noise they make, the ceaseless activity, and the amount they eat. I should like a scientific explanation of how a child aged ten can eat "thirds" of roast and two veg, currant pudding, and immediately follow this with a race round the field. I know that Edwin can do the eating but does he run back to the farm afterwards?"

Natural humour abounds — here is a selection from our social column:

Small child: 'Is that a 'ome up there?'

Helper: 'Yes, for awkward children.'

Chocolate Spread? No, you buy it in a cartoon.

Peeling spuds: 'E keeps on dipping the 'andle in the water, and rubbin it on the teddies an' making 'em green.'

Rosemarie, arriving today, is the grandmother of Benjy and John, and has been having monkey gland treatment for her one hundred and two years!!!"

Podex was a form of cricket cum stool-ball played with an Indian club for a bat and, either a tennis ball or a short stout stick for a ball. The game was so popular with campers and Spicelanders that it was difficult to regulate the team numbers; at times everyone seemed to be fielding. Nevertheless, I remember watching an innings of distinction played in late, very late, evening sunshine. Tom Henderson, a peace-time student of music, who must also have learned to wield the willow, struck the ball with elegant ease, and his cries of 'stay' or 'one only' as he controlled the running between the wickets might have echoed Francis Thompson at Lords —

'As the run stealers flicker to and fro,
To and fro:-
O my Hornby and my Barlow long ago!'

Two farming memories of this camp stand out. Before the camp began much equipment was carted from the house to the field, and some odd-shaped loads made precarious journeys along the narrow lanes. One load was built up on the wooden staging of the marquee floor, and the platform proved too wide to clear the gate posts at the top of the drive. To avoid dismantling and rebuilding the load, John Armstrong, whose physique matched his name, climbed into the cart and, like Atlas, balanced the structure on his shoulders, lifted it a few inches and for a few seconds, while the horse moved a few steps forward and cleared the gateway. John fell ungracefully in a heap at the bottom of the cart.

Water, always a problem at Spiceland, had to be carted in a large two-hundred-gallon tank from a spring in the village to the camp site — a distance of about a mile. This exercise gave trainees a lot of experience in carrying heavy buckets of water from the spring to the cart, and some experience of horse management.

The horse was June, and faced with a choice of going down the drive towards home or of continuing along the lane to the camp site, June decided that she would try for home. June's steadily increasing speed homewards in defiance of the trainee's determined efforts to keep her on course for the camp combined to turn the water cart over.

I was summoned to the scene by a breathless message that June was lying in the road with the overturned cart with Marjorie, who had been similarly summoned from the farmyard, sitting on June's neck to keep her quiet.

Murphy's Law decreed that the cart harness chain hook was underneath, and the chain held so tightly that the combined efforts of several could not free June. Someone arrived with a hacksaw, and soon one link was severed. Marjorie stood up, we all stood back, and with a shudder and a rattle, June also came to her feet and stood in a dishevelled array of chains and leather. June was unhurt, the cart undamaged, a false link repaired the chain, and mastery of the situation was restored as June was led firmly back to the spring and the water tank refilled.

In all two hundred and ninety-one children came to this camp. One group from Bristol arrived with a reputation and a history of violence. Jealous of their few possessions — one boy wore all his clothes, including his pyjamas, to prevent theft — they raided a neighbouring orchard within half an hour of arrival. Although under fourteen years of age they defiantly lit cigarettes and scattered matches and fag-ends. They were a group who had been sent for two weeks but, after three days, they had seen enough to realise that the helpers were strong enough physically to have dealt with them violently. They had expected violence to be answered with violence, and when that did not happen they changed sufficiently to become just children enjoying a holiday in the country.

By the fourth day there was a transformation, and for their second week they were joined by twenty secondary school girls who played no small part in a continuing process of civilisation.

A third camp, in 1942, was sited in the Top Path Field from which we had taken our first very thin crop of hay. To describe the field as even flattish would be a misnomer; but it was flat enough to allow Podex and other games. It called for no rent, and it had character. The uncertain stream which flowed along its boundary with the Drainage Field, had become more certain with the flow of drainage water, and a sadly wet summer ensured that there was a lot of water to drain. A protected and filtered pit was constructed in the stream to provide a primitive but effective cooler for storing milk and other perishable foods. Not protected enough. One morning a fine frog made a theatrical stage entry on to the breakfast table by leaping out of a jug of milk!

There were some fine trees in the hedgerows, which made the site secluded enough for the campers to make a small world of their own. They invented games of imagination to fit the terrain and the changeable weather. Fanciful names were invented for the tents, and the helpers played their part in the development of practical escapism.

The old rented site had been remote from the village, but this one was near enough for the village children to become welcome visitors and participants. A mile or so away lived a small group of non-conformist families whose homes clustered round a tiny chapel in a hamlet called Sainthill. They provided welcoming hospitality to a succession of campers who made the journey through what must be some of the most attractive country on the Blackdowns.

A moonlight ramble found a high point from which could be seen the distant sea reflecting a brilliant moon, and an early morning foraging party gathered mushrooms from the Drainage Field.

In September, the camp helpers looked back on a kaleidoscope of children and weather, with an accompaniment of noise and less noise, and benisons of cocoa which signalled the end of each tiring day.

CHAPTER 22

Gardens and Gardeners

The Spiceland gardens could be described as challenging, daunting or dispiriting. Certainly nothing about them was easy, but they could also be rewarding.

The front garden, of about an acre, sloped steeply from the south side of the house and, in earlier times, it had been a terraced pleasure garden laid out in beds and walkways. The Wayfarers had used it as a vegetable garden, and so did we.

The terraces had given way to an uneven slope with a few grass paths heavily infested with couch grass which spread greedily into the cultivated areas. The soil was one of the heavy marls which baked bricklike in the sun, and the southward slope made it into a sun trap. Good crops of cabbage, cauliflower, beans, peas, carrots and beetroot were grown, but at a heavy cost in man and woman power. There were only a few days in the year when the soil worked easily, and they were easily missed. At most times it was either too wet or too hard — the Devon climate with its heavy rainfall and hot sunshine saw to that. At such times heavy wear on garden tools and human muscles beat the clods into manageable texture. Hundreds of heavy buckets and cans of water were portered when planting out was followed by dry days.

Beyond this garden was a small neglected copse which had one or two fine trees, and lots of rampant brambles, nettles and other tough weeds. At some time in its history this area had been planted with hundreds of pheasant-eye narcissi. In the spring they flowered in a profusion of wild beauty — a beauty which, because it was totally unexpected, must have gladdened the hearts of those who experienced the first Spiceland spring.

Farther down the hill, hidden from the house, was a walled garden. It was split level, and divided into four large main plots. It had wide borders running the length of the walls against which grew some trained fruit trees, including a neglected and rampant fig tree which set fruits, but rarely ripened them. Entry to the garden was through a heavy door which reminded me of Robert Louis Stevenson's "Sire de Malatroit's Door" — but this door led to few adventures other than hard work.

The trackway from the house down to the door was too steep for the passage of reasonable loads of water or farmyard manure, though some of us attempted risky and sometimes wasteful deliveries with the small Construction made cart or a strong sledge — to the obvious discomfort and displeasure of the horses. Once again the rewards of cultivation had to be won by the application of hand tools, wheel-barrows, buckets and muscles. In the woody wasteland between the wall garden and Tinkers' Orchard, someone, probably Hugh, discovered a well, and in times of serious drought a chain of humans with buckets was employed to save endangered crops. It was a quiet mellow place in which to work, warm and scented when the weather was right, and sheltered when it was not.

The surrounding trees were the homes of many birds. Nuthatch, tree creeper, spotted and green woodpeckers all, at some time, made the repetitive chores of digging, raking, hoeing or fruit picking more of a pleasure. Once a meadow pippit nested in a hollow where the terrace wall had fallen. She watched me attentively while I hoed the bed close by, but did not leave her eggs. Other interesting creatures, like slow-worms and toads, made use of the sun and shelter, and added to the general interest of the place. Spiceland's heavy dependency on manual labour probably inhibited the use of the laboursaving devices and inventive ingenuity which could have made the wall garden a very much more productive asset. Hard work was to be welcomed not avoided. As it was the superb cos lettuces and other delectable vegetables, the baskets of gooseberries, raspberries, black currants and stawberries, which we picked for the kitchen, or sold to a local market gardener, were just a hint of the Victorian gracious living which the garden was designed to provide for "them up at the big house."

West of the path to the wall garden was a steep exposed orchard of neglected trees interplanted with market garden crops and, adjoining that, a triangular plot of about three-quarters of an acre of heavy arable land; beyond these two areas was the famous, or infamous, two-tine field which encompassed folly, despair, hope, and reward in one steep stretch of clay which is forever fixed in many Spiceland memories.

A succession of gardeners had to plan with Hugh how best to use these areas, and how to use the mainly inexperienced trainees, so that they got as wide an experience as possible of both farming and gardening practices. At the same time they had to make certain that the farm and gardens supplied

Spiceland's needs in homegrown food, and provide a surplus for sale to generate much needed income.

A series of evening lectures attempted to put the work of the training month into the context of a farm and garden year. They were simple, factual, liberally laced with anecdotes, and highly entertaining; but after hard days of unaccustomed labour, trainees sometimes slipped quietly into sleep. Nevertheless, much of the teaching, and most of the stories passed subliminally and effectively into Spiceland folk lore.

The first gardener was Rudi Weiss the Viennese refugee. I remember him most vividly as he laboured in the intractable front garden where I spent much of my working holiday in May 1940. Rudi was trying to conjure a tilth out of clods baked by a relentless sun at the same time as he was trying to keep earlier sowings of carrots, beetroots, onions, peas and beans thriving in near drought conditions. When he surrendered the first job to me, I noticed the mutilated fingers which were a legacy from his last months in Austria. He never talked to me about his experiences, but he did lament a lost dexterity which made him fumble simple operations, and spoiled his enjoyment in playing the violin.

It was as we worked together that he told me that he had once been administratively responsible for the Royal Parks in Vienna, and that the practical chores which he had once assigned to others, did not come easily to him. He shrugged his broad but stooping shoulders, and said "It must be". He could not hide his pedantic desire for order and regularity, nor could he disguise a wish to be growing more beautiful plants. He found it hard to bear with the ravages of pests and birds, and his quiet kindly nature could change to fierceness when he tackled them. I next saw and talked with him on the farm walk which preceded his internment, and after that not again until a Spiceland Reunion in the 1970s when the rough garden clothes had been exchanged for a dark suit, and the garden fork for a pen. The shy kindly man speaking English slowly and carefully with a marked Austrian accent was still there.

In November 1940 Charles Bubb, one of the early trainees who had many practical skills returned to work with Rudi but essentially to take charge of the market gardens. Although working with wood was his main interest, he hailed from a fruit growing and market gardening district of Worcestershire, and understood the possibilities, problems and pitfalls of commercial growing. He, probably more than any one else, realised how neccessary it was to plan and work for a surplus beyond estimated needs. In April 1941 he married another Spiceland trainee, Mary Quick, and they moved to the small farm which she had bought at Dunkeswell about four miles away.

But in those winter and early spring months, he had laid the foundations for the garden crops of 1941. He established cold frames in the walled garden where the seedling plants were raised in protected conditions for early maturity; introduced the two-tine fork which conquered the steep field, and generally left his practical mark on Spiceland's development.

Winifred Richardson, who succeeded Charles, brought a wide theoretical knowledge of horticulture coupled with practical experience which she applied with tremendous devotion and energy. Never content to explain and demonstrate what needed to be done, she led by example and did it herself. Because her skills in using tools had been developed by constant application and practice, and seemed to come so much more easily to her than to most, none of us realised just how much she overtaxed her strength.

In the years of 1941 and '42 the gardens and Tillage Field produced large quantities of vegetables of all kinds — more than enough for a community which often exceeded sixty people in residence. The surplus went to an uncertain market in Exeter through the good offices of a local market gardener. Uncertain, because he supplied his customers under contract and only needed our surplus when he himself was unable to meet his contracted deliveries, or when there were additional outlets — which he did his best to find. There were no large markets for vegetables and fruit in the south west and supplying the London market was a different sort of undertaking altogether.

Claude Turner and his extended family were a self- contained religious unit akin to the Plymouth Brethren but less rigid in dogma, and with some theological affinity to Friends. Hugh once came across the Turner lorry parked in a lane by a wood and, seemingly, unattended. He found Claude seated on a log and meditating on a Quaker pamphlet about silent worship.

The extended family were also the business, and they were knowledgeable and successful growers who worked together and tried to apply their religious principles to whatever they undertook.

Strong friendships grew up between the Turners and those of us who had regular contacts with them as a consequence of this marketing arrangement. Friday was market day in Exeter. Thursday was the day for carting our contribution to the Turner holding, where we were always well received, and where their own excellent field crops were open to inspection. One of the best ways of viewing the countryside is from the top of a load of crated cauliflowers.

Cauliflowers, or headed broccoli, were among our most successful crops, and sowings of Roscoff Nos 1, 2 , 3, 4 and 5 could secure a succession of fine curds from September to May. The abundance of leaves surrounding the curds were trimmed before crating and supplied a spinoff protein food for calves and cows.

Winifred also produced good bunches of early beetroot, carrots, broad and runner beans. It was when I watched her straighten her back after preparing a trench for sowing a new row of runner beans, that I realised how physically demanding it had been to take the big step from gardening to market gardening — even on our relatively small scale. I fetched a horse and the plough, set it to draw wide shallow furrows and together we planted the area by sowing beans in every alternate furrow and then raking the furrows to an even tilth. It was a clumsy operation for a big horse on relatively short rows, but it was effective, if not cost effective, and a great relief.

On another occasion I helped her to thin long rows of carrots after heavy showers had made the soil just right for the job. Even so the shuffling gait along the rows with our backs bent double as we pulled and bunched, and rushed to complete the job before the soil baked again, opened my eyes to what it was all about. Heavy lifting, pitching hay and corn sheaves for long spells — that I had experienced. This was different, more exacting, even fiddly, just as tiring, but lacking the rythm which helped to keep one going. I also learned that pulling carrots on a warm moist day created a scent which extended a generous invitation to the predatory carrot fly.

In July 1941 the ground prepared for leeks had baked solid, and there was no sign of rain. Winifred surveyed this with something akin to despair, but we solved it by making holes about eight inches deep with a crowbar, dropping a leek plant in each hole and then filling the holes with laboriously carried water. At the time it seemed like a defiant gesture but, come February and March 1942 of a hard winter, which spoiled many other vegetables, we dug, with nearly as much hard graft as it had taken to plant them, but with enormous satisfaction, magnificent leeks for ourselves and for market.

Appreciating help is not the same as admitting that, without it, the limits were being stretched too far. Winifred's character was such as to see help as a release to do something else — and there was always something else.

It is all too easy to identify those whom you think are holding back — and you can be very wrong about that. It is very difficult to recognise when others are on or over the limits. We were most of us working very hard and for long hours, but those of us who still had something in reserve, or, more likely, good powers of recovery, accepted too readily that that was also true for others.

The farm, with the fascination of caring for animals exercising a strong pull, with the opportunities for doing a wide variety of jobs which were outside the experience of most trainees, probably took more than its fair share of the trainee labour available. After all, most of us had some experience of gardening! Some trainees who were vegetarian had understandable objections to animal husbandry, and spent the whole of their "outdoor month" in the gardens. With hindsight it would have been better had there been more of them.

When, in the summer of 1942, Winifred's doctor cried "enough is enough" , and she left us to take up a post in Cumbria as a horticulture advisor, she had widened the scope of Spiceland's gardening immeasurably. Crops of many different varieties had been planted. New and improved varieties of fruit bushes had been brought in with the intention of propagating more, and extending the season and the yields. Some new trees had been introduced to the walled garden including Morello cherries on the north wall, and older trees had been pruned, reshaped, and secured to the walls. Even the neglected open orchard had been tackled and some of the trees regrafted. The ground had literally been prepared for something worthwhile. Unfortunately there was no one with Winifred's knowledge and ability to succeed her.

CHAPTER 23

Intimations of Change

Most Spicelanders were unaware that the year 1942 was one of crisis and change. The comings and goings of trainees and the openings for service went on unabated. The feelings expressed by Jo Noble in March of that year — that Spiceland had been there for ever and seemed to be eternal — were shared by most of those who were caught up in its flowing tide. Being a part of this seemingly ceaseless activity was, more than the place itself, Spiceland.

In June 1941 a report had been addressed to the Yearly Meeting of the Society of Friends stating in some detail what had been accomplished for, and by, the two hundred and twenty- four men and women who had, by that time, trained at Spiceland. The report had been well received. In the firm belief that Spiceland had a continuing role to play in the life of the Society, an appeal was made for money to repay the loans which had kept the Centre going thus far, to purchase the property, and to provide for running costs and future improvements.

Two thousand pounds was the sum hoped for, but in the financial climate of war time, this was probably too much to expect and, in the event, something over fifteen hundred pounds was received.

It was enough to encourage the Committee to exercise its option to buy the property and to set up a Charitable Trust with the object of "...expressing through service to the community the meaning and spirit of Quakerism and Christianity ...... and, in particular to undertake the training of persons in service-agriculture and relief work..........." The deed was drawn up by a layman, and there were later such difficulties about what those words actually meant that a legal interpretation was necessary. Fortunately the spirit of the intentions which the words framed was clear enough.

In January 1942 one member of the committee had said that the

Spiceland course was too practical, and that some thought should be given to the inclusion of intellectual studies. Most trainees wanted and needed training in practical skills. They equated themselves with their contemporaries who had been conscripted into the lower ranks of the Services, and wished to do comparable but non-military duties.

In fact the intellectual and academic qualities of Spiceland life were rich and varied. Staff and trainees from all walks of life, and from widely differing school backgrounds, had shared their intellectual experience in the same generous way that the practical skills of the actual course had been shared. Spiceland provided a very comprehensive education by association.

The committee member, who made brief overnight visits every quarter, could never have understood the quality of life enjoyed by those in longer residence. He was reflecting values, shared with many modern Quakers, which amount to an overemphasis on academic and intellectual matters. The end of the war was far away, but the Society was already receiving enquiries from people who were attracted by the history of Quaker involvement in relief work. The attraction was, in very large measure, because they thought of the Society as making a very practical expression of Christian love and understanding, and were anxious to join in any postwar work which Friends were able to undertake. But the enquirers were also indicating an overwhelming interest in work overseas. They too were reflecting a criticism of Friends, sometimes voiced within the Society, that Friends are always ready to travel in the service of their Lord — especially if it involves travelling abroad. These criticisms have substance, but are not entirely true or fair. Friends involvement in social affairs at home is well documented.

No doubt intellectual knowledge about European history, the varied cultures of the continental scene, languages, political economics, and study of the religious and spiritual bases which motivate Quakers could all be valuable, and might prove to be important ingredients of any postwar relief work. But these subjects were discussed in some depth as part of the informal structure of the Training Centre.

The harmonies created by learning to live and work in groups, respecting, accepting, even liking, peoples' differences, learning to distinguish between preferences and principles, and being prepared to compromise on one but not the other, which were the largely unwritten and unsung melodies of the Spiceland training, were not heard by Friends in London. Isolation on a spur of the Blackdown Hills was an important factor in facing a future which involved drastic change.

At the April 1942 committee meeting, John had to report that the numbers of men and women making applications for training were falling. This mirrored the nation's own achievement of full mobilisation, in that fewer C.Os were needing training and placement.

Apart from the serious thoughts expressed at Sunday evening discussion sessions and in Wallpaper articles, post-war reconstruction as a subject in itself did not take up very much of Spiceland's time. In May 1942, the heavy bombing of Exeter was a grim local reminder of immediate and continuing horror. Exeter was sixteen miles away, but the aerial activity was widespread, much of it in the skies above us, and the intensity of the attack seemed, from that distance, to rival anything experienced in the East End of London. Two of our number who were wardens of the old peoples' hostel into which the Friends Meeting House had been converted, and other Exeter Friends, gave stark accounts of human suffering, and of the destruction wrought in the city.

The Americans occupied an airfield at nearby Dunkeswell. The distinctive sound made by the engines of their Liberator planes was another night and day reminder of non-stop military activity. I once took a load of hay along the airfield perimeter road, and was processed through two American security posts. It was all very friendly apart from the Baroness Orczy scenario enacted when the first sentry prodded the hay load with his fixed bayonet.

At about this time I noticed that Prince, who with team mate Bonnie, had been working very hard, seemed sluggish and off colour. Hugh called in the Vet who examined the horse thoroughly after we had put him through a short spell of hard pulling. The Vet diagnosed the problem as being caused by the presence of tape worms. We were advised to starve Prince for twenty four hours; then drench him with a mixture of two ounces of turpentine mixed in a pint of linseed oil. Prince did not like being stabled alone for a day and a night, and whinnied with eager expectation when we arrived with his medicine which had been well shaken up in an old wine bottle. He could not have enjoyed what followed.

Hugh fastened a plough line round his upper jaw and threw the line over a beam above the manger. I am a short man and Prince was seventeen hands high — five feet eight inches at his shoulders. I climbed into the manger with the wine bottle in my left hand. Hugh hauled gently, but firmly, on the line to lift Prince's head high, while I grasped his nostrils in my right hand to force open his jaws and insert the mouth of the bottle towards the back of his throat. Hugh stroked Prince's neck with his free hand while I poured the liquid, and we waited for the swallow which would tell us that he had taken the medicine, and that all was well. Well, not quite well; I then had to stay with Prince and walk him up and down the farm road until he passed a motion containing the ugly looking tape worms which did tell us that all was well. The after treatment consisted of mixing a small quantity of common salt and flowers of sulphur in his daily oat feed for about a fortnight. He really was a more lively and eager horse after that.

The Semi-Perms met every Tuesday evening in John's office to discuss the composition of work groups, to assess the capacity of trainees to do the various jobs which were notified to us, and to work out priorities for the money and resources available. We all had to be fed, and the skills in planning and preparation exercised by Jo and Basil in meeting these needs called for little discussion and no argument. The day- to-day running of the household, laundry, clothing repair and like tasks were also basic and non-controversial, as were training in First Aid and sick nursing. Construction and the Farm were tough competitors for what ever else was available.

In the ruined house the reclamation of unused space and the improvement of rooms already occupied offered endless scope for a variety of building and construction jobs from which trainees could learn and gain experience. The under-capitalised farm, which was short of implements other than hand tools, offered an equal variety of jobs from which trainees could learn and gain experience, but was sometimes described by Bert Baldwin as a bottomless pit in which to pour labour and resources.

The farm obtained its working capital by charging the house for milk and vegetables supplied at prices above wholesale, but well below retail figures, and by supplying surplus vegetables to Claude Turner's market garden. We retained enough eggs to give Spicelanders whatever was the prevailing public entitlement — the rest were sold to an egg merchant. This gesture gave effect to a corporate decision not to benefit excessively from the farm.

It was sometimes claimed that food production was a public duty, and reclaiming a ruined mansion was not.

However, it was claimed with equal force that construction skills were even more necessary because more trainees went to work in jobs where they were required to build, repair, and maintain than went to work on farms.

Most issues were resolved with reasonableness and good humour, but Construction and Farm matters very occasionally produced tension, and with the degree of dedication which each department had for its own perceived needs, assertions of unreasonableness were sometimes made, and a blight would descend on all of us. We sometimes reflected that if people dedicated to seeking agreed solutions encountered such strains, how much more difficult it must be for those who did not even start with good intentions.

In fact Semi-Perm meetings were not conducted quite like ordinary Quaker business meetings, although we all did our best to get as near to the ideal as possible. John and Margaret, as Wardens, were directly responsible to the Committee for the conduct of Spiceland affairs. The Semi-Perms were consulted, but no minutes were agreed in open meeting nor did we keep a record of proceedings. John assuredly made notes, but it was understood that John and Margaret reserved a right to follow their own judgement.

Semi-Perm meetings could last a long time, and occasionally were then seen as a waste of time. Men watched enviously as women turned their time to good account by making and mending. Kenneth MacQuillen and I decided to take up knitting. Kenneth proved adept and made a very good sea-boot wool sweater. Less successful, I tried to knit a pair of socks with four needles, but, as the subject matter for discussion waxed and waned in interest, my concentration became patchy and more than once I found myself in need of rescue with thirty-two stitches on one needle and two idle needles.

A month or two after expressing her feeling that Spiceland was eternal, Jo Noble asked to be released to take up other work for the Society of Friends; then Helen Biller, a gifted linguist and Spiceland's secretary, and Kenneth MacQuillen, who was working on the farm, married, and they went to live in London — Helen to work in the B.B.C's Overseas Department and Kenneth to pursue further his discipline as a biochemist. Winifred Richardson, as already recorded, bowed to her doctor's warning that the Spiceland gardens were physically too demanding, and accepted a position as a horticultural advisor to Cumberland County.

The Semi-Perms were fulfilling their affectionate and prophetic description of themselves.

It was not all loss. Don and Jean Ironside, who were wardens of the children's hostel at Gerbestone Manor near Wellington, came back to Spiceland. Jean, a qualified Domestic Science Instructor, took Jo's place in charge of catering and nutrition, Don assisted Bert in charge of Construction and took over the Spiceland accounts.

Moving the Ironsides from Wellington to Spiceland provided another unusual carting job for Bonnie and Prince. Our "wagon" was a flatbottomed lorry with very low side rails and laides at either end for supporting hay and corn loads — not an ideal vehicle for transporting furniture and effects. The ten mile summer's day journey along the lanes to Hemyock where we crossed the Culm River, followed by a climb back on to the Blackdown Hills, and thence by ever narrowing lanes to the driveway of the Manor, was a wholly delightful holiday for me. For the horses not so; they did not enjoy travelling far from the farm nor did they like the separation of one pulling in the shafts of the empty wagon while the other tagged along behind on a halter rope; but we settled into a good rhythm and arrived well before noon to be greeted by Don and a group of curious children.

After a Basil doorstep sandwich lunch, we applied ourselves to the tricky task of loading furniture and bits and pieces on to the opensided lorry, and securing the uneven pile against movement. We achieved this with rope and binder twine, and contrived a series of Heath Robinson checks and counter checks, using clove hitches, half hitches and some other knots which are not described in Scouting for Boys. To bind the structure, a cart rope, with protecting sacking placed in strategic places, was thrown diagonally across the lot to produce something that looked like transport for refugees. By the time we had finished we had learned to respect the skills of professional removal men. The loading had taken longer than I had hoped, and it was mid-afternoon when I contemplated another ten mile drive along narrow lanes with many ups and downs.

The horses, rested and refreshed, were harnessed in tandem to the lorry and off we set, accompanied for the first hundred yards by children who may just have been hoping that it would all fall off. There we stopped for another inspection of ropes and load, to make sure that nothing had shifted, and to say goodbye. Bonnie and Prince now had their noses pointed towards home and were eager to be off. Despite the load, which was bulky rather than heavy, the return journey took no longer than the outward, but this time it was no holiday for me. I walked all the way beside the load driving the horses on a long rein, and dividing my attention between them and the safety of the Ironsides' precious belongings. It was a long day.

The staff changes were reported to, and discussed at the July Committee Meeting. With Jean taking full responsibility for catering, Basil filled the void caused by Winifred's departure, and temporarily switched his energy and abilities to the gardens — although gardening was far from being his favoured occupation. Spiceland life continued to flourish, and there was no outward indication that anything much had changed.

Jack Catchpool, a veteran of Quaker relief work during the Russian famine which followed the 1918 war, was a member of the Spiceland Committee , but was also the Secretary of the Youth Hostels Association. At that same meeting he suggested that, while offering training and experience to the smaller number of trainees to be expected in 1943, Spiceland should consider offering Youth Hostel facilities for young people in need of holidays. The suggestion was not warmly received but the possibility was put on ice.

Much more interesting, especially remembering the earlier comments about the too practical nature of our course, was an enquiry from the group of Friends responsible for the correspondence course for postwar volunteers. They thought it would be interesting and worthwhile to meet their correspondents in the flesh. Would Spiceland be willing to prepare and host two one week courses towards the end of the year? Would we not!

Of concern to Marjorie and me, was a later disturbing discussion with Hugh, who told us more about his long term concern for developing better understanding between town and country. He cherished a hope that he would one day be able to establish a farm which would welcome city-bred boys who were prepared to explore rural living with the intention of settling in the country. As a prelude to this undertaking he wanted to live in London and work for a spell with young Londoners. An opportunity might soon arise for him to do some youth work at Kingsley Hall in the East End of London, and he intended to ask for release from his Spiceland responsibilities. He rightly read the dismay pictured in our faces, and went on to assure us that he would not leave until, or unless, satisfactory arrangements could be made to replace him. The news raised some questions about our own future, especially as it might now be too late for us to complete the full training course. We should have to re-examine the priorities which only a short time previously had seemed to be almost too settled. However, there was too much work on hand for us to spend time in worrying about such matters.

CHAPTER 24

Post Warriors

The days we spent working with Albert on our boundary hedge were memorable and significant. Albert was known to have been hostile — he was the farm worker who had so nearly been run over by Reg Reynold's bicycle in the winter of 1940 — and his employer had, until very recently been more than reserved in his dealings with us.

Spiceland had been part of the local scene for nearly three years, and during that time there had been uneven progress from questioning toleration and hostility to acceptance, and in many of our relationships, real friendship. We were not only in ourselves a distinctive community, but were part of another — less easy to define because it was scattered over several square miles, but recognisable. There were tensions in both communities; but we had come to recognise that in order to maintain and improve the quality of life generally the resolution of conflict was as important to the larger group of the village and its surrounding farms as it was to our own small self contained group.

When things went wrong, Hugh was indefatigable in attempts to sort them out. It was all part of his concern for better understanding between town and rural communities and between pacifists and non-pacifists. His efforts to maintain and extend the area of mutual help and friendly acceptance were known to Spicelanders as "the social contacts" — a happily used phrase of understood inadequacy. They were a small scale expression of our belief that the same basic chacteristics of human behaviour are the common causes of conflicts; it is just that the consequences of failure to resolve them range from acceptable irritation to human disaster.

In the last three months of 1942 a great deal of thought was given by both the Spiceland Committee and the Semi-perms to the long-and-short-term futures of the Centre.

Whether there would be a postwar demand for the sort of practical training provided by Spiceland, augmented or even dominated by an intellectual element, could not be foreseen. While some of us were certain that there would always be a place for service inspired by Quaker commitment, others thought that the scale of relief and reconstruction confronting Europe and other parts of the globe by the end of the war would be so vast as to call for a new professional type of worker using resources far beyond our Society's reach.

Whether Spiceland would or could become the south western Centre for Quaker nurture that Friends in Devon and Cornwall desired seemed doubtful. The south western members of the Committee were glad to be a part of the work that was then going on, and they responded to the sheer beauty of the place when they were there, but they still shook their heads when they contemplated its geographical position in the north east area of Devonshire, and such a long, long way from Cornwall. Moreover they had never, as far as I know, sat down together and put on record what it was that they required at, and from, a Quaker Centre.

The trainees who worked on the boundary hedge and bank, were part of the last group to complete the full Spiceland Course. Continuance of full training for the small numbers expected after January 1943 could not be justified, and certainly none of the Semi-perms would have been prepared to be less than fully occupied. The Committee had accepted the responsibilities of ownership, and the farm, now producing usefully and contributing something to general upkeep, could not be easily abandoned. Jack Catchpool underlined his earlier enthusiasm for the provision of holiday accommodation for young people, and urged the Committee to use Spiceland, temporarily, at least, as an adopted Youth Hostel.

The Committee decided on a holding operation which would enable the trainees who did come to gain experience in catering and household management based on the requirements of the residents and Youth Hostellers, and in farming and gardening. They hoped that Spiceland would be asked to host short conferences for peace and religious organisations, and would continue to provide a place of refreshment for Spicelanders and other pacifists. The new and developing situation occupied much of the time at Tuesday evening meetings where we talked about our own futures in an atmosphere of friendship and encouragement.

Hugh was still anxious to take up the opportunity of youth work in the East End of London, and his Spiceland post of Agricultural Instructor had been advertised some months earlier. Marjorie and I had said that we were willing to help his successor to take over, but had recognised that he or she might make plans which did not include us. We hoped, in that case, to follow our original intention and work with the Friends Relief Service — despite the fact that we had never completed the full Spiceland course.

John and Margaret occupied a flat on the first floor, with private access from the partially restored staircase which, in the Earl's day had served the Rector's part of the mansion, but which, in our day, ascended mysteriously from the back door to a still ruined wing in the north west of the building. Their always accessible front door opened on to a gallery which overlooked the central hall and led to the Quiet Room. Outside their front door was a handsome Grandmother Clock which ticked away the minutes and beautifully chimed the quarter hours. It had been presented to them by the Highway Clubs, but it was appreciated and enjoyed by everyone as being part of Spiceland. The Quiet Room, the gallery, and the area round the entrance to the flat was always peaceful, and in sharp contrast to the bustle of life everywhere else. There was no written or unwritten law about this — it just happened.

Informal conversations with John could occupy a long time, with well-considered thoughts framed in few words punctuated by long thoughtful silences. It seemed to me that, like the peaceful area round the entrance to the flat, they just happened. I can only remember having one formal interview — but I suspect that even his informality was well-considered beforehand, even engineered, to hide a sensitivity which could be, and sometimes was, misunderstood by youth's impatience. One such conversation happened when, walking together along the gallery after morning Quiet Time, we approached the entrance to the flat and stood uncertainly outside. The conversation started with comments about the clock chimes, and continued as we changed positions to lean over the balcony and watch the comings and goings in the hall below. The substance of the occasion cannot be adequately conveyed by a report of what was said.

John told me that few of the applicants for the farm vacancy had qualifications which matched Hugh's, and those that had, were looking for an opportunity with career prospects beyond the duration of the war. John was certain that it would be unreasonable in prevailing circumstances to encourage them. He then said that none of the other applicants seemed to offer as much experience and expertise as Marjorie and I already provided, that we had become part of Spiceland, and — "how did we feel about running the farm?"

We talked to Hugh, and discovered that he had already seen the applications and discussed them with John. He thought that we could manage, and supported the invitation. Running the farm was one thing — and a big one — describing ourselves as Agricultural Instructors was something altogether different. We were enthusiastic amateurs with some experience — interested enough to have read avidly some of the prolific wartime output of books about farming — able, until now, to turn to Hugh and milk his brain with questions, willing to ask our neighbours for help, advice and instruction but.........

Just as John himself rarely gave instant answers to questions, he did not press others to do so. After much thought and more talk, we told him that, if the Committee were willing to appoint us to manage the farm, and to give such training as we could, without giving us the formal title, we would happily have a go.

The wish to be part of any operation which would keep Spiceland alive and ready to fulfil a long-term future played the major part in reaching this decision. Another factor was that we had been members of the Youth Hostel Association for many years, and had a lively appreciation of what the movement had done to broaden, intellectually as well as physically, the horizons of thousands of young townsfolk like ourselves.

Slowly the plans of other Semi-perms took shape; But there was still a joyous burst of Spiceland activity to come before any "tents" were folded.

The last full group of trainees covered a wider age range than its predecessors. There were youngsters who had completed their last year of schooling, were approaching their eighteenth birthdays and the age of registration for military service, and older men and women, who had been reserved by occupation or were in the upper age registration groups. Of course there had always been a spread of ages but the difference this time was pronounced. It made absolutely no difference to the spirit in which they lived, worked and played. If anything, the knowledge that they were the last of a line, and were responsible for the last editions of Wallpaper, for the last Christmas party, for maintaining a tradition, intensified the zest with which they approached everything.

The children's party and pantomime were as good as ever before, and the adult entertainment shared with the village was a charivari of real talent and music hall corn — mixed with boisterous enthusiasm and received with generous applause. The village and its children had come to our earlier shows with a mixture of curiosity, misgiving, and shyness, but to these they came with happy expectation.

On Christmas Eve 1942, some of us went carol singing and villagers stood in open doorways to listen as we took up strategic positions along the village street, and outside the cottages on Ponchydown hill. Our last hoarse medley was "sung" at the bottom of the hill outside France Farm House, and was blessed with a gift of apples from farmer Reid.

The last trainees overlapped the two seminars arranged for those postwar relief volunteers taking the Friends Service Council's correspondence course. This provided another blend of age, experience, and interest which was quickly absorbed into the Spiceland atmosphere. The lectures and discussions were generously opened to all of us, and very much shortened versions of the basic Spiceland catering, construction and farm courses were integrated with the special material prepared by the F.S.C. The Quaker connection with Cadbury provided an interesting preview of the shape of things to come. From their Research Department they sent quantities of dehydrated vegetables — beans, carrots and potatoes — for experimental cooking and comment. Early generations of Smash may well have made an appearance on Spiceland tables!

Two guest lecturers, who were also volunteers, were Professor Plimmer and his wife — notable nutritionists of the day. Their lectures were simply delivered as well-planned duets in which a wealth of information was presented and illustrated on wall charts with a fund of quiet humour. Amongst their audience were some Post Warriors — as the course members were quickly dubbed — who were "human guinea pigs" in an extended series of experiments conducted by Dr. Kenneth Mellanby into the effects on health caused by vitamin deficiencies. They had voluntarily accepted a regimen which excluded, as far as possible, certain specified vitamins. One man who excluded vitamins A and D from his diet over a prolonged period, experienced such a general deterioration in his health, including loss of his hair, that he could not be accepted for work overseas when that opportunity eventually came. His slow recovery demonstrated that reserves of those particular vitamins could not, certainly at that time, be quickly restored.

One of the Post Warriors was a very talented, super-charged, American woman with command of several languages. Not a Friend herself, she had a rather critical view of what she regarded as Friends lack of professionalism, and did not appreciate the primitive Spiceland background to the course. During Hugh's lecture on elementary farming principles and practice she took exception to his description of the cultivation of corn crops. She said bitingly that corn, which in her native language was maize only, was not grown in England, and that only in America was it grown well. After a barrage of protest she accepted gracelessly that in Britain the word corn was used to describe cereal crops generally. Sitting in the audience I found this hard to bear. I was there because Hugh had arranged that after his talk we should give a demonstration of farm implements in use. Our two ploughs, cultivator, horse hoe, and harrows had been assembled in Tinkers Orchard and, on a pleasant winter's day, we walked down Mendham's Lane with the horses jingling their loose harness chains and blowing breath vapour into the cool air, to make a picturesque rearguard to a motley crowd.

The intention was that while Hugh talked about the implements "on the ground", I should plough a few demonstration furrows and then offer to let anyone who would, "have a go." Bert Baldwin had once said at one Semi-perms meeting, that there is a basic need for everyone to lay a brick and plough a furrow. Tinkers' provided our only easy stretch of ploughing and one by one the Post Warriors had the satisfaction of driving a plough although, like my own tutor of a year earlier, I called the words of command to the horses. There was one exception. When our critic stepped forward to grasp reins and handles I loosened the all important "wang" and the, so far, simple operation became discernably more difficult as the plough became a live thing and slewed violently out of the furrow. I never explained the incident, or talked about it, and I am not proud of it.

Another of the guest lecturers was a German historian whose purpose, in a series of evening talks, was to describe the pre-war social and political backgound in Germany, and to suggest the possible and probable difficulties and opportunities which could confront postwar Europe, and be encountered by relief and reconstruction groups. He was looking forward to the emergence of a democratic Germany. He spoke excellent English, quietly, but with an underlying passion for the hoped for good things, and a fierce detailing of what might thwart his hopes and expectations. When he had put a series of thoughts before us he would introduce his own explanations with the phrase "and hold and below ......" So well did he hold his audience that no one betrayed by smile or whisper his idiomatic error. His contribution to the seminars was marked at the end by the gift of a small token. As he slowly opened the package offered to him he said with an equally slow and engaging smile "Lo and behold ......"

Soon after the departure of the Post Warriors, the last regular trainees, some former trainees, the Semi Perms, and a few visitors had a celebration of their own in the form of a sort of Edwardian drawing room concert. Basil Goodey's father, Tom Goodey, was not only an eminent nematologist, but was also in demand for his fine tenor voice. Accompanied on the Steinway by Ronald Masters who was one of a long line of Spicelanders who were also gifted musicians, his selection of songs and ballads were the chief entertainment. Hugh and I provided the comic relief with the last of our fictional representations of an encounter between a college agriculturist and a rustic farm servant.

The following weeks saw the curtain fall on the end of Spiceland's first act, and rise again on the beginning of its second.

John and Margaret Hoare left to work for the Society of Friends in Birmingham, Basil Goodey accepted an appointment at Rothampsted Agricultural Research Institute, and he and Joan left to live in Hertfordshire, Bert and Hilda Baldwin moved to Welwyn Garden City where Bert re-entered the building trade, Brother Oswald returned to the Order of St. Francis, and Hugh went to the East End of London to work at Kingsley Hall.

Don and Jean Ironside shared our interest in the Youth Hostel movement and, equally, our feelings that Spiceland must be kept alive, not only in the minds and hearts of Spicelanders, but as a physical place with which they could identify, and to which they could come for refreshment of body and spirit. They were appointed by the Committee as Wardens of Spiceland, and the four of us sat down to work out our plans for action.

Farm policy had to be modified so that we had a more economic unit with fewer people to work it. The number of livestock had to increase if we were to improve and make better use of our under grazed pastures, cash crops had to be a more important consideration. A greatly reduced emphasis on the variety of crop and activity, which had been necessary features of the training centre, would go some way to make simplification possible. None of us knew just how much the residential population would fluctuate, or if and when the flow of youth hostellers would start. The house must be supplied with an indeterminate quantity of farm and garden produce, and we had to budget for over production in hope that we could sell the surplus.

Tom Burke had completed his prison sentence, and had returned to Spiceland to work on the farm and recover from that experience. He had been resident over Christmas and during the Post Warrior seminars. He thought that a spell of hard outdoor farm work was just what he needed and agreed to join us. Sid Harrison, former Old Markonian and member of Winchmore Hill Meeting, who had made the cycle journey to Spiceland with us in the winter of 1941 was working and "living in" on a nearby farm. He agreed to take over the garden and market garden side of the venture.

Planning the "House" was much more difficult. There were so many imponderables. Maintenance work on the building, office work for both Spiceland and the Youth Hostel, catering and cooking for how many? A fully occupied Spiceland could now accommodate ninety or more folk. Although every youth hosteller was expected to perform some duty task before leaving, some more permanent help was certainly needed. An offer came from Doris Rutter and Hilda Pullen who had worked together in Midland City Centre youth work before coming to Spiceland as trainees, and who had since then been working for Friends Relief Service in London. There was a snag. Don and Jean were thinking in terms of one extra helper, but the offer was a joint one and Hilda had expressed a preference to work outdoors.

Although, like all other Friends Service workers, we worked on a small pocket money and clothing allowance, the staffing costs of running Spiceland were yet a serious consideration and we talked long and hard before accepting the unplanned extra. On many counts and in many different ways it proved a wise, good, and fortunate decision.

CHAPTER 25

The Youth Hostel and Farm

The most obvious change in the new pattern of life was the smallness of the resident group, and the absence of people who had made significant practical contributions to our spiritual and physical wellbeing. The mansion which had hummed with the almost ceaseless activity of many, now echoed to the footfalls of a few, who could not fail to be conscious of an emptiness, of past events which could not be repeated, of space aching to be filled. Sunday morning meeting for worship had fewer than twelve, and drew deeply on a well of silence. Because there was no longer a flow of trainees between the activities of House and Farm to maintain a coherent whole, there was a risk that the two small groups could go their separate ways.

When once a flow of hostellers had been established, the mornings and the evenings would again be times of hustle as travellers arrived, booked in, were fed, given the freedom of the house, bedded, fed again and sped on their several ways. A hustle of brief encounters!

Lunch time was the opportunity to maintain the traditional Spiceland shared meal, preceded by the single stroke of the table bell — the undeclared sacrament. It was also a time to relax, to have fun, and enjoy one another's company, but not often for more serious exchanges. We agreed that four o'clock tea — when the day's horse work was done, but with the afternoon milking and stock feeding still to do, when the vanguard of hostellers was still some slow steep miles away — should provide the opportunity to have our quiet time together, and hold our moot session. It was a good idea and worked well between pressure-enforced breaks, but it did not supply all the answers to problems of harmonising the disparate functions of House and Farm.

Soon after Christmas, Hugh went to London to take stock of his new undertaking. Within a day or two of his departure Marjorie drew my attention to the fact that Benjie the bull was slobbering over his food, and shaking his head up and down as if something was worrying him. We could find no cause and as the condition persisted for a day or two, we sent for the Vet. Our own Vet was away, and his brother from Uffculme, a very jolly man with a rich vein of humour came in his place. He diagnosed the trouble as wooden tongue, which he said was a fungus disease probably picked up from eating thistly hay — a distinct possibility. He suggested that Benjie should be given a drench, once a day for a fortnight, consisting of a pint of water containing a solution of iodine. Then he looked at me and said "He's a big bull and you're a small chap — you could try two pints every other day." I laughed, and replied that if a daily dose was the best practice that is what we would do.

We had drenched cows many times, but Benjie was a different proposition — I could not pin him against the wall with my shoulder. Each day we mixed up the medicine and put it in the old wine bottle kept for this purpose. Benjie was given a small feed of oats, and while his nose was buried in the manger, I grabbed him by the ring in his nose. With two fingers of my right hand through the ring I could exert enough pressure to make Benjie raise his head. Marjorie stood by with the bottle, and handed it to me when I had manoeuvered his head into the best position for inserting the neck of the bottle, directed at his throat, into his mouth. While I poured, Marjorie massaged Benjie's throat until he swallowed. Once that happened the job was done, and I could let go. We only failed once, and Benjie sprayed all the medicine — which seemed much more than the pint — in a great fountain above his and our heads.

Not long ago I heard one of the TV Vets say that this treatment was all that was available until after the war, and that it did little good. In our case it was very successful, and when I recall that daily wrestle with seventeen hundredweight of bull, I am very thankful that it was.

During the next three years many people, for many diverse reasons, came to Spiceland to share our life and board. One of the earliest was the artist son of an Edinburgh pacifist clergyman. He came to us in search of peace and quiet after a long period of debilitating internment in a French North African prison.

He spent many hours, warmly wrapped, sitting by the south facing Common Room window enjoying the benison of some welcome winter sunshine. His artist soul slowly responded to the ever changing panorama of cloud shadows chasing sun gilt patches across a quilted landscape of valley fields and distant hills. Eventually he asked for paper and crayons, and soon afterwards he welcomed conversation. The tautness went out of his system and he told his story, not in one burst of exciting narrative, but in short spells of recollected incident slowly remembered.

One day he watched the harnessed horses as they were led past the house and up the drive on their way to plough, and he recalled a pre-war commission to illustrate a farming biography by Crichton Porteous. He described how he had been taken to wild places in the Derbyshire hills, bleak outposts of agriculture, to sketch in black and white the author's memories of stone byres, desolate farmsteads, horses at rest and at work, men and beasts bent to the chilling wind; — all drawn as end pieces to the printed chapters of Porteous' rural life. On other days he talked of Edinburgh and Scotland, and in due course, of the harsh more recent past.

He had shared in good measure his father's thoughts about war and peace but, restless and undecided about what should be his own response to the outbreak of war, he had joined an unarmed merchantman as its radio operator. The master of the ship was already famous. His exploits while shipping cargoes of food to Barcelona during the Spanish civil war had earned him the name of Potato Jones. The ship sailed without escort, and at night without lights, carrying a cargo for besieged Malta. One night they sailed unknowingly into the fringe of an Italian convoy. A hastily hoisted Italian flag saved them from close investigation, but not from an attack on the convoy made by British aircraft. The ensuing mayhem enabled them to slip the convoy and sail on alone. They reached Malta, unloaded, and set off on a perilous voyage in search of another cargo.

Luck deserted them when the ship was strafed by a German plane and blown out of the water. Two or three survivors roped themselves to some floating wreckage, and luck returning, they were washed up, after what seemed to be an age of interminable foodless, waterless, hot days and cold nights, on a stretch of Algerian beach which was the only hospitable landing place in miles and miles of inhospitable coast. And so to an inhospitable French prison.

Prison life took its toll — insanitary, boringly inactive, climatically enervating, deficient in nearly everything which might have made it bearable — it was relieved only by the prisoners' patient efforts to while away the time with useless games, and to make friends with lizards and insects as they sat in a compound of whitened dust with but scarce shade from the unrelenting sun. His release followed the British/American landings in North Africa at the end of 1942, and brought him eventually to our part-restored mansion on a spur of the Blackdown Hills, and to gentle restoration.

At this time the farm herd consisted of four milking cows, October the fourteen-month-old heifer born in 1941, a beautiful roan heifer calf born triumphantly to April the aged practice cow, and Benjie the bull. Two other winter born calves had been, disappointingly, bulls, and sent to market. The four cows and October were all hopefully in calf by courtesy of Benjie, who was eating his head off with no early prospect of any more work. He was a splendid but uneconomic asset.

On the farm at Stentwood where Benjie had been boarded out for short spells, and nearer home, on Mr. Mendham's farm, some handsome young animals were evidence of Benjie's ability to sire good stock, and there were many favourable comments about his prowess. We were not altogether surprised when Cecil Snell paid us a visit one Sunday afternoon "to look a-round loike."

Cecil had often been very helpful to Spiceland with advice and in practical ways. In the hard winter of 1941 when we were desperately short of animal food he had let us have the residue of his swede crop. He was broad-shouldered, immensely strong, and red-faced from long days spent out of doors in all weathers. He could be both slow-and-quick tempered, but despite one or two brushes, like the one when our pigs had rooted in his corn field, we were very good friends.

I had once tried to explain to him some of the intricacies of tax procedures, and how they affected farmers who were becoming very prosperous after years and years of low incomes during which tax returns hardly concerned them. I had then to explain why I would not wish to make his return for him — including the fact that I valued his friendship! He had wisely decided to employ a good accountant!

We stood for some minutes in the bull shed, watching Benjie eat his way through a bundle of hay, before Cecil said that he would be doing us a favour if he had t'old feller down at his place. When asked if he meant that he wanted to buy Benjie he replied "Summat of that sort though oi be'ant thinkin' bout money." Devon farmers were great ones for swaps and bargains, but we needed money rather than some animal that Cecil no longer wanted, and that I was not expert enough to value. Benji was now nine years old, and cows "with calf at foot" were selling in Honiton market for thirty-five to forty pounds. I said that as far as I could tell we would not need Benjie for some months — perhaps a year, and I would sell him for thirty-five pounds if we could have free service from him when the time came. I had weeks earlier discussed with Hugh the possibility of parting with Benjie, and he had suggested the likely price.

There was a long silence. I felt churned up inside and hoped that it did not show. When I am nervous I talk. I reminded him about the contagious abortion, which was why Hugh had bought Benjie in the first place, and confidently said that it could not be passed on through the bull, and that in any case we had experienced no more trouble. "Nay t'is in the' grund." Cecil lapsed into another long silence as we walked back to the house and into the Common Room. I threw away any claim to be considered capable of striking a hard bargain by telling Cecil about the wooden tongue, and how we had cured it with iodine drenches. Cecil said that he was not bothered about wooden tongue — "'tis of no account." There was another long silence, and convinced that any deal had now fallen through, I said that we were fond of Benjie and could probably feed him till the spring. He let out a huge bellow of a laugh — a laugh that had become familiar to us over the years — and said he'd pay my price if I'd knock off the cost of transporting Benjie to his place. Confidence returned, and I said "Full price and — I'll deliver Benjie into your farmyard." We shook hands.

The next morning we searched high and low, but without success, for the bull pole which Bert had made for the several four mile road journeys that had been made to and from Stentwood. We did find a short stout oak staff and drilled a hole in it through which we threaded three thicknesses of binder twine. With a lot of head shaking on Benjie's part, and some patient skill on ours, we passed the binder twine through the ring in Benjie's nose and tied three very careful reef knots — our insurance against any trouble on the way. A last feed of oats calmed Benjie, and assured him of our goodwill, before we led him out into the farmyard for the last time. He stood there majestically sniffing the winter air for a while before Tom Burke took the honour, and the staff, to lead Benjie down the copse lane, along the bottom road, and on to Halsbeare Farm.

Benjie, as always, behaved impeccably and walked into the Snell farmyard where he stood sniffing new smells with his nose curled, and his head lifted high. A crouching, snarling, farm dog with bared fangs and an ugly look came out of the cow shed where Cecil was still doing his milking and sat crouching on a barely discernable three-legged stool. His head was tucked firmly into the flank of a cow, but was turned sideways the better to see what was going on. Apprehensive about the dog, which was belly creeping nearer and nearer and snarling ever more threateningly, I asked Cecil to call him off. Cecil laughed his great laugh, and said that the dog wouldn't hurt a fly, but that the one behind me would have my leg off at a word. Sure enough a second dog was crouched almost at my heel, but was completely relaxed and looking from me to Cecil and back again, waiting for that "word."

Cecil finished milking his cow and asked me whether I had changed my mind about the bull. I said no, and that I'd brought him with me. An astonished Cecil shot out into the yard and saw Benjie, now on the far side, making slow circles round Tom as he held him there steady with the aid of the nose ring and the binder twined staff. The episode did us no harm, and the story soon became "brought him down with a stick and a bit of string."

Benjie served Cecil well, and in a year or two the Halsbeare young stock bore the unmistakeable stamp of his head shape and his roan colour.

In many ways the farm dictated its own work pattern. Four cows gave more than enough milk for our reduced numbers, and for the first time we were in the business of selling milk to the Duchess of Devonshire Creameries and receiving a modest but welcome monthly cheque from the Milk Marketing Board. Determined to build up a herd, we bought two heifer calves, one of them by Benjie, to rear with April's calf and enjoyed having young stock around which were Spiceland's own. Teaching calves to feed, by giving them fingers to suck, then coaxing them to lower their heads into a bucket and to draw milk, not from mother cow's udder but from an altogether different angle, establishes relationships which are hard to describe, but which are part and parcel of the rewards of small-scale farming.

Tom got on with the ploughing, and earned compliments for his work on the Drainage Field — visible for miles around — where our main crop potatoes were to grow. But he learned the ropes, as I had done, in small, secluded, Tinkers Orchard — well away from critical eyes. We had great plans for Tinkers. Mr. Turner had told us that early potatoes marketed in the last week of May, or the first week in June, would probably make £30. a ton. We chitted seed, Epicure and Sharpes Express, by sprouting the tubers in trays on top of the beds in the vacant dormitories, and planted them out in March. We hoped to gain six weeks by this means.

Tinkers with its rich store of poultry manure fertility produced a splendid crop, but not by the last week in May nor the first in June — we were too far up the hill for that — and we had to be content with modest prices, and forego the dreams of avarice.

Sid, with help from me, got stuck into the garden and market garden work, but how we wished that we had spent more time working with, and listening to, Winifred. In our zest for speeding things up to grow early crops we mollycoddled seedlings under glass, lost them to "damping off", and learned some other very painful lessons. We were saved by a mild winter, and the kindly sheltered wall garden, where our outdoor and later sowings prospered. The winter and spring of 1943 were so mild, despite the snow of New Year's Eve, that rows of runner beans, planted between the trees of the decayed orchard by Winifred in 1942, and left in the ground all winter, survived and sprouted afresh to give a second crop, and to teach us that the tuber roots of beans can be harvested and stored — if the game is considered worth the candle.

With Benjie gone we had to think about a replacement, because our neighbours would still hesitate about letting our cows visit their land and their bulls. We could not use Benjie for much longer — October and two other heifer calves were his own daughters. I had maintained Christmas card contact with the farmer sons with whom I had spent my boyhood holidays — the Bucknell Boys — and I wrote to the eldest at his farm near Reading and told him what I was doing. He showed the letter to his father, who remembered kindly the days I spent playing in his orchard and working in his fields and cow sheds. I received a brief letter — more of a line — to say that a pedigree dairy shorthorn bull calf would be put on a train at Reading for collection at Cullompton.

We collected this generous gift, which made the journey from Cullompton to Spiceland, appropriately enough, on the back seat of the bull-nosed Morris. We called him Brutus, and he prospered. We bought a strong tether so that we could select for him the best of our undistinguished grazing — much of it not in our fields but in unfenced areas near the house — and he grew big and strong. Too strong for his and our good, because one evening, when he was barely seven months old, but very much aware of his growing strength, he broke loose as he was being brought in for his feed of concentrate, kicked his heels high in the air, and made a dash for his stall and the expected goodies. He slipped on the cobbles at the entrance to his shed, and grazed a hind leg. It looked a superficial wound, but in the morning he was obviously sick, and our hastily summoned Vet sadly diagnosed a soilborne disease called Quarter Evil and known locally as Black Leg. Inoculation as a youngster would have given immunity, but there was no local history of the disease to warn us, and the injections given after infection proved of no avail. In a few hours Brutus was dead. His short life had been full of promise and excitement, and it was no consolation to be told that wellbred animals were more susceptible to the disease than others.

Of course we tried again, with a second pedigree calf from the same source, but Tolstoy never grew as fast or developed the fine conformation and power of his predecessor. It will always be a matter for regret that we did not rear a replacement for Benjie, and that the high hopes conjured by Brutus foundered, not at Philippi, but Blackborough, and not by falling on his sword, but by falling on his own doorstep.

The Youth Hostel officially opened at Easter 1943, but a steady trickle of hopefuls began to arrive as soon as the Handbook giving details of our location was published, and the advance bookings for the Easter week indicated a full house — especially cheering for us all because the Committee had arranged to meet then for a progress report. The signs were that Spiceland was likely to become a very popular hostel, and the signs were not wrong.

Easter itself taxed all our resources. Don and Jean were laid low by a virulent 'flu bug, and retired to bed leaving Doris to cope with the carefully laid plans for the flood tide of visitors. Marjorie left Food and Pigs to Hilda — the first bonus from the partnership — and became the kitchen and laundry maid. Her memories are of putting tray after tray of Doris-prepared food into the Esse ovens, and taking out tray after tray of appetising meals, cutting seemingly endless slices of bread, serving hungry hostellers from a table at the dining room entrance, washing up, washing up, laundering in an old fashioned dolly tub the piles of sheet sleeping bags which were part of hostel life in those days, and hanging them out to dry on the laundry patch.

I had the altogether more social job of booking the hostellers in, collecting their membership cards and fees, and providing the initial welcome. How difficult it is for visitors to the hilly south west to translate miles on the map into cycling and walking times. 'Phone call from Sidmouth: "I shall arrive a bit late, can you save me a meal? Its about sixteen miles — shouldn't take much over the hour." Oh more than hopeful hosteller, if he did but know how long and steep the hills, how narrow and rough, and, without signposts, hard to find, were the lanes 'twixt there and Blackborough!

Yet our inaccessible situation, the battered but still impressive Egremont pile, the glorious views stretching on the best days from the Quantocks in the northwest, over Exmoor and Dartmoor to Woodberry Down in the southeast, made for a youth hosteller's paradise. To this, House and Farm did their best to add a welcome and warmth of hospitality which encouraged many of them to come back time and again, and some to enter even more fully into the life of the community.

CHAPTER 26

Allercombe

Pressure of outdoor work was always heavy — and even in bad weather there seemed to be something which could and should be done. In days past Hugh, Marjorie and I had sometimes talked about, and wistfully looked forward to, those long winter evenings when we should be free to read some books, and catch up with our letter writing. Winters came, but not the long winter evenings devoted to reading and writing. There was so much else to do, and yet, we did read and write. The Quaker weekly "The Friend", "Peace News", "The Manchester Guardian Weekly", "The Farmers' Weekly" and the "Farmer and Stockbreeder" were our weekend diet, but not all of it was thoroughly digested. We had neither the time nor the money for a daily paper, and relied on the BBC for our daily dose of what it was considered necessary for us to know. On occasional evenings we enjoyed group reading, as something that we could do together while we darned our socks and repaired our clothes, but may have shied away from as individuals — Trollope was our favourite antidote to the twentieth century and we moved happily through nineteenth century Barsetshire in the company of Dean Arabin and the widow Bold. I must also have read a great many books and pamphlets about farming which are even now in my bookcases. They stir memories when the pages are turned.

My favourites were the Clifton Park System of Farming by Robert Elliot, and a Penguin Special — Ley Farming by Stapledon and Davies. The first was published in 1898 and reintroduced to readers by Sir George Stapledon in the 1940s. Both men became, and have remained, rural sages to me. Another book which influenced me considerably, despite initial scepticism, was Sir Albert Howard's Agricultural Testament, which I found to be compelling reading. These works could be read now with profit. What the writers had to say then is important now — and to a greedy world which is only beginning to wake up to the consequences of what it has done and is doing, their wisdom has application far beyond the boundaries of farming. Too many farmers have ceased to be husbandmen, and are merely miners of our steadily deteriorating soil. They are partners with "science" in the destruction of the environment, and what they produce affects the health and well-being of all. The books should be taken off the shelves, dusted and reprinted.

I suppose that the interplay of reading with the day by day involvement in the work of our own small farm and the more productive farms of our neighbours, coupled with my Old Markonian-based social attitudes gave rise to the questioning ecological approach to life which I have developed over the intervening years. Once, during the slump of the thirties we had walked through a neglected farm in Hertfordshire and found a long-neglected deserted farmhouse and some empty cottages. There was evidence of last meals, abandoned utensils, unraked firing, even jackets draped over the backs of chairs — a sort of Marie Celeste on land. I had later on come across a quotation from Oliver Goldsmith's Deserted Village which seemed apposite then and seems just as relevant now:

"Ill fares the land, to hast'ning ills a prey,
Where wealth accumulates, and men decay,"

Early in March 1943, I had my first visit from the War Agricultural Committee men, who called at the house and were directed to the Tillage Field where I was ploughing. Clothing was always difficult, with shortage of money proving a bigger problem than rationing. We used everything we could, and on what was an unusually warm day, I was wearing an old hockey shirt and shorts. I must have offered an incredible sight to the two prosperous-looking farmers who stood in the field gateway and watched me as I drove the plough away from them to complete a furrow at the far end of the field before turning on the headland to come back towards them.

They did not try to hide their laughter, but they were friendly, and enquired after Hugh with evident respect and interest. They wanted to walk the farm with me, and I unhitched the horses, tied them up separately, threw some sacking over their sweating backs, and gave them some hay which I had brought for the midday break. A compliment about both the ploughing and the horse care put me at ease, a sweater covered the garish shirt, and we set off. Tom's ploughing of the Drainage and Top Path Fields also pleased them, and they were astounded by the growth of wheat in the Middle Path Field.

The thick matted old turf which had been ploughed two years earlier, and had caused such trouble in 1941, was now well rotted and had improved the texture of the heavy Keuper Marl soil out of recognition, as had the many cultivations which were carried out for the potato crops. There were years and years of stored up fertility which was only now being fully released. In the earlier stages of the rotting down process, nitrogen is actually taken out of the soil. The very mild winter had ensured steady growth of the seedling wheat which was several inches tall. One of the men said that, if it were his crop, he would graze it with sheep. We had no sheep, and I asked whether cows would do. They both agreed that it was worth a try, as long as the soil was not too wet — cattle being heavier on the hoof than sheep.

Heads were shaken over the ragged hedges and broken banks; their one really sour comment was that we should have made better use of "all that labour" but then, their understandably singleminded farming outlook could not be expected to understand the wider implications of Spiceland training. They softened again when we came to the hawthorn hedge at the bottom of the old coach road, said that we were learning, and acknowledged that a lot of work must have gone into reclaiming Tinkers.

On the way back to their car, I talked about our poor pastures and the lack of any field from which we could take a good hay crop. I asked whether I could undersow the oats in the Tillage Field with a grass and clover mixture to establish a good ley. It was against wartime policy to allow arable land to return to grass, but they understood the problem, and said that they would allow a one-year ley which must be ploughed again in 1945.

They were busy men who had farms of their own; they walked and talked fast, and in little more than an hour, I was back at the plough.

We had received an allocation of artificial fertilisers, together with a permit to buy them from our local agricultural merchant, but when I looked at the prices and our slender resources, I knew that we could not afford them. I would not, at that time, have refused them on organic farming principle, but would have used them to boost our potato crop and to give our one year ley a good start. A commercial farmer would, no doubt, have borrowed the money from his bank, and prayed for a good harvest. We had promised the Spiceland Committee that we would manage on what slender capital was already available. The most we could afford was four tons of lime which was heavily subsidised and cheap, plus some small quantities of phosphates.

Lime is not a fertiliser. It sweetens the soil and helps to unlock the treasure house of goodies that is already there. There is an old saying that lime makes a rich father and a poor son. Our lime arrived on a morning when everybody except me was busy elsewhere. The lorry driver, who was anxious to get away as soon as possible, pulled up near to the field gate, said that he had orders not to drive into fields, that he was ruptured, and that I must handle all the sacks myself. The lime was in tough, but vulnerable, paper sacks holding one hundredweight each. With a sack truck, the driver wheeled each sack to the tail board of the lorry from whence I carried it, cradled in my arms and pressed against my middle, through the gate to a spot where I could lower it gently and make a stack of sacks. The driver said nothing at all until he wheeled the eightieth, and final, sack towards my lime sore arms and grasping hands when, with a ghost of a smile, he said "That's the one you'm lookin' voor maister."

With the help of a borrowed spreader we quickly shifted the lime on to the waiting furrows before too many of the paper sacks had spilled their irritating, penetrating contents.

In late April when the oat seedlings were a few inches high, we lightly harrowed the field to disturb and kill the annual weeds, and then sowed our grass and clover mixture. The tiny seeds would germinate and grow under the protection of the oat crop, and our ley would be well established by the time the oats were harvested. Mr. Percy, the owner of the "fiddle" for broadcasting cereal seeds, and other interesting implements, lent us a seed barrow which had a chassis like a wheel barrow with a long narrow hopper eight or more feet long mounted upon it. Small holes in the bottom of the hopper trough allowed the seeds to trickle on to the earth. A long axle, furnished with small round brushes, ran the length of the hopper, and was rotated by a geared shaft driven from the barrow wheel. As this rather unwieldly contraption was pushed to and fro across the field the revolving brushes "fed" the tiny seeds towards the exit holes and secured a very even distribution.

It was not an easy job. The barrow was heavy and it was difficult to keep the wide hopper approximately level and steady, balanced as it was on a single large-diameter wheel. It was important to cover all the ground and not to waste the expensive seed by covering some areas twice. It was easy enough to mark out the field with sighting sticks the right distance apart, but not so easy to push the barrow and keep it straight for the whole length of a field which, although providing one of our better stretches, had its share of ups, downs, and sideling knaps, not to mention the large grit stones which were a feature of the Greensand soil.

Once sown, the seeds were pressed into the receptive earth by rolling the field with a Cambridge roller, and thus the foundation of our 1944 hay crop had been well and truly laid; but what about 1943?

Mr. Kelland of Allercombe Farm, where, in January 1941, I had spent a disastrous day of failure as a hedger, bank repairer, and maker of no faggots, was a very sick man. Allercombe means "valley of the alders" but aller had another, local, meaning — evil. They talked of aller beasts and aller situations.

Edwin, Ron Amsden, and Doreen Hill — all Spicelanders — had worked long hard spells at Allercombe, and had helped to keep the farm and the family afloat. Indeed Edwin and Doreen developed a strong affection for them which was just as strongly reciprocated. Ron and Doreen had both "lived in" in the dark, gloomy, and disease ridden house; but all had moved on to other work — Doreen after sustaining a broken collar bone.

One day in early May, I was more than surprised to get a message that Mr. Kelland wished to see me. I had not been in the house for over two years, but found that in summer the living room was much as I had remembered it to be in winter. It was dark, and a smoky fire smouldered on the open Devon hearth. There was a pleasant smell of burning wood, but there was no movement of air, and as I stood there what had been pleasant became oppressive — like incense. Mr. Kelland was sitting, half reclining, on a couch and was enveloped in a blanket which he held up over his shoulders and gathered under his chin. Although still in his early forties, with grey hair and a hunched shrunken figure, he looked an old man. His wife, who was also a sick person, said nothing, but took the four-year-old twins — who looked pink and well and as bright as buttons — out of the room. Donald, the teenage son who had brought the message, stood by the couch.

Mr. Kelland asked me if I would make his hay for him because he was not well enough to attend to things himself, he did not want to bring in one of the contractor chaps, and, in any case, he could not afford to pay one. He spoke very slowly and was very short of breath. He looked at me through blue eyes which were too bright. My own were moist, and I was more than a little touched that he should have sent for me when it was well known that he had not set any store by my abilities. I told him that he was not to worry; although we were hard pressed ourselves we would do what we could, and it was early days to be thinking about mowing.

I reported back to our tea-time get-together, and we agreed that, difficult as it was bound to be, we must help, and, I had to admit that it would be good experience. Nevertheless, I was very thoughtful. I had no real knowledge about the family's financial situation. Mr. Kelland would not want to pay very much for what would demand a big effort on our part, and might not be able to pay anything at all. I suddenly remembered that the grass field at the bottom of our copse was part of Allercombe Farm, and that it was Mr. Kelland who had rented the field to Spiceland for the children's summer camps. It was a long way from the rest of his farm, at the bottom of a steep hill, and a bit of a nuisance to him.

I waited a few days before making another visit to Allercombe. I went firstly to assure Kelland that we would make his hay, but secondly to bargain for some of our own. I said that we would mow his grass, make and carry his hay, if he would stop grazing the camp field and let the grass grow so that we could mow it for Spiceland. For a brief moment he was stirred by thoughts of a bargain and struggled to make a haggle. As soon as it was mentioned, that field became worth a lot of money, and I became a very hard man in Mr. Kelland's eyes. But no cash would pass, and that fact was as important to him as it was to us. I promised faithfully that we would not mow a blade of grass for ourselves until his hay was safely gathered in; in any event the grass would hardly have grown long enough or thick enough so to do. We shook hands.

Soon afterwards I 'phoned Stentwood to make arrangements about our shared mower only to be told that the sharing was at an end, and the mower could not be spared. I had thought that the money spent on repairing it had given us part ownership, but it was a matter for disappointment rather than bad-tempered argument. I had to accept the situation with a smile and a semblance of good grace.

I cycled over to Halberton, near Tiverton, to see Twose, the Agricultural Engineers who had repaired the old mower. I hoped that they might have a second-hand implement for sale. They had not, but they did have a brand new Bampton horse- drawn mower in stock, price £28. The repairs to the other one had come to more than £20. Prudence deserted me and good sense prevailed. I bought it.

In 1941 a Friend, Ronald Smith, who was at that time Director of Sparsholt Agricultural Research Station in Hampshire, had visited Spiceland to advise Hugh and the Committee about farm development. He had also walked round the farm with me and had said, among other things, that we needed stronger tackle to rip our matted pastures apart and to put some weight into our cultivations. Spiceland had no money to buy new implements, and good second-hand tackle fetched good prices at farm sales. Hugh had made do with some light harrows we picked up at a farm sale and made them heavier by weighting them with heavy logs, and with what we could borrow. We were still in that situation when Bob Lake, our blacksmith, offered to make some heavy drags for £12., and with a second rush of blood to the head, I said "Yes."

At the next meeting of the Committee I was gently, but very firmly, reprimanded for spending on capital goods without consulting the Treasurer. I doubt very much whether, if I had asked first, he would have agreed to spend, but my failure to ask was not devious, it was due to the enthusiasm of the moment and a different perception.

In his younger days Mr. Kelland had enjoyed a reputation as a good judge of horses, and an equal reputation for schooling them. Doreen loved horses and had shown considerable aptitude for working them while she lived at Allercombe. In the late summer of 1942, during a spell of remission from his illness, and while he was enjoying a rare burst of energy and enthusiasm, Kelland had bought two lovely working mares which he called Madam and Lady, and a roan cob called Tommy. He had refurbished his trap, and for a few weeks, with Doreen driving the spirited Tommy, and Mr. Kelland sitting admiringly beside his pupil, the trap became a familiar sight in the lanes round Blackborough: but alas, no more.

The first Allercombe meadow was cut in early June. Mr. Kelland wanted his mares to work, but was unsure whether to trust us with two lively underworked beasts. We compromised and teamed first Madam and then Lady with Prince, and pulling the new brightly painted mower, they made a splendid sight and did a splendid job. The weather was fine, it was a good crop, with thick bottom grass, and we turned it with a swathe turner on the second day. On the third afternoon we horse-raked the crop into long lines across the field, so that the breeze could blow through, and the sun should not scorch the "green" out of the grass. We hoped to start carrying the hay on the fourth day and finish on the fifth, and intended to start cutting the second meadow on the fourth morning.

On the third evening, with many hours of double summer time daylight to go, Donald said his father wanted to see me. I was ushered into the same dark room, but with a shaft of sunlight making a path through the shadows. Mr. Kelland had sent for, and was holding a handful of the part-made hay in his hand. He smelled it and fondled it and said that it was good. He said that he felt that there was rain in the air, and that we ought to start carrying straight away.

Sidney Harrison was with me and we both argued that the main bulk of the crop was "doney" — too moist to stack. It would heat up in the barn and spoil. The couched and worried man started to fret. It was his hay, and we bowed to the inevitable.

Tom Burke and others joined us when we hitched horses to wagons and fetched the first loads from field to barn. The forkfuls of hay felt heavy on the forearms as we built wagon loads. We were worried, and filled two sacks with straw and placed them near the middle of the stack to make "chimneys". We gave Donald the job of pulling the straw sacks upwards as the stack got bigger and bigger. The idea, from an old practice, was to make two vents which would allow the heat from the sweating hay to escape.

There was a shower in the night. It was of no real significance, and would not have spoiled the hay in the field, but it did give Mr. Kelland cause to think that he was right, and we had to press on. The crop was carried too soon, and it did heat up, despite the straw bag chimneys. A week or so later we turned the stack from one bay of the barn into another to reduce still further the fire risk. The sweat poured from us as we laboured on a hot day and under a hot corrugated iron roof. The very act of disturbing the hay allowed air into the mass and, if fire had been smouldering somewhere, it could have burst into uncontrollable flames, so there was some anxiety and a touch of fear about our actions. All was well, but the result was dark brown hay that was very sweet smelling and, no doubt, very sweet to the taste. Cattle ate it greedily but much of the food value had been lost.

In the meantime the second meadow produced some very good hay, and having discharged our undertaking, we were free to cut the camp field and make some for ourselves. We were now well into July and the weather was unsettled; there were long uphill treks to haul each wagon load along the lane to the church, and a difficult stretch from there down the steep drive and into our farm yard. It was time consuming; with only half the field carried and safely stored, we found ourselves looking anxiously at a lowering menacing sky, and quickly borrowed a horse sweep to work far beyond the light of double summer time to stack the other half in a sheltered corner of the field near the copse. As we covered our treasure with a tarpaulin we heaved great sighs of satisfaction and relief.

It had been a hard slog, but we had made a lot of hay, some of it for ourselves, and gained a deal of experience in the process. We had carried the main responsibility in spite of, or perhaps because of, the bedside directions.

We woke that night to listen to the sound of heavy rain, but not for long: tiredness overcame, sleep conquered.

PLATE I: *Seed sowing with a barrow*

PLATE II: *Allercombe Farm*

PLATE III: *Spiceland from the farmyard*

CHAPTER 27

Some Soldiers An Officer (Ret) and Some GIs

The vicar of Kentisbeare was tall, elderly, distinguished-looking, and a very kindly gentleman. He was a scholar, and had written a short history about the locality and its Egremont connections. He was also responsible for air raid precautions in Kentisbeare and Blackborough, and these duties brought him to Spiceland on a number of occasions to inform us, warn us, reprimand us, and to warmly invite us to his church services. We liked him, and I think that, after a little initial, and understandable, awkwardness, he liked us.

During 1943 the military activity in the west country increased considerably, and even our remote corner did not escape. There was almost ceaseless air traffic at Dunkeswell with US Liberator planes a rather graceful, if ominous, feature of our skies, and army vehicles of all types were occasional, and sometimes uncertain, travellers along our narrow, winding, and hilly lanes. Once, when I was out late and alone, walking across the very rough field between the old coach road and the House, I investigated some quiet movement and subdued voices emanating from a clump of trees and bushes. I found a small patrol of very young soldiers who were on a cross country exercise, orienteering with the help of map and compass, but more than a little lost. We chatted for a little as I pin-pointed where they were — but they resisted directions, and rightly insisted that they work out a route for themselves. The countryside at night is not silent. The sounds of moving and grazing animals, of creaking and soughing trees, of running water, hooting owls, the soft but penetrating squeaks of small animals, and other sounds for which there is often no certain explanation, can be eerie, and even frightening. So too can be the weird suggestive shapes made by trees and odd buildings looming out of darkness into shadowy light. The soldiers confessed that being lost, coupled with this awareness of the mystery of the night, had made their exercise a scary experience — even for men in training.

We walked together up the old coach road, and they were amused when I told them that it was known to us as the Burma Road. We parted company at the top of the drive where they picked out the church steeple as a necessary guide point, but, when they looked in the direction that I was to take, they saw the dark, stark, and forbidding silhouette of the Spiceland chimneys against a very pale light. I told them that I worked there, and that it was a Quaker centre for training pacifist relief workers, and presently a Youth Hostel. They accepted that I was a conchie without comment. It seemed that it was just another, and a different job from their own.

One day the vicar called to tell us that there was to be an "incident" in Kentisbeare to test the response of the village to an air raid with civilian casualties. He was sure that if there were an actual need we would respond in any way that we could, but he was not at all sure that we would be willing to take part in a mock exercise. He was seriously lacking in people with any first aid training or experience — if we could send a first aid party to demonstrate on the labelled volunteer injured, who would be scattered about the village houses and street...........?

The late afternoon and evening were frantically busy times for the House, with hostellers arriving at all times and meals to prepare and serve, so the outdoor staff and the two or three farm trainees brushed up their rusting first aid training, and went into Kentisbeare on the appointed day with a store of bandages and splints used on the old training course. It was a quiet warm summer evening, and a quite unreal setting for tragedy, yet all over Europe and much of the rest of the world such unlikely places were in very fact theatres of war. The labelling had been done very thoroughly, and provided a sterner test than we had expected, but we survived the scrutiny of a visiting inspection group, gathered up our equipment and returned home. We hoped that we had at least helped the Vicar, but were very conscious that the update had revealed how superficial our own practice had become.

Not long afterwards the Vicar called again. He asked us to become a standby first aid unit, not part of the official ARP set-up, but able and willing to use the bull-nosed Morris and our skills and equipment, if tragedy should strike our little corner and its two small villages. Don readily agreed, but told the Vicar that our tiny petrol ration ran so precariously low that we could not always guarantee to be mobile. Don suggested that we should be issued with a reserve two gallon can for use in emergency. The Vicar had no power to authorise such use of scarce rescources, but promised to send on the request to "them".

A few days later Don received a letter from a high- ranking, but retired, military gentleman who lived in a nearby village. He was willing to authorise Spiceland to hold two gallons of petrol provided it was kept in a sealed can and a secure place; but before issuing the permit, he wished to interview a responsible person from the Centre, and would like such a person to call on him at seven o'clock on .... The address was "The Cottage", Craddock.

Once again it was an inconvenient time for Don. Marjorie and I took an evening off, and cycled the four miles to Craddock where, because it was down hill nearly all the way, we arrived well before the appointed time. We dismounted and walked round an attractive village with parkland nearby. We recognised the estate from which we had brought loads of hay from Commander Metters. But it was not Commander Metters whom we had come to see. It was a warm summer evening, and I remember particularly a group of lime trees in full flower, scented, and haunted by thousands of bees. We admired and inspected the scatter of wellkept properties, but could find no place that was called "The Cottage". Eventually, in fear of being unpunctual, we had to ask for directions, and were pointed someway along a lane in the direction of Uffculme to a gracious house in a large and well kept garden. We allowed ourselves a smile at the expense of whoever had decided on such a modest description of the property, walked up the garden path bounded by masses of what could truly be described as cottage garden flowers, and knocked on the very substantial front door.

A maid answered our knock. She was not dressed as a maid, but there was little doubt about the trim appearance and the quick efficient movement. We were, or one of us was, expected, but it was strange to be announced as Mr. and Mrs. Smith when we had been Stanley and Marjorie for so long that we had almost forgotten that there was a formal world. An "acre" of plain blue carpet with the deepest pile of any into which our feet had previously sunk, stretched in front of us; at the far end was a large desk, and behind that, an elderly, distinguished-looking, man dressed in tweeds. He said that it was good of us to come, but he did not rise, and he did not ask us to be seated. He asked a few questions, said that he was satisfied that we were trustworthy, thanked us for being willing to help, and said that a coupon would be sent to us. He rang a bell on the desk to call the maid and to indicate that the interview was at an end. As we walked back, but not backwards, across the carpet, my roving eye noticed an extended fishing rod draped gracefully as a wall decoration, some country scenes in gilt frames, and a uniformed portrait hanging over the door by which we had entered, and were now departing. We walked down the garden path, and stepped out of the pages of "England Their England", and into our own world.

We retrieved our bicycles and enjoyed the much longer, in time but not distance, journey from the valley to our home on the hill.

In August and September Spiceland hosted another Post Warrior Course. The principal speakers were guests invited by the Friends Service Council, but Jean dealt with the section on catering and diet, as she had done on the earlier courses, and I took over Hugh's talks and demonstrations on elementary farming. I did this with trepidation, and pointed out that I was an insurance clerk rather than a farmer, and that the theoretical material was not my own preparation. Nevertheless, the group entered into vigorous discussion and later enjoyed the practical field work — Tinkers Orchard again — and so did I.

There were also Regional Conferences for the Peace Pledge Union and the Fellowship of Reconciliation. It was good to be joined again by like-minded people, and, although we were too busy to attend the sessions, the larger meetings for worship enriched by the presence and ministry of John Hoyland, Patrick Figgis, George Ll. Davies and others were an inspiration. On one occasion we made a special effort to open the old Spiceland Meeting House where we were joined by visitors from Exeter, Wellington and Taunton Meetings. The between session hum of eager conversation in the Common Room and on the Terrace, recaptured some of the atmosphere of times past.

The wheat crop in the Middle Path Field had prospered. In the spring the too forward winter growth had been grazed by the cows who had relished a change of diet and an early bite of green fodder. It had then tillered well and grown strongly. The upper part of the field had been sown with Garton 60, and the small steep area at the bottom with Little Joss. In growth the two varieties showed up in marked contrast; Little Joss being a red wheat with a long straw and a much darker colour in the ear. The crop was ready to cut by mid-August, but it was the first week in September before we could get our contractor to bring his tackle. The corn was ripe in the ear, there was little moisture in the straw, so we decided to carry and stack the sheaves without delay. We shared real satisfaction, even excitement, in contemplating our first bread corn harvest.

But the Devon weather clerk decided otherwise. We woke to be

greeted by steady rain and a warm windless day. It rained all day, and visits to the market garden areas to watch thriving green crops did nothing to raise our spirits. It was Saturday, and a visiting Committee member persuaded us to take him to Honiton in the afternoon. I do not think that he wanted to go, but felt that we needed to be taken away from our misery. He also insisted on taking us to a cinema to see one of only three films that we saw during the whole of the war. It was an adaptation of A.J.Cronin's novel "The Keys of the Kingdom" with Robert Donat as a Catholic missionary. Why should I remember that as well as the teeming rain?

Sunday brought no comfort. More steady rain culminated in a violent thunder storm which kept me awake all night as I thought about the havoc being wreaked in the Middle Path Field.

Two or three flattering mornings of pale sunshine were followed by afternoons of more rain. There was little that we could do but get on with other work and feel glad that ours was a mixed farm. It was the week of the Peace Pledge Union Conference, and one of the delegates was George Maddaver who farmed extensively at Looe Down near Liskeard in Cornwall. He was in his seventies but strong, knowledgeable, and experienced. There was a day of sunshine, and after lunch he came with us to the field to inspect the sodden sheaves standing in their rows of stitches — we had at least replaced the fallen and kept them upright to minimise the damage. The outer parts of the sheaves were drying in the hot sun, and a steady vapour was rising from the ground, but the insides of the sheaves were soaked with the accumulated rainfall. Maddaver lifted a sheaf, held it across his knees, and thrust his strong thumbs into its centre. With a quick twist of his wrists he turned the sheaf inside out and said "that's what we've got to do. They'll never dry out unless."

It was very hard going but many hours later most of the sheaves had been turned and re-stitched. Some were so wet that the string bind had to be cut, and the whole sheaf spread out to let sun and breeze do its best. The weather held, and Maddaver cut some of his conference sessions to help us carry and stack. Some of the grain was spoiled, and some shed in the field because it was so ripe, but much was saved. The crop had given much satisfaction in its sowing and its growing, but much disappointment in its harvest; I shall never forget the sleepless night of thunder and rain during which much of its value slipped away; but I shall remember always, Mr. Maddaver's determined rescue operation which restored hope and faith.

In late September we received a visit from an American army unit. An officer and some GIs arrived in a truck. The officer wanted to know what sort of training went on, and asked to be "shown over". The visit was not accidental, but I do not know what purpose lay behind it. It may be that it was a "reccie" to find billetting accommodation, or it may be that they were security sensitive, and wanted to investigate the strange community which existed so close to an important airfield. Certain it was that no refusal was expected or would have been respected. The "ask" was a command, and the party was in the entrance hall before an invitation could be made. They walked briskly through the rooms, and as the use of each one was announced – Common Room, Dining Room, Kitchen, Dormitory, Quiet Room – the officer said "What d' ya know fellers!" without expecting, or getting, any reply. The walk through the farmyard was more relaxed, as was the brief visit to the wall garden. We grew no flowers, but some clumps of mis-shaped chrysanthemums and some Michaelmas daisies had survived in front of the house. The officer asked what they were, turned to his patrol, and said "What d'ya know fellers – Mickey Mouse daisies!" They piled into their truck. The officer was the last to climb into a seat by the driver, but as he turned to swing himself up, he noticed a bush heavily laden with sloes growing in the hedgerow. "What d'ya know fellers – winter cherries!" I cried "No!" and tried to restrain him as he grasped a handful and pressed them into his mouth. Just as quickly he spat them out again. "Bitter as gall" he cried, swung himself into his seat, raised one hand in token of departure as the truck roared up the steep drive. I have sometimes wondered whether a report of this visit was filed somewhere in the US Army records, and if so, what it actually said.

As Christmas approached there was a suggestion that American service men should be invited to share the festival in English homes to promote a spirit of entente cordiale. How it reached Spiceland I cannot remember, but Don duly received the 'phone number of a US welfare unit. With lots of goodwill, incredible naivety, and an unaccountable belief that we could somehow be considered a typically English household, we 'phoned an invitation which was surprisingly accepted. Our own holiday numbers were small — one or two former Spicelanders, two farm trainees, one or two hostellers making return visits, and our working group — little more than a dozen. At tea time on Christmas Eve we were joined by four US airmen who arrived in a jeep.

The evening meal was a gastronomic triumph of skill and ingenuity over rationing, but the table conversation revealed what we ought to have known, namely that the US forces were used to a wide variety of foods and luxuries which had virtually disappeared from wartime Britain. Stentwood had a contract for the disposal of the air base kitchen waste, and after allowance had been made for some exaggeration, the description of what came daily past the sentry post defied reason. Certainly the Stentwood pigs fed well, and citrus fruits were not unknown on the Stentwood breakfast table. Nevertheless more than justice was done to the Spiceland board, and there were no complaints.

After the meal we decided that despite our small numbers we would repeat the carol singing of the year before. Our guests came too. It was not quite their scene; they quickly deserted us in favour of the warmth of the Ponchydown Inn, where surely the hospitality flowed in a broad stream, and probably at Uncle Sam's expense. It was very late when they returned, very much the worse for wear, to an anxious Spiceland. They were noisy and restless, but very determined in their search for the feminine company which one of them asserted had been guaranteed by the welfare officer. The attractive members of the household were hurriedly withdrawn from circulation, and the menfolk accompanied the guests on a belligerent, but fruitless, search of the landings and corridors. Eventually tiredness and alcohol overcame desire, and they went to bed.

They slept late; but when they did appear all was sweetness and light. Some very attractive Spicelanders re-appeared, and organised the sort of

Christmas day recovery exercises that any other family might have enjoyed, — leisurely walks near the house, special Christmassy "forenoons" on the terrace, inspection of the farmyard, and a prospect of distant views, were all enjoyed. Comparisons with homes in the States were made. Photographs of wives and children appeared miraculously from pocket books and forage cap bindings, and were shown, sheepishly at first, as if expecting indignant criticism, but proudly at last. No one mentioned church services, although one confessed catholic said that he should have gone to midnight mass. Christmas dinner was marvellous, and the King's speech and the radio filled a somnolent afternoon. But as the day passed and evening approached our anxieties returned.

Then Don had a brilliant idea, and organised a family party which started with Tom Burke, dressed in a white coat and with his face suitably masked, performing an abdominal operation on a reluctant Christmas dinner casualty. The victim was hidden under a white sheet, and fearsome knives and saws, borrowed from the Construction room, went to work under the sheet, accompanied by a series of sharp commands to attendant nurses. A succession of unlikely objects were extracted from the patient, and proudly and triumphantly displayed by the amateur surgeon. Pure improvised slapstick. The ice was broken, charades followed, and then all the other games that memories could conjure. No one mentioned the Ponchydown Inn, and we had no alcohol, but a "good time was had by all."

On Boxing morning our guests returned to base, but before the jeep departed with a display of extravagant driving, one, formerly elusive, pretty girl, tried her skill on the four-wheel-drive, direct steering, machine which had quickly, but briefly, become a familiar feature of the Spiceland landscape.

CHAPTER 28

Tom Burke

The owner of the steam tackle which had threshed our first harvest had decided that he could no longer risk his aged traction engine on journeys to the remote farms on the steeps of the Blackdown Hills. It was not easy to find another outfit willing to take over, but a farmer who lived a few miles away invested in some tackle of his own, and purchased a brand new heavy-duty diesel-engined tractor to provide the power. He agreed that if we combined with our immediate neighbour, Mr. Lane, to make a worthwhile stint he would "see us right." Mr Lane had a small farm at Sainthill, a hamlet on the far side of our hill spur, where he lived; but he was also the tenant of about thirty acres of land which bordered our driveway and belonged to Coombe House — a desirable residence opposite the church. With the exception of one wet, rush-infested, meadow which fed the springs and reservoirs of our water supply, these acres were fairly level, very fertile, and well farmed.

Mr. Lane was a small man, wiry, strong, and very active despite his more than seventy years. He and a younger brother, who rarely spoke, but moved around the farms like his shadow, did all the work on the two holdings with very occasional help from a third brother, Leonard. Leonard had no fixed occupation. He was immensely strong, and turned up at any place where a day's work was on offer, and where heavy lifting or prolonged effort was called for. But he relaxed and replaced his expended energy with too much liquid malt for his own and other people's comfort. Despite his occasional quick temper, he had a ready smile and was a very likeable man. He had skills as well as strength, and could fork sheaves with great dexterity to within inches of where they were required by a stack or load builder. He also contrived a more than passable haircut for a matter of pence.

In 1940 Mr. Lane had told Hugh that he did not need help, and did not understand conscientious objection. But he had lent us his roller, had given advice when asked, and now readily agreed that we could work together at threshing time. The tackle arrived in Christmas week and we enjoyed the first of many joint ventures with the Lanes. We benefited greatly from their skills and experience, and they from our youth and energy. I worked with Leonard at the back end of the machine where the threshed grain pours out into four bushel sacks. We quickly established an understanding as we unhitched full bags, replaced them with empties, moved the heavies on and off the scales, weighed them, tied them, and swung them on to a flat-bottomed wagon. There was one nearly sour moment. The owner's son was young, big and strong. He supervised the machine operation and moved round with the oil can. He watched Leonard and me for a time, fixed me with a hostile eye and grasped a fifty-six pound weight in each hand. Slowly he raised the weights to shoulder height, paused, and then pressed them upwards to arms length above his head. He put them down, straightened up, took several very deep breaths, said nothing but looked at me again. Leonard laughed, but then he too looked at me, not with hostility, but with a smile of encouragement, and I realised that he expected me to respond. There was a moment when I thought that my wrists would give way before I could put the weights back on the ground. They held; I also did some very deep breathing.

At Christmas Tom Burke said that he wished to leave the farm to work once again with people. It was a great blow to lose someone who had mastered many farming skills, and was physically strong, but his decision did not come as a surprise. A noticeable and growing restlessness had been apparent for some time.

The Spiceland community was made up of individuals cast in moulds of great variety, and Tom was one whose mould was larger than life. He was born in the East End of London, and came to Spiceland via the Highway Clubs and a warm personal friendship with John and Margaret whose work at the Clubs had kindled his respect and admiration, and some of his aspirations and ideals.

As a boy leaving school in the depth of the 1930's depression he had found employment in a brewery where his weekly wage was augmented by a free issue of beer. The degrading effect on the work force of liberal access to alcohol, and the "trading" in free issue beer which went on, sickened him and led him to total abstinence. To leave a job voluntarily was to forgo the small but essential dole. Prudence and protest combined in the action of overturning a pile of crates in the brewery yard to secure dismissal.

Tom told me this story soon after James Hudson, a Quaker, and former

Labour member of parliament, with a twin concern for peace and abstinence, had visited Wellington Meeting to speak about temperance. Tom said that he found Hudson's case too theoretical, too moral, and so dogmatic that he felt like making a visit to a local pub to down a protest pint! Tom's own objections were based on personal observation and close involvement.

Tom was one of that first batch of trainees who threw themselves into the hard physical work of building construction and farming, where his strength was more than a match for most. He also entered fully into the rich common room life of ideas and argument, where his very presence challenged those from differemt backgrounds, and where he would emphasise his spoken contributions by striking his chest defiantly to proclaim himself, with good humour, as "The Great Burke" — .

When the London Blitz developed he returned to the East End, and worked for and among the homeless in situations which were often dangerous and demanding.

Not only a pacifist, he opposed the right of government to conscript, and refused to register for military service or to exercise his right to state the grounds of his objection. The Law caught up with him and he was brought before a court at Taunton where reluctant magistrates sentemced "a hero" to serve a prison sentence — he was at that time working at the home for evacuated children at Gerbestone Manor near Wellington. Part of his sentence was served in Dorchester prison where, from a precarious perch at a high window he could see a small frame of Hardy country. From the prison library he borrowed, read, and absorbed the Hardy novels. By one of those odd quirks of human behaviour the main resentment of his pacifism came from a fellow prisoner who was serving his own sentence for desertion from the army.

After prison Tom worked on a variety of Friends Relief Service projects and returned to Spiceland between jobs. One of his between job stays at Spiceland coincided with a request from a neighbour, Robert Veale, for help with a day's threshing, and Tom's known prowess ensured a warm welcome when he arrived at the farm. Robert took him by the arm and talked enthusiastically about the stack of fine quality malting barley which was going to show a handsome profit. The war time price of wheat was controlled, but that of malting barley was not!

Tom stopped in his tracks, and said firmly that he was not going to help thresh a stack of malting barley. For a total abstainer this was a "no" job. He turned to leave the scene and walked back up the hill. Robert pursued him — beseeching a change of mind, commending his worth, appealing to team spirit — but all to no avail until he succeeded in sowing seeds of doubt by asking "Tom, what about the malt for the children's cod liver oil and malt?" Tom hesitated. He loved children, and had worked with many of the deprived and under-nourished. "Is it the same malt?" he asked. Robert gained confidence, and grew lyrical in his assurances as he realised that he was on to a potential winner. He led Tom back to the waiting machine and its attendants.

After the war Tom worked in Quaker relief teams in Germany. First in Oldenberg where they were mainly involved in the re-settlement of refugees from Silesia and Pomerania, but also in helping the Control Commission to re-establish local government; then in Hanover refugee camps, and the huge concrete bunkers which had become home for many footloose German youths who had been wandering since the end of the war. This second team worked closely with German Quakers in organising youth clubs, sewing rooms, and in the teaching of English. Their efforts to build bridges of reconciliation included organised visits by some young Germans to Britain, with intent to expose them to something very different from their experience of growing up in wartime Germany. The team, which included two American Quakers, kept together for two years.

On his return to Britain, Tom was accepted for training as a Probation Officer — his prison experience being accepted as a positive qualification — and he eventually headed the probation service in the county of Middlesex.

Tom's departure left no one to keep the horse work moving steadily, and, mistakenly, we decided to make use of a contractor. Much good ploughing weather was lost in waiting for someone who never came, and our under-used horses got fat and frisky. We came to our senses in time, and Sidney and I neglected some of the market garden chores to share the horse work. There is more satisfaction in doing than waiting, and no greater satisfaction than a day's ploughing. The land and sky scape, the smell of freshly turned earth, the flocks of birds rising at the approach of the horses before settling again to continue their search of the furrows for grubs and other delicacies, the occasional buzzard wheeling overhead in a long range search for small mammals or in hopeful expectation of separating a young rook or jackdaw from its flock, the companionship of the horses with their snorted reminders of an expected meal break or of the approaching end to the working day — all make a collection of enduring memories of action, sight, sound and smell that time cannot dull.

That winter provided spells of hard frost, and a few brief, but heavy, falls of snow. In one of the frost periods we were asked to open a clamp of potatoes to help meet a temporary market shortage. The clamp was in the Drainage Field, and an impatient driver insisted on taking his lorry into the field "to save time." Once loaded, the heavily laden vehicle stuck in a gateway patch of thin mud — thawed by the sun. Rather than lighten the load all the known dodges were tried — old sacking, hedge trimmings, straw bundles, were thrown under the spinning wheels to encourage grip; but the thin mud became deep mud, and the wheelspin worse. I have never been able to understand why the resistance to off loading is so strong in situations like this — and I am not guiltless — but the person who suggests doing so is nearly always derisively over-ruled. It is like Passepartout in Verne's "Round the World in Eighty Days" who suggested that the passengers in a train confronted by a weakened bridge, should walk across before the risk of driving the train over at full speed was taken. The very idea is too commonsensical to be taken seriously, and is cowardly and defeatist into the bargain.

Everybody stood around while I fetched the horses. "A bit of a pull loike at the front 'll shift it." The sacking was replaced, faggot wood was pushed in front of the driving wheels, Bonnie and Prince leaned into their collars, the chains tightened, they gave all they had, and it nearly succeeded, only a slide slip of the driving wheels defeated them. Part of the business of getting the best out of horses lies in knowing when you are asking too much. While they took a breather I insisted that about a ton of the load be taken off. It was enough. All the aids were spread over the mud once again. The driver started his engine once more, but used a higher gear, and as he engaged the clutch, the horses pulled again to shouts of encouragement. The wheels bit just long enough for the combined effort to shift the load on to better ground, and the lorry drew away. It took little time to put the twenty sacks back on the lorry, and we were left to ponder on the waste of time and energy that had resulted from trying to save time in the first place.

It was a very different scene when the postman brought his small van through several inches of snow, and then got stuck on the sharp bend in the drive where the gradient was one in four. Prince hardly noticed the effort required to pull the postvan out and haul it the rest of the way to the church.

There were some unhappy times with horses. One morning only Bonnie and Prince answered the morning call, and they were unusually agitated. Search in half light revealed that Fanny, of uncertain age and half blind, had fallen into a dry ditch and could not move. She had severely damaged her back, and the vet eased her pain with a single shot. She was old, and her end was sad, but retrieving her body from the ditch was most distressing for Marjorie and me, and for Bonnie and Prince, who were very agitated while they performed this last office.

I am sometimes told that I attribute to animals, especially horses and cats, powers of thought and reason which cannot be justified, but I try not to go beyond my own experience. One morning in the winter of 1943 I went to collect the horses from their field, but on that occasion, only Prince and Fanny were waiting at the gate. I opened the gate, left them to find their own way to the farmyard, and with some misgiving, went to look for the missing Bonnie. It was fairly dark, but a muffled whicker led me to a spot in the hedge at the bottom of the field where it adjoined Snell's farm. Bonnie was rear-end on in a shallow dry ditch, with his head and shoulders thrust into a thin part of the hedge which had been bodged with barbed wire. He had no doubt sought better fortune on the other side, and had got himself well and truly tangled. He was not struggling, and seemingly had not struggled, because he was not lacerated and appeared to be more ashamed than distressed.

I got into the ditch, forced myself up the broken bank and into the hedge, found his head, fondled his ears, spoke soothing words, and tried to assess the situation. One strand of wire was across his neck, a second was between his front legs and dangerously near his ticklish underside, the lower strands were wound round his lower legs and hoofs. Now that he was found I did not want to leave him to fetch wire cutters. I grasped his forelock and laid my arm along his neck. Then I put my boot firmly on the second strand, using the heel to trap it, and slowly forced it downwards. Pushing his already drooping head further down, I used my arm and his forelock to guide it through the widened gap and so released his head, neck and shoulders. Slow release of my foot pressure on the wire was a nightmare, because the foot on which I stood was unsteady, and the lower wire returned to its former menacing position on Bonnie's underside; but Bonnie remained still, and I now had two free hands to manipulate the wires round his hooves which he lifted when asked, and when I pulled on the loose hair round his fetlocks. With his feet free, the strand of wire between his front legs became the last desperate obstacle, but we were both standing on uneven ground in the ditch.

Once again I trapped the wire in the heel of my boot, and once again forced it downwards. Bonnie had now to be persuaded to lift his foreleg on the far side high enough to clear the taut wire, and then put it down again on the near side. With my right shoulder underneath, and pressing firmly into,

Bonnie's left shoulder, I stretched down to grasp his fetlock while balancing with one leg on the ground and the other on an unstable wire. As soon as he felt the upward pressure on his hoof he lifted and leaned — he weighed considerably more than half a ton — and in seconds he was finally free. As we walked up the field towards the gate Bonnie repeatedly pushed his nose into my back with a nuzzling motion. Was he trying to say something? When we reached the gate Fanny had wandered down to the farm, but Prince was still waiting there. Was he trying to say something?

The incident was not over. We had borrowed a circular saw from a farmer in Ashill, and had promised to return it that day. Later in the morning Bonnie was harnessed to the low-slung two-wheeled cart which Construction had made, and the sawbench was loaded on to it. It was pretty heavy, so I promised Tom that I would follow half an hour later on my bike in case there was no one about at the farm to help off load. With the sawbench delivered and unloaded, I quickly set off again for home, leaving Tom to follow with Bonnie and the empty cart. I looked back briefly to see Tom standing, legs astride in the middle of the cart, and holding the reins like a charioteer. The first half mile was fairly level but was followed by a mile and a half of twists and turns with slopes of varying steepness as the lane eased its way up the Blackdowns. Tom said afterwards that as soon as he had given Bonnie his head he had set off at a steady trot in pursuit of my bicycle, and that he kept going all the way without urging or encouragement. In some steep places I slowed to a walk, and Bonnie caught me up by the church at the top of the drive. He was a big strong horse pulling a light unladen cart. Of course I do not know what powers of thought horses possess, nor do I know what went on in Bonnie's mind that day, but I know what I like to think.

Towards the end of winter 1944, Sidney reported that Prince was sluggish and seemed to be in pain. Mr. Roberts, our vet, was away, but his brother, whose surgery was in Uffculme, once again came speedily, and explored with hand and arm the horse's back passage before deciding that there was a blockage which called for a strong purgative. As he prepared to blow the medicine pill down Prince's throat with the aid of a blow pipe, he told us the old story that every vet must learn — that he must blow quickly, and before the horse! He then said that Prince must be kept on his feet, and on the move until the medicine took effect. "Horses," he said, "Can give up hope too easily, and must not be allowed to lie down in this condition." We took turn and turn about in leading Prince up and down the farm lane and round about the house and grounds. We talked to him encouragingly, stroked his ears, caressed his muzzle and generally helped him to believe in us and himself. It was well past mid-night, when I was leading him yet again down the farm lane, that he stopped and delivered a large motion. Then he relaxed, shook all his muscles, and moved on with a new freedom. It seemed that he had sought a change of winter diet by eating some hedge twigs which had knotted inside him. Within a few hours he was back at work.

I cannot remember the date on which Don opened a locked drawer in the office and found that it contained farm "bits and pieces." Marjorie and I examined them, and recognised, among other things, some newspaper packages which contained medicines for a cow, November, which had died from digestive disorder long, long ago. I remembered that Hugh had sent me, on my bicycle, to Mr. Robert's house in Cullompton to fetch the packages, which the vet had described as a powerful last hope to save her. Each little homemade packet had contained one dose of a powder which we had mixed in water, and poured down November's throat out of a bottle. She had died soon after the first dose, and Hugh had evidently locked the remaining packets in a safe place. Should we burn them, bury them, pour them down the drain? No, we must telephone Mr. Roberts and ask him if he remembered what was in the packets. Hugh had not locked them away without good reason.

When I described the packets, and recalled my late night cycle ride to collect them, Mr. Roberts remembered them at once. "Good Lord!" he said, "Wrap them up carefully and bring them back to me. There is enough strychnine in those packets to wipe out your training centre. I said at the time that it was a last gasp effort!"

Spiceland had had one or two adventures with poisons, dating from Rudi's first order of pesticides leading to village rumour. In 1941 Construction had disturbed a hornets' nest in in the roof, and Bert had decided to destroy the dangerous insects with cyanide gas. He tackled this from outside the building by ascending one of the longest assembly of wooden ladders I have ever seen. He introduced the poisonous substance on a long improvised ladle, and then added some liquid to activate the gas. It was only when he returned to earth that he told us that we need not have worried about his ability to balance on ladders, and that the real danger arose because he had no sense of smell, and could not be sure that he had activated the gas.

More than once I had to sign the poison book to obtain small quantities of chloroform to put down farm cats who were in distress from injury or sickness. We had a comfortable air-tight box into which we placed our casualties before introducing the chloroform on a cotton wool pad. The chemist always asked me to describe exactly what I was going to do and how, before he would sell the substance.

We enjoyed good relations with our vet and his assistants. Their visits were nearly always at times of anxiety or sadness, sometimes of tragedy, always with unwelcome financial consequences; but we enjoyed talking to them, and I think that they enjoyed talking to us. Certainly their bills never seemed to reflect all that they might reasonably have charged, although there were times when we were hard put to it to find the money. I well remember our first use of M and B as a treatment for mastitis in cows, and how, with some of the precious powder left over, I used some of it to treat a farm cat which had 'flu, and some more to apply to the wound of a cat which broke a leg in a gin trap. In both cases there were remarkable recoveries, although the latter cat, Pentecost, only survived to make the same mistake again and pay for it with his life.

With the coming of spring nothing gave greater pleasure than the lush growth of clover and rye grass on our new ley. We had never had an early bite before, and although the main purpose was to make hay, I was tempted to give the stock a treat. I knew it had dangers, and there were strict instructions that it was for a few minutes only on that first day. There were two or three trainees who had come to us from Hugh's work in the East End of London, and they had been given the job counting the minutes, and then of rounding up the small herd and driving it to rougher pasture. So excited were the animals by the unaccustomed luxury of eating clover that one of the cows got separated from the others, and got "blown" before she could be rescued. She had to be chased up and down the drive until she had belched herself into comfort.

While this was going on I had visions of Hardy's Gabriel Oak puncturing Bathsheba Everdene's sheep to relieve the same condition. Fortunately the exercise did the trick and the first day was also the last of this experiment.

In the course of 1941 and 1942 there were one or two outbreaks of foot and mouth disease in our area. Fortunately the disease was arrested a mile or so short of us and, apart from extra precautions with disinfectants, restriction of cattle movement, closure of markets, our greatest distress was to watch from our hill top eyrie, the burning of corpses which followed the slaughter policy designed to limit the spread. One of the victims was Tom Perkins whose son, Harry, owned a caterpiller tractor with which he did some of our ploughing and harvested our corn crops. Tom Perkins had a fine herd and the slaughter hit him hard emotionally. In the six months after the slaughter, during which no cattle could be kept on the farm, Harry ploughed many of his father's fields and no doubt some of the old pasture benefited from the treatment.

When the time came for restocking the farm the shortage of good beasts for purchase took most of the pleasure out of the task, and after a few months Tom Perkins, who was nearly eighty, decided to call it a day and sold up. I went to the sale. It was fine and sunny. A very good crowd gathered — some to purchase, some out of general interest, but many because Tom was wellknown and well-liked, and the occasion was something in the nature of a send-off. The auctioneer rang his bell to summon the laggards, and with a feeling of wellbeing brought about by the fine weather and the good crowd he said: "Tom is a good farmer, he has done so well, that he has decided to retire while he is still a boy. He has instructed me to offer to you fortunate people a share of his good fortune.........." With this happy start I am sure that he created an atmosphere which encouraged participation and, at the end of the day, a satisfactory sale.

It is not just the farmers, the farm workers and their families which make up the rich tapestry of country life. The vets, the blacksmith, the hay and corn merchants, machinery engineers, the peripatetic dealers who work in the margins, and the auctioneers — all contribute. The auctioneers are powerful men who use their wide knowledge of people and events. The public part of their work conducted in market places and at sales reveals them as people of many parts — actors as well as salesmen who can use all the arts — "Gentlemen, you can see for yourselves that this fine cow could supply a city......."

Treating the 'blown' cow

CHAPTER 29

Births Death and a Wedding

On a cold, clear-skied, Sunday evening in March 1944, and after more than a week of doubts and uncertainties, Marjorie said that she thought her time had come. Don 'phoned the nursing home in Wellington to warn them of our coming, and we piled into the bull-nosed Morris with me hugging the small suitcase which had stood for some weeks already packed with the listed necessary articles. Don and Jean were in front with Don driving; Marjorie and I were in the back seats. All of us were well wrapped against the cold night air which washed freely around the passengers in that roofless open tourer as it purred up and down hill on its ten-mile journey. Don had thoughtfully made sure that the lights were in working order and suitably masked against the blackout regulation. We must have looked very much like the old cover design on Ordnance Survey half-inch touring maps as we made our way along the west country lanes. But, however beautiful the setting and romantic the style of our progress, our thoughts were cast on very different matters.

In far off 1939, a consultant had told us that a family was unlikely, and a birth probably difficult. The current wisdom was that children, certainly a first child, should be born before the mother attained thirty. At twenty-nine we had ventured, and the first forecast proved incorrect — Junior had entered our consciousness almost at once. The second forecast had been put out of mind, but Marjorie's modest less than eight stone, had grown to eleven stone and the babe was already a fortnight late by the charts. The goodbye in the blacked out nursing home porch was like something out of Dickens, with waiting staff hovering in the shadows. Our reluctant departure was the surrender of hostages to fortune.

The weather had entered a dry spell of warm sunny days and cold frosty nights. Stentwood had 'phoned for help with threshing some barley which they hoped was of seed quality, but I had turned them down, preferring to lift a few rows of potatoes the harvesting of which had been frustrated by winter rains and which were now a hindrance to cultivation of the Drainage Field. Don, who 'phoned my reply, said that it was not well received, and potato "ground-keepers" had been unfavourably contrasted with seed barley. The real reason for my refusal — standing by for news from Wellington — did not seemingly enter into the reckoning.

Strangely, the winter frosts and snow had little spoiled the potatoes snug in their ridges and under old straw which had been strewn across the narrow strip of field. The work of lifting, bagging, and carting in warm sunshine was demanding enough to banish anxiety for a time, but phone enquiries which gained no news — only injunctions "not to worry" — did little to make the long wait bearable. Tuesday was "more of the same", but the job was finished and the narrow strip properly ploughed by late afternoon. I had been told to 'phone again at six and there was an anxious vacuum of empty waiting time, with no more pressing practical tasks to hand after the horses had been fed and watered.

A fresh, sweet, and friendly voice answered my, by now stereotyped, enquiry with a surprised "But didn't you know! A baby boy! born at eleven this morning!" .... "Yes, of course you can come and see them." I made light of the ten mile cycle ride to be with them, but the Sister's pride in the nine-and-a-half pound baby, red-faced but peaceful, despite a gash near his eye — was not mirrored in Marjorie's pale face and exhausted eyes. However, the smile came.

The twenty-mile return cycle ride became part of the evening round for nearly a fortnight; and there were other welcoming and encouraging visits by Wellington Friends, by the staff of the nearby Quaker Home for elderly evacuees at Oldway, and by staff from the children's home at Gerbestone Manor. Eventually Dr. Griffin pronounced Marjorie strong enough to come home, but it was several months before he told me how near to disaster we had all been. I had not 'phoned to tell him that Marjorie was at Wellington. I had thought the nursing home would report progress and need. He had arrived on a routine visit to find her exhausted, and at the end of her tether after a prolonged labour, and the baby not delivered. Marjorie's own recollection is of being beyond knowing or understanding, when his shouts for action echoed round the ward, and she was dimly aware of his coat flying and his shirt sleeves close to her as she passed into oblivion; from eleven o'clock and for some hours before I heard that fresh young voice of surprise, Marjorie and Adrian had lived — but only in the margins.

From that time on, babies and young children became an important ingredient of Spiceland life. We had become acquainted with the birth of calves and pigs, and were familiar with the needs of animals for warmth, shelter and enough suitable food of balanced proteins, carbohydrates, trace elements...... It came as something of a shock to find how little we knew about human mothers and babies, and to find out that mothers, like cows, could suffer from mastitis, as well as over- and under-production of milk; that babies could be allergic to what was on offer; and that the current handbooks were uncertain guides and not blueprints.

The hard graft of spring work on the farm suffered unexpected, but necessary, interruptions to nurse a fever and dolly-tub the nappies. How fortunate that the days were long and light, and physical strength seemingly on tap. There were good times too, with the baby asleep in his pram in the farmyard, and the ceaseless movement of a farm day all around him — or lying awake under the shade of the noble trees on the front lawn watching the movement of leaves and branches gilded by the sunlight above him.

Hugh Flatt had made a welcome return to Spiceland. His work among young people in the East End of London had cemented his desire to establish a farm of his own where he could practise good husbandry, and provide background and training for townsfolk who wished to make a change to country living. His intention was to make Spiceland a base and work freelance on local farms, but with freedom to look out for an available farm which would suit his purpose. Although he worked long days away, he brought back with him a breath of times past with serious discussion laced with fun and laughter.

Soon after his return he invited a young pacifist farmer from the Lincolnshire fens to stay awhile, to look at west country farming, and comment on his own project for small scale farm training. He introduced him as a "carrot king" — an allusion to one of the prolific crops harvested from his large level fields of black fen soil. He walked up and down our small sideling knaps expressing his disbelief, but also his respect for the growing crops. Even the larger valley fields which we overlooked from our hill top heights, and which sometimes excited our envy, were small by his eastern England experience.

We walked down the copse track to inspect the hay stack in the camp field. Mr. and Mrs. Kelland had both died, the family had dispersed, and Allercombe Farm was to have a change of tenant. We had to move the hay, and I was balancing in my mind the relative value of attempting several small loads up the short but very steep copse track, against larger wagon loads hauled two miles round the still steep, but kinder slope of the road. The walk demonstrated that there was no choice but the long haul, and once again, our guest commented on the problems of "marginal farming", but he did thrust his arm into the stack and pulled out a sample of cool green hay which he fondled and smelled before declaring it as first rate meadow hay. Discouragement and appreciation went hand in hand as this highly successful commercial farmer from broad acre country shared his wisdom — and his fears.

We walked back through the wood, and proudly showed off our badger setts with the telltale signs of lively occupation, before making track for home through the market garden field and a stand of winter kale. Some yards ahead of us I noticed movement among the tall stems and dived instinctively forward to come up with a fine cock pheasant. Sadly, he had been the victim of a rabbit trap and a broken leg, which he had vainly sacrificed for short-lived freedom. He was gently but firmly despatched and carried to the kitchen.

Before our guest's departure, Doris prepared an epicurean luncheon of roast pheasant and of such culinary artistry as few of us had experienced. At the end of the meal our visitor, who was tall, handsome, and something of a charmer, leaned across the table, and said to Doris in words of honeyed appreciation "Would that you could cook for me always." I have no reason to believe that this memory of mine was noticed by anyone else or had any significance; but not long afterwards, to everybody's delight, Hugh and Doris announced their engagement and sealed it with — a chicken ring!

Hay for the winter was not our only stock-feeding problem. The poor steep pastures burned up in high summer at the first hint of a dry spell. One of the daily chores I had shared with the Bucknell boys in summer holidays on the farm at Reading was to cut and carry a load of green maize — six feet tall, thick juicy stems, surmounted by a top of sweet green leaves — to feed to the dairy cows in their mangers at milking time. I had not seen it grown locally in Devon. There was probably no general need in an area of high annual rainfall and good grass. In 1943 I had asked our local corn merchant about it, and he had obtained a quantity of expensive, but aptly named, White Horse Tooth Maize seed which we had grown on a market garden strip near to the house and farm yard. The crop grew and prospered just as I had remembered it, and cows, horses and sows all enjoyed a welcome, succulent and nutritious addition to their diet.

In 1944 we sowed again; but this time in the Top Path Field — a long way from the regular passage of people. It was very discouraging to find, on my daily visit to the field, that the bright green seedlings were being bitten off at ground level, and left to wither in the sun. A dawn visit revealed a pair of crows as the culprits, and Mr. Mendham lent me his twelve bore shotgun. I rose before dawn, concealed myself in the hedgerow, prone and uncomfortable, and waited. Nothing happened. Nor did the crows come on the second or third days. On the fourth day, hungry and cramped, the unused gun beside me, I was amazed to see a big buck rabbit come out of the bank, sniff the air, and make some cautious jumps away from me and into the open field. I thought he had bounded out of range but decided, in a sort of desperation, to have a go. I took careful aim and fired.

At the same time as the rabbit jumped in the air and fell flat on his back, a great shout of human anguish came from the other side of the hedge. Jack Trump, Mr. Mendham's man, who was walking down the Burma Road on his way to work, had all but jumped out of his skin. In fact he was in no danger — my shot had been directed away from him, but neither of us had known of the other's presence. Jack refused to believe that I could have hit a rabbit at all, and certainly not at long range. We walked across the field together and dissolved in laughter as we watched helplessly while the rabbit proved his existence by getting to his feet and leaping to safety. There was great consolation in that the maize seedlings survived.

Towards the end of May we cut and carried our first crop of clover and rye grass hay. We cut early because the weather was right, and because we hoped to take at least one more cut before we ploughed the field in the autumn to honour our agreement with the War Agricutural Committee men. Its bulk, texture and sweet smell made it a pleasure to handle, and carting it home gave us immense satisfaction.

In early June we helped a neighbour, Mr. Scott, who had bought Tom Finch's smallholding, to make hay on those very fields where we had helped the taciturn old soldier in 1941. An RAF man, who had enjoyed a hostel holiday at Spiceland the previous year, was making a return visit, and asked if he could help with the hay. We worked side by side in the warm sun, enjoying together, without words, the distant views, the scented grasses, the wheeling swallows — and all the other haymaking ingredients; but in the evening he came to tell me that he had had to 'phone his base, and must cut short his holiday. His face was grave as he added that a new form of aerial attack was expected. A few days later we began to hear stories of unmanned planes — flying bombs.

The farm day was long. We milked the cows at half past five by the clock, and double summer time ensured that in mid-summer light was in the sky until well past eleven so that chickens and ducks were reluctant to roost much before midnight. Even so there were never enough hours to do what needed doing, and between milking and roosting it was hard graft. The house day was shorter, but had spells of intense activity with seventy or eighty breakfasts and evening meals to prepare, hostellers coming, going, and milling around in the mornings and evenings seeking information and attention. They often arrived tired, hungry and late. There was a load of paper work including complicated rationing regulations, advance bookings, many time-consuming small money transactions, and the everpresent unrelenting chores of a large house. And it was all indoors.

Very few people wanted to do farm work, but paradoxically nearly everyone envied those of us whose work was out of doors. It would be idle to pretend that there was never any tension. To ease the situation the farm staff organised the after-breakfast washing up, with the help of those hostellers who chose this as their "job", and took over the lunch time washing up (when there were no hostellers), so that house staff could get out of doors and enjoy exercise, rest and refreshment afforded by the unfailing beauty of the panorama.

We could all, farm and house alike, have been forgiven if the issues of the wider world had washed over us, yet despite the pressure of immediate tasks, the war was never far from our lives. There was the ever present noise of the Liberators and their graceful but ominous passage across our skies. There was the news from scattered and variously occupied Spicelanders, and our contacts with those who shared our lives but not our attitudes. A friend and colleague of prewar was killed in North Africa and we went to visit his family in nearby Tiverton to share memories and grief. Mr. Lane's family had become close friends, and one of his daughters introduced me to her husband of a few days when we met at the foot of the Beacon. Two days later he was killed on a Normandy beach.

In June I went to London for a meeting at Friends House, stayed overnight with my parents in North London, and experienced at first hand the eerie terror of the flying bombs. The unmistakable sound of the engine, the brief silence following the cut-out, the explosion and then the questioning anxiety about where? In the mid afternoon of the second day I was waiting at Paddington station for the coaches of a Taunton train to be brought in from a siding. Tea was being served with every indication of normality from a station kiosk. I found myself drinking tea and talking to a woman bound for Tiverton, and waiting for the same train. There was a Tannoy warning before a bomb droned overhead, cut out, and exploded with what seemed to be awful nearness. Instinctively, if mistakenly, folk had looked upwards at the station canopy as the thing passed over, but catastrophe was not here. There was nothing to be done except wait for the train. I manhandled her heavy suitcase into a compartment, and before long we were steaming westwards. The outward calm masked inner turbulence.

My companion was bound for a new job as house matron at a boarding school, and as we approached Taunton she became anxious about changing trains. I assured her that there was no problem because my stopping train for Cullompton would also stop at Tiverton Junction. While we were waiting for this connection she sought reassurance from a porter who said that the train about to leave from the next platform was for Tiverton Junction, and he bundled her and her luggage into the departing train. I followed suit. As we rattled over the points I knew that we were on the wrong train, but we could do nothing until it stopped at Crowcombe. There the porter told us that there were no more trains that day, and that he was about to shut everything up. He suggested that we walk across the fields to the road, and beg a lift back to Taunton. It was a long and uneven walk and a very heavy case. I was grateful for the comparative ease with which I could now carry heavy weights on back and shoulders. We were rescued by a coal lorry whose driver good-humouredly squeezed us into his cab. Matron must have been very late on her first day at school.

It was this visit to London which triggered off some unexpected requests from mothers with young children for safer accommodation in the country. They were impossible to refuse, but they added a new and sometimes uncomfortable and uncontrollable dimension to the already complicated household arrangements. Mothers, babies, young children, and hostellers all have different needs, and often made their demands at the same time! In June the second indigenous Spiceland baby was born. To Don and Jean a son — John.

In August 1944 the Peace Pledge Union held a Summer School at Spiceland, and a number of people prominent in the Peace Movement, including a much loved and respected Quaker, Maurice Rowntree, were invited as lecturers. Maurice had visited Spiceland on other occasions, and was familiar with its situation. His journey was delayed because of the illness of his wife Maud, and because he had travelled via Bristol to visit a daughter who was expecting a baby. He came to Cullompton by a late train and made his own way to Spiceland, where he arrived after most folk had retired for the night.

He sat and relaxed for a time by the big Esse cooker in that most comforting of Spiceland places — the kitchen. He talked with a bed time straggler, who made cocoa and found some simple refreshment for them both, and who said later, that Maurice had confessed to being very, very, tired. They said good night and parted. At night Spiceland was very dark, partly because of our concern about infringing blackout regulations, but mainly to avoid activating the diesel engine which charged the batteries of the lighting system, and which chugged into vibrant and expensive life when lights were switched on. On his way to bed, Maurice, questing a toilet, opened a rarely-used cellar door and fell, unwitnessed, to a sad and terrible death which was not discovered until the following morning.

The discovery plunged the whole place into questioning grief. On Don fell the added responsibility of dealing with the police enquiry and the subsequent inquest. In the absence of any members of the family, Don had also to represent them, and to inform Maud of the tragedy. He was no doubt buoyed up by the support of the community and by those attending the Summer School, especially people like the Rev. Pat Figgis and John Barclay. The police and the coroner were particularly sensitive and helpful in the days which followed.

Maud asked that Maurice should be laid to rest in the old burial ground by the Spiceland Meeting House. She herself was too ill to travel. Mr. Leat, the Kentisbeare wheelwright, was also the local undertaker. He was more than willing to help, but said that he was now too old to dig a grave so I travelled with him to do the heavy work under his supervision.

It was a hot August day and the droning of insects, the occasional sounds of lowing cattle, of bleating sheep, as well as the myriad scents of the countryside mingling with the smell of the deep dug soil, were all insistent reminders of burgeoning life beset by death. Our wheelwright was a deeply religious man and a perfectionist. The grave had to be exact of measurement and of depth before he was satisfied; but when we had made the site trim and tidy, and gathered our tools for departure, he paused, and said with evident concern that it should have been dug on a strictly east west line and that he had failed to ensure this.

We sat down on a bank, and I tried to assure him that no one would be critical or offended by what he regarded as his failure. I explained simply the Quaker understanding about death, the Society's attitude to ritual and the sacraments, and our desire for simplicity. He eventually accepted my assurance that we had no need to start our work again. Many years later, when he was a very old man indeed, he said that he was still troubled, but he made this confession with an understanding smile.

A Quaker funeral meeting for worship, like our other meetings for worship, is based on silence but it is open for any person present to break the silence with spoken ministry or prayer. We meet to give thanks for the grace of God as it was shown in the life of the Friend who has died. The small meeting house was filled with people who had come from far and wide, many of them not Quakers, and some distinguished far beyond the Peace Movement. They came to share their grief in a deep silence, and their tributes were spoken simply.

The wheelwright and I stayed to complete the burial. While we were at work I was approached by a man who said that he represented the Devon and Exeter Gazette, and that he understood that the deceased had been a distinguished man, and many of the mourners distinguished people. Would I write an article for his paper? Some days later the Editor telephoned to thank me for what I had written, and said that he would like to print it because he had found it full of interest; then he added that he was sorry that he could not do so, because what really interested his readers were the names of mourners attending the funeral. Was he an editor of little faith?

The trauma of the events of August had served to obscure some other interlocking events which were to produce far-reaching changes in our personel.

Hugh and Doris were planning to marry in the autumn and had settled, not without difficulty, on a farm between Okehampton and Holsworthy. The fields were flattish, no pun intended, but the soil was heavy and held water. Cecil Snell, who went with Hugh on a visit of inspection, came back and muttered darkly about the lack of stinging nettles, of which Spiceland had an intractable abundance against which we waged a protracted war of attrition, but the presence of which Cecil regarded as necessary evidence of fertility and human occupation.

The departure of Doris would call for new house staff. Doris and Hilda had worked together in youth clubs, as Spiceland trainees, in Friends Relief Service and then as Spiceland Semi-perms. It was the breakup of a good partnership — for the happiest of reasons — but a breakup nevertheless. Hilda felt the pull to make a decisive move for herself, and to return to social work in particular. She decided to apply for training as a Probation Officer. By working on the farm Hilda had entered a tied occupation, but the Ministry of Labour readily agreed to release her for such worthwhile service, and she planned to leave as soon as possible after the wedding. Without Hilda's presence during the time of Marjorie's pregnancy and Adrian's birth, life on the farm would have been difficult indeed. In saying goodbye to her we had also to be thankful that we had accepted the joint offer from Doris and Hilda in the first place.

A married couple, Stanley and Dorothy Musk, who quickly became established and affectionately known as the Muskies, joined us: Dorothy in the house, and Stanley, who was a quiet and painstaking man of many skills, some of which he had acquired while working in Lea Valley greenhouses, in the gardens.

Don and Jean were also facing the need to move. The birth of their son had been followed by Jean contracting puerperal fever, and Don had added, and increasing, responsibilties for his widowed and unwell mother. They reluctantly, but rightly, decided that they needed a more settled life than continuing voluntary service could provide. An opportunity offered for work in Bristol and they too planned to move sometime after the wedding.

A Quaker wedding is solemnised at a special meeting for worship during which the couple make simple declarations which are recorded on a certificate. At the end of the meeting the certificate is signed by all those present, and provides a happy record of the occasion — and a reminder to everyone of those years past when all Quaker weddings were illegal, and the signatures of witnesses important evidence when, as sometimes happened, parties outside the Society tried to dispute the marriage. A meeting for worship for a Quaker wedding can be held at any place where Friends customarily meet for worship. The presence of an outside registrar is not required and, of course, the Society has no priests nor ministers. There is no ceremony, and the declarations are simply and happily made in the presence of a gathered meeting.

The Spiceland Quiet Room had been the centre of our worship since 1940, and the East Devon Monthly Meeting of the Society readily agreed that the wedding could take place there. So, in the company of their families, friends, farming neighbours, villagers, babies and children, Hugh and Doris made their declarations at a memorable gathering of joyous worship.

Afterwards we shared two marvellous wedding cakes magically conjured out of wartime rations, baked and iced — one by Jean and the other by Doris herself.

CHAPTER 30

Autumn to Spring

Don decided that the chimneys should be cleaned before the onset of winter and before the need arose for good log fires in the Common and Quiet Rooms. After some discussion, it was agreed that we should try to do this by using a chemical preparation rather than face the inevitable mess from amateur application of rods and broom. Good strong fires were built up, and the proprietary cleaning agent applied — according to the printed instructions. The fires were allowed to die away and we all had feelings that it had been just a little too easy.

At about midnight, Godfrey Whitwell, who occupied one of the small rooms, Faith, Hope, or Charity which had been constructed out of the old chapel on the third floor, roused us because he thought he could smell fire above and beyond his sleeping quarters. Don removed one of the plywood panels which formed the ceiling of the room, to clear a way into the empty space beyond — an eerie darkness festooned with cobwebs and inhabited by bats and jackdaws. Don is several inches over six feet and I am only five feet six so I went up the ladder, balanced myself on a substantial beam, and switched on a torch which quickly revealed smoke plumes drifting away from the chimney stack, and from a hole which was the point of entry for the beam on which I was straddled!

The fire was not yet serious. There was a lot of smoke, and a dull glow emanated from the tough old beam where it protruded into the chimney itself; but there were no flames. Don passed up a fire extinguisher in exchange for the torch, and I confidently banged the nob on the top. Nothing happened. Repeated efforts produced no reassuring stream of whatever the heavy canister contained. With no light I had to pass the canister back for inspection or replacement by another. As I waited I could hear muttered reading of the instructions, and then a shout of triumph. "You have to turn the thing upside down and it works automatically!" Back up it came and in very few minutes it had done its job. Don's thorough investigation on the following day revealed a bad piece of repair work which had been carried out long before Spiceland's occupation of the building. The old beam was now supporting nothing but itself and could be removed and the chimney brickwork repaired.

Shortly before the close of the full training scheme in January 1943, and at a time when the Friends Relief Service was equipping hostels for evacuees, Spiceland had been allocated a standard of timber for making furniture. The intention was to train Spicelanders in the use of tools and make hostel furniture in the process. The valuable and scarce pine timber had been carefully stored on racks under cover in an outhouse near the back door. Two Spicelanders who were working for F.R.S., and of whom Godfrey Whitwell was one, had returned to Spiceland to convert this timber into cupboards, bedside cabinets, and many other useful items which were collected and distributed to widely spread hostels. Godfrey, a quiet modest man, was both craftsman and artist in the use of wood. He had trained with Gordon Russell, and good design as well as good workmanship were the hallmarks of the simple utilities which left the Spiceland workshop.

Some months before the fire in the roof served to demonstrate the need to know how to use equipment as well as to have it handy, we had been close to another serious fire. The wood ash from our generous Common and Quiet Room fires was a valuable source of potash fertiliser which was accumulated in a forty gallon drum placed near the back door, and covered with a lid to preserve the qualities of the ash from the ravages of the weather. The drum had been placed in position long before the timber racks had been made. Except when emptied it had never been moved, and its lid was made of wood.

One dark night in the early months of 1944 I went to make the last round of the farmyard and cow sheds, to see that the animals were comfortable and that all was well. As I left the house I was greeted by a pleasing fragrant scent of wood smoke; but it should not have been. My nose led me to the drum, all but filled with ash, some of it still hot, and to its lid which had caught fire and fallen smouldering into odds and ends of timber debris lying around. It took only minutes to tread down the small threatening flickering flames, and to fetch water to douse the back door area. The drum was moved to a safer place and we pondered the value of jobs like those of a night watchman who sits and broods, who walks about a bit, who peers and sniffs and only rarely does.

The weeks before Don and Jean's departure were weeks of concentrated activity for all of us. Another harvest gathered and threshed. In addition to the two cuts of clover hay we had what seemed to us generous supplies of oats, beans, maple peas, and barley, with plenty of straw — some of it fit for cattle feed, but some of it battered by weather during our usual experience of delayed cutting and a long gathering. We had again been able to sell some millable wheat, and our association with the Lanes had again lent us skills and experience in return for willing energy.

Mr Lane had harvested a splendid field of wheat which our local corn merchant bought for seed. Pressure for early threshing and delivery had resulted in the stack being built in the field some yards from the field gate. A strong team was assembled for a hard day's work, and Leonard Lane and I found ourselves once again at the business end of the machine manhandling the four-bushel, two-and-a-quarter hundredweight sacks, — measuring, weighing, tying and stacking them ready for the lorry man.

When the lorry driver did arrive at the end of the day, he took one look at the prospective load and said that there was no way that he was going to drive into the field and risk not being able to get out again. There were fourteen of us, but age and histories of hernia, reduced the number who could shoulder-carry the heavy sacks from field to roadside, down to two — Leonard and me. There were plenty of willing hands to ease the sacks on to our backs, and to shout encouragement as we made the uneven journeys across the stubble, and to set up the cry of triumph "Ther's the one you'm lookin' fer!" as the last sack was loaded.

A Youth Hosteller from Australia, who later watched our own threshing operation, told me that Australians would never stand for the anachronism of the four-bushel sack. He said that they would have had a platform and used two bushel sacks which were more easily, and more quickly, handled. The sacks used in our part of England were supplied on hire by The West of England Sack Company based in Bristol. Emboldened by what he had said, I wrote to the Company when paying the hire charge — the sacks did not come cheaply! — told them of my experience, and suggested that the time had come for fresh thinking. The Company replied that the four bushel sack had been acceptable in Britain for a long time and provided a useful standard of measurement by both volume and weight. They added that it might interest me to know that the standard sack in Egypt was six bushels! The combine harvester was yet to come.

Although we had taken two cuts of hay from our grass and clover ley there was still a lush growth when the time came to plough it in. I was tempted to make some silage, but the asbestos sheet contraption we had used in 1942 had not survived intact. Don suggested that we partition off a section of the swimming bath — a thirty by ten foot pool, which had been constructed by the Wayfarers, but only very rarely filled because of our chronic water shortage. He constructed a barrier of corrugated iron sheets on a wooden frame and erected this in the deep end. The lush growth wilted and trod down into a much smaller volume than we had hoped for, but it proved a successful and palatable winter feed for our growing young stock.

The long notice of intended departure which Don and Jean were able to give, ensured that there was no hasty search for their successors. Continuity of spirit and purpose was achieved when Dick and Joan Steel, who had been trainees together in 1941, and who had later married and worked in Friends Relief Service, came back to Spiceland as Wardens. The team was further strengthened when Godwin Arnold, another Spicelander, who had worked in Ham Green Hospital and later in an F.R.S. hostel in the North West of England joined the Semi-perms. He was an embryo architect who brought with him practical skills and a variety of experience. He was also an accomplished musician, and when it was discovered that Stanley Musk was a more than competent flautist, the Common Room was occasionally and agreeably filled with splendid sounds from the works of Mozart, Bach and Haydn. Sounds which seemed to please the infant Adrian as he lay in his pram or sat attentively in his play pen.

The war years gave a great stimulus to public interest in food values. Full employment and rationing ensured that more people than ever before enjoyed nourishing food — the grumbles about shortages and boredom came mainly from people who knew very little about poverty. Knowledge about vitamins, proteins and balanced diets was increasing and information was more widely disseminated. Making sure that babies and children got enough of necessary foods was a national priority. The value of rose-hip syrup as a source of vitamin C was advertised and recipes published. Our hedgerows offered a plentiful supply of good quality rose-hips, and the Spiceland babies and children benefitted from hedgerow walks and subsequent boilings. Wild fruits, herbs and roots were in demand as sources of medicines. Once there was a demand for dried dock roots, and a seemingly good price was offered for them. Docks were very plentiful in some parts of Spiceland, and it was relatively easy to pull them when they were in flower and the ground was wet — a not uncommon juxtaposition of events.

We pulled hundreds of them, both because we needed to get rid of them, and because we hoped to make something out of such unwelcome growth. We spread them out on the cow shed roof and invited the sun to cure them for us. The huge bulk steadily reduced in volume as the water content evaporated, and the price per ton looked less and less attractive as the days passed. In the end we were hard put to it to fill a sack or two and a ton of dried dock root became a desert mirage.

To Godwin we were indebted to a revival of reading aloud during long winter evenings as we sat in the Common Room darning socks and making do. Mrs. Scott often joined us for these tranquil sessions which might have been lifted from a Victorian drawing room — an impression heightened by the fact that once again our choice was Trollope.

Not long after Dick and Joan arrived, we were faced with one of our periodic water crises. Although water was present and flowing in the upper reservoirs, the flow between them and the holding reservoir in Big Field had stopped. Mr. Reynolds, the Cullompton ironmonger, had a long association with the Spiceland water system, and had advised and helped on several occasions in the past. He came at once, and we walked the fields along the probable line of the pipe, looking unsuccessfully for tell-tale signs of trouble until we reached the point where it was known to go under the drive and enter Big Field. Mr. Reynolds said that there was nothing else to do but dig back from there towards the upper reservoirs. We found the pipe almost at once and, whether by luck or judgement, found the break and the leak a few yards farther back, near the boundary of Mr. Lane's field. The tell-tale signs of a water leak had inconveniently disappeared by discharging inconspicuously into a ditch. Dick sectioned and repaired the broken pipe, and we hurried to inspect the holding reservoir and watch with enormous relief as the water first trickled, and then flowed to restore the house supply.

However, Mr. Reynolds shook his head over the condition of the pipe and warned us that it could happen again. He repeated earlier advice that the system should be replaced with modern asbestos pipes of two inches diameter. The November Committee meeting agreed; the pipes were ordered and delivered at a cost of £97. In March 1940, at the dawn of Spiceland's story, a working party from Sidcot Friends School had helped to make the building habitable. One of the dormitories was named Sidcot to perpetuate the memory of the gifts of labour and community spirit. Now another working party from that School agreed to come in March 1945 to dig the trench, to lay the pipes, through which could flow the water of Spiceland life. In due time the pipes were well and truly laid.

Unfortunately Dick contracted a particularly unpleasant attack of conjunctivitis while the operation was in progress, and far from seeing through a glass darkly, he could not see at all. We drove over the hills to Hemyock with Dick semi-prostrate on the back seat, his head shrouded in dark towelling, and in an uncharacteristic state of painful misery, — to see Dr. Griffin. Godwin, the architect, became the on-site organiser and general encourager as the, far from easy, tasks of digging the trench, removing the old and laying the new, and making good the terrain were completed. So iron was replaced by asbestos.

Trapper Wright, whose cottage overlooked the reservoir field, kept a watchful eye on the proceedings, and gave his verdict: "'T weren't no good a doin' at all — I tell 'ee that that there asbaastaas 'ent no good, and wont last 'ee. Thee should 'ave done a prapper job."

Hilda Pullen's departure to join a training course for probation officers had aroused considerable interest, and the syllabus had been examined very closely by Sid Harrison. Pre-war he had been a very dedicated member of the staff of one of the big banks, but the break brought about by the war had stirred new awareness and new interests. I had known him for many years and recognised the signs that accompanied each new interest — a detailed examination of theory and practice, and a restless wish to be doing something about it. His terms of exemption from military service were fairly wide, but by working on the land he had entered a wartime tied occupation which was unlikely to hold him when the war ended. Once again the Ministry of Labour considered an enquiry with sympathetic understanding, and replied that no objection would be raised if he were to be accepted for training as a probation officer.

By the end of 1944 the farm staff was reduced to Marjorie and me, with Stanley Musk tackling the heavy demands of the gardens. From the end of the full training course in January 1943 there had always been a few people who had come for farm experience, and had stayed for short or long periods before going on to other work. Most of these were "men (and women) whose righteous deeds have not been forgotten...." but there were others "...that have left a name behind them, to declare....." One of these was Molly King, who developed pacifist convictions while serving as a Waaf. She disobeyed orders on grounds of conscience, and was eventually allowed to state her case to the Bristol Tribunal where she was supported by Rev. Mervyn Stockwood, at that time a priest in Bristol, but later the Bishop of Southwark.

How Molly came to Spiceland I cannot remember, but it may well have been the result of a suggestion made by the tribunal chairman who knew Spiceland's background from his experience of the many Spicelanders who had appeared before him. An effervescent nature thrust Molly into every Spiceland activity with an enthusiasm which sometimes led to misunderstanding, but she was good for us, and did well many things which the rest of us could not. When the Charities Organisation sent to us, for sanctuary, Gracie, a thirteen-year-old girl who had been found living rough among the ruins of blitzed London, Molly befriended her and helped to build some confidence by working and playing with her. Molly had been an art student and was an imaginative painter. She understood Gracie's insecurities, and could enter with her the dream world of phantasy which had been fuelled by creeping in through the exit doors of London cinemas to live in a world of celluloid pretence.

While at Spiceland Molly met and married another late farm trainee, Dennis Bullock, and together they eventually left to gain more experience at a community farm near Dulverton. Molly was generous by nature, and in addition to the practical contribution made by her presence, she made a welcome donation to the farm finances.

A number of trainees came as a result of Hugh's work at Kingsley Hall in the East End of London, including one man, Fred Rollason, who stayed many months and changed our perspectives on many aspects of life. His upbringing had been rough. He had only partial use of his left leg and arm, where foot and hand had been damaged by illness or injury in childhood. Despite this he had acquired a laboured dexterity of movement which defied his disabilities. He had known violence, and had been taught to box by a father who thought that to be a necessary accomplishment in an unfriendly world. A brother had died as the result of a boxing blow. He described a different, and hostile, view of the probation service; of being tempted in the interview room by seemingly carelessly "left" sums of money or other portables. He was an omnivorous reader and loved ballet and music of all kinds — but especially trad jazz. A prized possession was his trumpet, which he practised in an old hen house far removed from the house and unappreciative ears.

Compensating and generous gifts of grit and determination had fashioned a physically awkward but well rounded self-educated person — prepared to talk and philosophise about anything and everything, to shift laboriously a manure heap, to tramp willingly across uneven fields to see that young stock were safe and well, or to fetch the cows for milking.

Another long-term resident who balanced a lack of physical strength with deep thought about the nature of life, became a somewhat maverick disciple of Rudolf Steiner. His vegetarianism caused him to view the farm with deep suspicion, but he gave long spells of help in the house and in the gardens. He accepted milk, but allowed it to sour before using it in his highly individualised diet which included selected grasses in salads. He studied the growth of weeds and plants generally, and developed theories about their presence in any particular place being an indication to man of the sort of composts which would best suit different soils. He built long low heaps in scattered spots of the estate, and paid great attention to the vegetable material which he put into them. They quickly became known to the rest of us as Rudolf Steiner graves, and they eventually rotted down into small quantities of good compost.

People of mixed ability and enthusiasm supplemented our own amateur skills and growing experience. Without them we would have done some things differently, some of them more quickly, and generally with less debate or explanation; but many other jobs would have been done less well or not at all. The essence of community is being able to put in what one can without grudging, and accepting what others offer graciously. We were often a long way from doing that, but we always recognised our differences — sometimes seriously but often with laughter — and respected one another.

With the growth of the Youth Hostel a new group of folk were captivated by the atmosphere of the place and the beauty of its surroundings. They came back time and again. A small number of these gave short term help on the farm, but one in particular came to our aid in the Summer of 1945 with a long stint stretching beyond the end of the war. During this time he became a close friend as well as a willing and able farm worker.

Dennis Wall was a Bristolian who had several times cycled to Spiceland for short hostel holiday breaks. He was physically strong, and had a natural affinity with animals. He quickly learned to milk cows and work the horses, who accepted him as a familiar friend. At the outbreak of war he had been an apprentice butcher. He was a pacifist and at the onset of the blitz volunteered to drive an ambulance and do other hospital duties. He took his driving test on a very heavy ambulance constructed on a Rolls Royce chassis, and was tutored by a very exacting instructor who had an intimidating habit of stopping the vehicle on steep hills, placing a match box under a rear wheel, and demanding a perfect hill start.

Surprisingly, a number of hostellers booked for Christmas, some Spicelanders came home, and with the evacuated families with young children it all combined to make a comfortably full house and a joyous festival. There was a fine Christmas tree decorated with coloured silko discovered in a village haberdasher's store, other improvised ornaments, and a quite splendid dolls' house which was somehow secretly constructed in the work shop.

The wartime shortage of toys was made excitingly good with wooden artifacts — trains, boats, bricks, and other imaginative creations fashioned from timber off-cuts, cotton reels and other "waste" materials to designs prepared by Nancy Catford for use in wartime nursery schools and creches. They were made at the Workshops of the Nursery School Association and of Friends Relief service at Haddo House on Parliament Hill. Her book "Making Nursery Toys" had been published in March 1944 and is still treasured.

Nancy Catford's father was a member of the Spiceland Committee, and earlier in the year Nancy had visited Spiceland to observe the activities of our badger colony with the intention of making sketches for nature paintings. Her observations were made at night, from a tree perch selected during a day time reconnaissance. Her tour of the copse had started from the workshop, where Nancy had selected a piece of discarded wood a few inches long and, perhaps, three inches thick. A small party walked and talked its way through the copse to the badger sett, and as they walked Nancy whittled away at her piece of wood with seeming carelessness and a small knife. Later on, from the workshop waste box, a delicate wood carving of an owl was retrieved to give wondering pleasure to many children over many years and to become a treasured possession.

Although a pantomime was now beyond our resources, there was the traditional swinging party for the village children. The "Big House" was now more firmly established as part of the life of the local community, and on rather different terms, than it had been for fifty years.

CHAPTER 31

The Final Year

The winter of 1944-45 was another hard one with heavy falls of snow, one of which proved too much for the roof of our farmyard barn. Fortunately it was well filled with hay and straw and the collapse of two struts and a cross beam was arrested by the contents. We were able to improvise some supports and rearrange the corrugated sheets to keep everything dry. Getting the ground ploughed, tilled, and the crops sown was hard graft and Stanley Musk and I had to work as a pair and alternate between the gardens and the farm to keep everything moving. The "herd" was growing — the young calves of 1943 were now young heifers with calves of their own. We had not been able to lay down another ley for hay, and I had fallen back on the idea of growing a mixture of oats, barley and peas to cut early for hay, or to grow on to early harvest and then cut while there was still good feeding quality in the straws.

The Bottom Path Field was providing food for thought, but looked unlikely to provide much in the way of edible food. It was a poor pasture on very heavy marl, and local memory said that it had never been ploughed. When Harry Perkins ploughed it with his caterpillar tractor the signs of earlier shallow ridge and furrow ploughing going diagonally across the field were clearly to be seen, and when Harry retrieved a small donkey shoe thrown up by his own work, we speculated on how many long years had passed since the soil had last been disturbed.

The field was sown with wheat, but germination was slow and uneven: came springtime and the field looked very bare and unhappy. The probability is that the old turf had taken too much out of the soil in its rotting down process, and had been too successfully competing with the wheat seedlings for nitrogen. Wireworms and leather jackets had also been busy. I wanted to plough again and try something else, but the War Agriculture Committee men quoted the old saying "A plant a stride let 'un bide" and refused to treat it as a crop failure.

I wondered whether they were influenced by a story that was going the rounds about a farmer who had wished to grow barley on one of his fields, but was ordered to grow wheat. He delayed sowing until mid-winter, sowed thinly, claimed a crop failure in March, ploughed quickly, sowed barley and reaped a good harvest. He received a subsidy for sowing the wheat in the first place, and the price of wheat was controlled but that of barley was not.

At the November 1944 committee meeting I had raised the subject of Spiceland's long-term future, and had put forward a number of ideas based on the thoughts and feelings of the resident group. The intention was to sharpen perception of what role, if any, Spiceland — the place — could contribute to the post-war life of the Society of Friends.

The constituent bodies had joined together in 1939 to promote a shared project, begun at Carclew and continued at Spiceland, which would further their separate, but interrelated, long-term concerns. The war had focussed Spiceland's activities on an immediate need to provide training for pacifist men and women, and to promote initiatives which would help them to find satisfying and worthwhile service as an alternative to military service.

Over three hundred men and women had passed through Spiceland. They shared a common purpose, they shared hopes, fears, joys, and sorrows. They lived, worked and played together, and in doing all this they forged a fellowship and a community which was, to them, the real Spiceland. It existed independently of place, but was, nevertheless, sharply identified in all their minds with the ruined mansion of stuccoed brick, built for the Fourth Earl of Egremont on a spur of the Blackdown Hills, and on seventy or so acres of woods and fields which were the setting in which it had all happened.

A sub-committee was set up to examine the ideas, to consult with the constituent bodies, and to report to the March committee. The future of Spiceland "the community" was never in doubt, the future of Spiceland "the place" most certainly was.

When the committee met in March 1945 it was clear that the concerns which brought the constituent bodies together in 1939 had been fundamentally altered by war and the passage of time. The ideas put forward in November were thought to be eminently worthwhile — in particular the need for a Quaker Conference Centre in the south west of England; but it was at last recognised that the farm, as a farm, was seriously under- funded, and that more money must be spent on the fabric of the building. The thought was expressed that the sheer hard work, the ingenuity and the improvisations which had enabled Spiceland to flourish during the war would not be sufficient for the Centre to flourish in peacetime.

Architects had many times examined with professional interest the gaunt structure of soft brick and stucco. One architect served on the committee, several more and some student architects had been among the trainees. Their many pronouncements had varied between hopeful optimism and gloom and doom. In particular there had been fears that the tall chimneys could not be expected to withstand many more years of winter gales, ninety-mile-an-hour gusts were not unknown. Now the opinion of yet another, independent, architect had been sought and he advised that urgent repairs, and some demolition, should be carried out to ensure that the building remained weatherproof and safe.

The committee concluded that in the climate of the war, which was still raging, and with so many other worthwhile projects in need of money, an appeal for funds was not justified, and was unlikely to succeed. They put on record their recognition of a deep-rooted fellowship that had grown up among Spiceland staff, trainees and visitors, but at the same time recognised the compelling nature of the facts which had been presented to them. They agreed that the use of Spiceland as a Youth Hostel and Conference Centre should terminate on October 31st 1945. At the same meeting it was reported that there were fewer evacuee mothers with children in the house, but that advance bookings for Youth Hostel accommodation were being received in greater numbers than ever before, and two conferences had been arranged to take place in the summer.

Nearly fifty years on the building and its chimneys are still standing. The urgent repairs and partial demolition were not carried out.

The event of the spring of 1945 was Roland Wood's sale of stock. He was very troubled by his landlord's decision to sell his farm, and was convinced that he could not afford to buy it at prevailing prices. He thought that he could just about manage to buy half. With some trepidation he agreed with his landlord to buy the whole farm, and then arranged to sell the house and the upper fields to Mr. Scott of Coombe House, to retain the lower fields for himself, and move with his family into Beacon Cottage — the former home of Tom Finch the retired soldier — which was empty and also the property of Mr. Scott.

Roland was a rare judge of animals and a good stock breeder. Having started with one breeding sow and one heifer his policy had been never to sell animals unless forced to, and then never his best. He distrusted money, lived very much off the produce of the farm, and put everything he had into the improvement of the farm and his livestock.

Marjorie and I stood by a very sad Roland as his beasts came into the ring for auction. Prices had been rising for several months, but he was quite unprepared for the high bids which now came — thick and fast. Before half the stock had been sold he realised that he had become a relatively wealthy man, and could have bought the whole farm. He stopped the sale to preserve for himself some of the animals which were exciting such interest. Nevertheless, Roland honoured his promise to Mr. Scott, who moved into the farmhouse and put Coombe House on the market. The thirty acres of land belonging to Coombe House were farmed by Mr. Lane, and the consequent change of ownership was to have serious consequences for him, for Spiceland, and for the village.

The first intimation that something fundamental in our village life had changed, was a 'phone call from the police station in Cullompton. The attitude of the police towards Spiceland had mellowed with time. In the early years blackout problems, not all of them confirmed as valid, a car lighting offence, a bonfire not properly dowsed, the little matter of Reg Reynold's clash with the special constable, the suspicions about Rudi's purchase of poison for pest control, had all contributed to a certain wariness on both sides.

Police from Cullompton had been present at the Kentisbeare first aid exercise and their attitude had thawed considerably. So much so, that the sight of the old bull-nosed Morris in Cullompton High Street could conjure a smile and a greeting. On one occasion when I had parked outside Reynolds' ironmongery store, a sergeant had reminded me that because the car had no rotary arm to remove — it had magneto ignition — one front wheel should be chained and padlocked to the chassis to comply with the wartime regulations about immobilising unattended vehicles. He did not prosecute. Nor did another officer who, leaning in friendly fashion with one arm along the windscreen, said to me "I would never suggest that your vehicle was other than completely roadworthy, but, although it is an open tourer with views all round, you are required to have a serviceable rear mirror. I can't see yours."

The key 'phone call came on a Saturday morning. The station sergeant said that he had just been told that Mr. Lane was threshing corn, and that he was sending a policeman up to see that everything was in order; would I slip up the road and make sure that the wire netting to prevent the escape of rats, which was a requirement of the law, was in place before the policeman arrived on his bicycle!

I dashed up the hill and was greeted by old Mr. Lane who thought that I had come to lend a hand. "T'is only a liddle piece — two or dree hours at most. Didn't think to trouble 'ee. We c'n manage." I explained about the netting, and in no time at all the threshing contractor produced the coils and set the wire in place. The contractor shook his head and said "'twas but a morning's work — which was why we ordained a Saturday." I stayed to help finish the work, and to see the arrival of the policeman who, warm after his six mile journey ending with a slog up the one in four final flourish of Ponchydown Hill, was glad of a draught from the cider jar. His comment that his journey was all for nothing, as the job was seemingly being done right and proper, with his added comment that we did not want any trouble "did we?" said everything.

When all was done, Mr. Lane explained to me that the new owner of Coombe House was an American who had thought that, as the owner, he could take possession of his land as a matter of course. Neither the right of a tenant to remain on the farm unless dispossessed for bad husbandry, nor his right to claim compensation for disturbance, had been properly explained to the newcomer and he found the situation very hard to accept. He had blown his top, and announced that he would make things as uncomfortable as possible. 'Phoning the police about the wire — how had he known about that regulation? — was just one of many acts calculated to cause inconvenience and unhappiness. To the locals, including the police, he was a "furriner". Could it be that Spiceland, or at least the semi-perms, were no longer "furriners" but locals?

Not long after this incident the newcomer came to visit us. He refused our invitation to come in, and stood with one foot on the doorstep addressing us as if we were a public meeting. He said that he understood that we were Quakers, and went on to say that, when he had been a member of the American Expeditionary Force in 1918, he had had good cause to be thankful for the Friends Ambulance Unit who had saved his life. He then said that he had discovered two reservoirs on his land which supplied water to our house, and that he needed a lot more water than his own supply could furnish; He was sure that, as good Quakers, we would recognise his prior claim and announced his intention to install a pump so that he could draw water for himself.

Our reply that we too were always short of water, and our explanation that the water rights were long-standing and dated back to when all the land was part of the Egremont estate was badly received. He loudly expressed his bitter disappointment at our lack of charity, said that we had destroyed his long standing admiration of Quakers, got into his car, and drove fiercely up the steep drive.

At some time on the following day our water supply failed almost at the moment that Mr. Lane arrived to say that the field adjacent to our reservoirs was flooded. The pump had been installed, but was being used to bring discomfort to both of the perceived enemies at the same time. Dick played the role of mediator, the flow of water resumed, and the floods receded. Reluctantly we asked the Spiceland Trust solicitor to examine the deeds, and write a formal letter to our neighbour about his future behaviour. Thwarted, and inwardly fuming, he remained prickly and uncomfortable. More was to come.

May 8th 1945 was a glorious early summer day. As I cycled along the lanes enjoying the sunshine, the scent of the hedgerows, the ever-changing views of which I never tired, I was unaware that it was also V.E. Day and had other glories. I was on my way to call on a pedigree poultry breeder to collect some clutches of Rhode Island Red chicken eggs and some Khaki Campbell duck eggs. Marjorie had decided to rear more birds. The poultry breeder lived alone and I was the first person that he met that day. He took me by the arms and we danced merrily in front of his bungalow door for some minutes before he realised that I was mazed by his antics, and did not know the cause of his unrestrained joy.

He refused to discuss business. The fact that the war in Europe had ended was all that was to be understood at that moment, and I could join readily in that. He said that it was a day for doing nothing, and made some tea. We sat outside the bungalow enjoying the sunshine, drinking the tea, talking and laughing. It did not last — working with and caring for livestock has its own compelling disciplines and its own set of priorities. Before long we were inspecting his flocks — free range in large netted paddocks — and eventually he got round to packing the clutches of eggs which I had come to collect.

Before I left, he raised a forefinger to his nose in conspiratorial fashion, and said that there was one more thing that he wished to show me. He led me to a small barn and opened the doors to display the front end of a 1912 Talbot motor car. The rest of the vehicle, which was later revealed as a two-seater open tourer, was covered with straw bales for protection. He told me that he had acquired it just before the outbreak of war, and that his ambition was to restore it for a vintage car rally. I met him only the once, and treasure the hour or two which I spent with him. I hope that he got to Brighton.

The rest of the day is a somewhat confused memory. The eggs were bulky: the return journey was a walk with a bicycle supporting a light but fragile load balanced across the handlebars. Preparations for the evening's influx of hostellers were unchanged, and farm and garden work was still being done. But everything continued in an air of suppressed excitement. At sometime during the afternoon a group of ladies from the village arrived to ask whether the village could hold a bonfire party on Beacon Hill. They added, rather wistfully, that they thought we might not like it on our land, but it really was the best place. We replied that we shared the general gladness that the war was over, at least in Europe, and that, of course, the Beacon was the best place. We hoped that they would help themselves to "sticks" — in Devon anything from a thick tree trunk to a twig is a "stick" — and we were glad that they had come. In fact we were humbled and touched by a sensitivity of feeling that we could hardly have expected.

We stayed away from the actual party, but the hostellers joined in the festivities, leaving us to celebrate in our own quiet way, and to watch from afar as the countryside lit up with scattered flame. Tom Hood, writer of comic verse, lived in Winchmore Hill in the 1830s and attended the same Quaker meeting where I encountered Friends a hundred years later. He was no doubt a critical, somewhat cynical, attender, but he was sympathetic and wrote some lines of unusual seriousness about a Quaker celebration of peace. I came across the verses while browsing through John Hoare's copy of Hood's collected poems. I had been searching for some comic verse to read at an evening of light entertainment.

"And is it thus ye welcome Peace!
From mouths of forty-pounding bores?
Oh cease, exploding cannons, cease!
Lest Peace, affrighted, shun our shores!

O mild should be the signs and meek
Sweet Peace's Advent to proclaim!
Silence her noiseless foot should speak,
and Echo should repeat the same.

Lo! where the soldier walks, alas!
With scars received on foreign grounds;
Shall we consume in coloured glass
The oil that should be pour'd in wounds?

The bleeding gaps of war to close,
Will whizzing rocket-flight avail?
Will squibs enliven orphans' woes?
Or crackers cheer the widow's tale?"

CHAPTER 32

Closing Down

The first practical impact of an uncertain future came at the end of May — haymaking time. The field of mixed oats, barley, and maple peas had grown well, and it was time to act if we were to cut it and make hay. I hesitated. If Spiceland were to close altogether and we sold the farm animals, there would sadly be no call for hay. A ripened cereal crop would be easier to sell — and more profitable. On the other hand I had always wanted to try my hand at what was, for our part of the country, an unusual — text book — hay crop. While I was still undecided, Mr. Broom of Ponchydown Farm, called to say that his grass mower had broken down, that he was ready to cut, and could he borrow ours? Our neighbours had always been so willing to lend their equipment to us that it was good to be in a position to respond in turn. It was also a good reason to vacillate. We unbolted the horse pole from the mower and fitted Mr. Broom's tractor bar in its place.

A few days later Mr. Broom returned the mower, and in return for the loan, offered to cut our crop with his tractor. It was a glorious summer evening and Dennis Wall, the pacifist hosteller who was giving, and enjoying, his long spell of farm help, looked at me with mute appeal. He was keen to set about it. I shook my head. The July committee meeting was short weeks away and there was so much else to do — the daily chores of milking, food and pigs, the market gardens — especially the market gardens which were supplying large quantities of all kinds of soft fruit and vegetables to feed the large numbers of appreciative hostellers and residents. All these jobs called for immediate, pressing, action. I acted out of character and we made no hay.

The forty acres of rented land had been leased to us at a nominal rent for two years, and the rent for subsequent years was subject to negotiation. The elderly owner was difficult to see, and even more difficult to deal with. He would not name an acceptable rent, but rejected the sums suggested to him. I think that he had hoped to sell rather than lease, and thought he was holding a gold mine instead of some sub-marginal farm land. Local farmers described him as a "witty" man by which they meant, someone who lived by his wits not by laughter. I travelled by the Friday bus from Kentisbeare to Exeter to consult a solicitor who had been recommended by an Exeter Friend.

The solicitor was more used to dealing with city properties and matters ecclesiastical than with farm properties and leases. His interest could not be aroused, and he advised me to go on trying for a settlement by personal bargaining rather than by involving lawyers. He said that west country farmers never gave anything away except advice — which was usually worth nothing anyway. He thought our man would enjoy bargaining and would come round eventually. I went away disappointed. I am not good at haggling, and am naturally happier with a Quaker's "fair price."

I wandered round the old City until it was time to catch the bus back to Kentisbeare, and in a greengrocer's shop noticed some beautiful solid heart Lobjoit Green Cos lettuce which we had sent to market the day before. They were priced at a shilling each, but we had been paid a mere ninepence a dozen! It was not one of my better days.

Help and advice came from what I would once have thought to be an unlikely source. A few days before the committee meeting, the War Agricultural Committee men made one of their periodic farm visits, to appraise what had been done and to agree the next year's cropping plan. It was another lovely summer day, and when one considers the generally high rainfall pattern of our west country weather, it is remarkable how often the fine days chose to adorn those that were memorable for other reasons. The hilly pastures had not yet dried out and looked at their flattering best. The herd, with its calves and heifers now numbering fifteen, was grazing the Big Field; they too looked well and were a source of quiet pride.

We walked amongst them on our way to the Tillage Field and en route for the Burma Road which had become the established pattern for a farm walk. As we walked I told them about the coming closure and my difficulty about the rent of the forty acres. That Spiceland should take the fields in hand had, I think, been one of their own suggestions in 1940. They were disappointed. They had a responsibility to make sure that the reclaimed land did not deteriorate again, and that our own fields were not neglected. Rather wistfully I said that I could not offer any cropping plans because I was not likely to be responsible beyond October.

By this time we had reached the Middle Path Field where an even crop of Star oats was ripening towards an early harvest. In the Top Path Field the hay mixture of peas, oats, and barley also looked good. Spiceland crops had so often promised well in past years, and then suffered the ravages of late cutting and west country weather. "Your stock look well and there is enough feed in this one field to see them through the winter. Your green crops are good, your potatoes promising — there's still a lot that needs doing, but you've come a long way; further than we'd have thought. Why don't you take it on yourself?" I told them that the farm capital was under £500. and that over half of that was in interest free repayable loans. I tried to explain the maintenance and pocket money basis on which we had all worked at Spiceland, and how this applied to Quaker relief workers in general. By further process of question and answer they began to have a clearer understanding of what had been done and why. They showed genuine interest in what had happened to the trainees, and the conchie camp which they had first visited in 1940 was seen in a somewhat different light.

They soon realised that Marjorie and I could not command the resources to continue farming Spiceland by and for ourselves, and that, keen as we were, it was not only the farm that had sustained our interest. There were the other Quaker activities of which Spiceland and its farm were only a part.

We strolled on down the Burma Road and came to the eyesore of the failed wheat crop in the Bottom Path Field. In some curious way I was glad to see it. It somehow restored the balance from euphoria to the reality of our amateurism. Tinkers Orchard always interested them, as it had always inspired me — a small secluded plot which seemed to overflow with riches, and which this time carried a heavy crop of grey winter oats and cattle beans. "You could double your stock." was their comment as we walked up Mendham's Lane to the house and their car. They gave me the name of a Land Agent who would see us right about the rented acres, and probably help with arrangements for other farms to take them on. They thought my offered rent was not far out, but guessed that it would come to a few pounds more before the matter was settled.

We shook hands. They paused to say again that they thought it was a great pity. They supposed that I would go back to London when the war was finally over (at that moment nothing was further from my thoughts!) and that too was a great pity....... We never met again.

The July committee appointed the Land Agent, and after meeting him and talking things through, I felt free from worry on that score. I addressed myself to gathering in the crops and winding up the business of the farm, but, as if to invest those tasks with the air of unreality which I felt inside me, Spiceland life was burgeoning!

The hostel was busier than ever before, and the belief that the end of the war was near, had given new zest to the hostellers, visitors, and many other folk who came to stay. There was a Young Friends Conference, a regional Peace Pledge Union Conference, and in September, a national PPU Summer School — all of which went with a swing and engendered such enthusiasm that it was difficult to think that Jo Noble's words "Spiceland seems to have been here for ever and will go on for ever" were just not true.

The July election and the return of a Labour Government was a great event. Never a Churchill admirer, I had listened with disbelief and foreboding to a pre-election speech in which he foretold the doom and disaster which would follow the election of a government led by people, who more than the members of his own party, had been the backbone of his administration. It seemed a shabby dismissal, and revealed that deep down he believed in two nations — not the one nation he had purported to lead. Politics is the art and science of people living together, and to that extent I am a very political animal, but I have never felt happy with the rules and constraints of party politics, and wish that more MPs were prepared to "Cross the floor" on issues about which they disagree with a party line. Nevertheless, I was overjoyed by the voters response — hardly muted by the local fact that Tiverton had remained firmly Tory.

The sight of the Bottom Path Field haunted me until the end of July when we gathered what little grain there was for poultry feed. The stubble was ripped about with heavy harrows and then a turnip drill was borrowed from Mr. Percy. On August the first I drove the drill round the lane from All Hallows Farm to the Burma Road and on the way met Mr. Sansom, the new tenant of Allercombe Farm. "Where be you to?" he shouted. "I be drilling turnips!" I shouted back. "You'm a main bit too late — thee'll never get a crop." "'t is a catch crop, — quick growing." I countered. "I suppose you read 'bout that in a book?" We enjoyed the joke.

Mr. Percy had told me not to hurry about returning the drill, but that evening he 'phoned to ask for it back — Mr. Sansom wanted to borrow it to sow some turnips!

An extra petrol allowance, and a request by Margaret Hoare that her Austin Ten, which had been in wraps since 1943, should be re-commissioned, encouraged us to make a "family" outing to Sidmouth. We had lived in Devon for five years and knew eighty acres like the backs of our hands, several hundred acres very well indeed, but most of the County hardly at all. The trees crowning the top of Woodberry Down were clearly, and beckoningly, visible from our dining room window. I had many times longed to go there. Sidmouth was only sixteen miles away — as many hostellers had told us when 'phoning to say that they "wouldn't be long."

It was wholly delightful to watch children, who had never before seen the sea, enjoy sand castles; and grown ups, who had but distant memories of such joys, relaxing together in summer sunshine; the three-car cavalcade's two journeys through the lanes — the first in excited expectation, the second in happy recollection, set the seals on a marvellous package.

The success of the Youth Hostel prompted the committee to make an offer to sell the Spiceland buildings and equipment to the Youth Hostel Association, but after long consideration, the Association decided not to purchase, but to rent the building for one year — until the end of 1946 — with an option to purchase then.

At a special meeting in August the Committee gave every possible encouragement to the YHA to take the Hostel over as a "going concern" and to buy the equipment at an attractive price, but this offer was not accepted. The YHA decided to bring in their own furniture and equipment — a decision which meant that, not only the farm, but that all of Spiceland as we had known it must go under the hammer. These decisions made little difference to the hectic bustle of summer activity, and thoughts about the personal futures of the remaining Semi-perms were pushed out of mind to await calmer autumn days.

I hardly remember how we cut and carried the harvest. Stanley and Dorothy Musk left Spiceland to take up a joint appointment at a Sidmouth guest house which was looking forward to post-war holidays. I sorely missed Stanley's quietly exercised skills, his determination to see a job through, and his willingness to work in all weathers. Without the unflagging energy and enthusiasm of Dennis Wall, occasional help from Spicelanders making valedictory visits, and the support of the Lane family it would have been a heavy burden. As it happened, that combination of forces plus the exercise of skills and experience which had accrued, almost without notice, from five years of toil in the fields, made for an easier than usual harvest, carried, threshed and sold — with a generous retention to feed our stock and horses until the October farm sale.

Five acres of potatoes posed a more difficult problem — not many people really enjoy "tettie howking" — pride yielded to necessity — I asked for help from the Land Army. In two long days of September sunshine a small group of cheerful hardworking girls picked spuds up as fast as Bonnie and Prince could plough them out.

With the heavy work of harvest done, there was time to relax in ways which we had denied ourselves for a long time. The PPU September Summer School was in lively residence with some socialising after the serious sessions. The neglected table tennis table came into use; Dennis found an attractive visitor partner and quickly showed that he was no mean performer — at table tennis that is. He persuaded Marjorie and me to join in, and the four of us developed a fairly good standard in a setting of high spirits and much laughter. So much so that we were challenged by the Summer School to a match — Spiceland v PPU! I had always enjoyed playing games for fun, and because I was never good enough to be pressured into high performance areas, the fun persisted. Marjorie had been a considerable athlete, and had known the pressures of coaches and team selectors to change style and train hard — for the good of what? She came to despise the desire to win at any cost, and asserted that competitive sport did nothing to benefit, and a great deal to harm, the wellbeing of mankind. She never knew the score, had to be told when to change ends, but yielding to Dennis's pleading, she enjoyed the speed and excitement of the play, and shared the praise when Spiceland won a glorious victory!

The farm sale was a sorry affair. The day was wet and miserable, the auctioneer arrived late, and the animals we had cared for, and in some cases reared and loved beyond the claims of husbandry, made a sad procession which brought me close to unashamed tears before the end of day. I could hardly bear to part with the horses who had been my daily companions. Lovingly groomed for the day, and moving well, they did me proud. Bonnie was bought by Mr. Sansom who had laughed at, but copied, my book learning. He would, I thought, treat Bonnie well. Prince was bought by an elderly farmer from Plymtree way, who had come some days before the sale to watch him in action. I hope that he too was used well.

Hardest of all to part with was October, the calf Marjorie and I had brought into the world in 1941, whose mother had nearly died of milk fever, who followed Marjorie around like a familiar friend, and who had already had one calf and was now near to being a mother for the second time. She had a special place in our affections and she seemed to look at us through liquid eyes with something near reproach.

Blackborough village had grown out of the business of quarrying grit stone from the Beacon Hill. The original villagers had been "brought in" — they were not farming folk, but miners, and were regarded as foreigners for many years after the quarry work had ceased. The war and the farming prosperity it had engendered, had helped the village to find a new identity and develop a spirit of community with the surrounding district. The war over, they decided to work together to build a Village Hall, and called a meeting in the village school. The American Newcomer at Coombe House went to the meeting, and offered a piece of his land and his full support. A committee was formed, but he was not elected — a returning soldier son from one of the larger farms "over towards Sainthill" was preferred as Chairman, and a disappointed aspiring Squire withdrew the offer of his piece of land — and his support.

The village had not forgiven him for the threshing incident, nor for the other little unpleasantnesses, including interference with the water supply, with which he had hoped to gain farming possession of his own land. Fate was to play another, and final, blow. A heavy duty tarpaulin fell off a passing lorry just outside the Coombe House gate. He wheeled it in; nobody could be certain that his intentions were not honourable, but he delayed long enough for someone to suggest to the police that it was "larceny by finding." Coombe House once more went "up for sale."

The last committee meeting to be held at Spiceland was on November 4th, 1945. A number of Spicelanders made nostalgic journeys to be there, but it was a rather wistful gathering which roamed down the lanes of memory, and shared, more buoyantly, future hopes and plans. Dick and Joan were to return to Friends Relief Service. Marjorie and I agreed to remain at Spiceland until the new YHA wardens arrived, and to deal with the sale of the furniture and effects. At Dick's suggestion a gift of some of Spiceland's tables was made to the new Village Hall Committee, and the children's camp equipment was given to a Spicelander who organised youth clubs in the Chalk Farm area of London. The minutes record other helpful disposals, and reports the progress which the Land Agent was making to ensure that the War Agricultural Committee's wishes about the use of the land were being observed.

Dick and Joan insisted that we have a holiday before they returned to London, and it was agreed that we should spend a few days with Hugh and Doris at their farm at Halwill. The bull-nosed Morris was prepared for a long journey, and the feeling that we were going on an expedition was heightened when Dick made the last minute addition of a spade and a rope. "Tis November, and 'ee can't trust west country weather — 'twill likely snow over they hills!" he cried in mock dialect. In the event it was mild and muggy, but we enjoyed new scenery and the rare freedom of being just ourselves — a mum and dad enjoying a family outing. As we left Cullompton, at the spot where the road runs parallel with the railway, a Great Western express thundered by and eighteen month old Adrian's whoop of delight was an early demonstration of his developing and abiding interest in iron horses and the joys of the railroad.

Reunion with Hugh and Doris was also great fun. Doris, Marjorie and the infant Adrian spent happy hours together and Adrian, using domestic articles like patty pans for toys, contrived to hide them in some of the many "hidey holes" provided by a farm house. But it came as no surprise to find that Hugh had offered to help a neighbour move home and farm, and that our personal exchanges were mostly contrived between loading and unloading lorries with what the farmer euphemistically described as "bits and pieces." There came a time, long after light had gone from the sky, when everything, including the farmer, his wife, his wife's mother and the children had been moved to the new house — a house that the wife had not seen before the day of the move. Everything that is except the cows! I found myself late milking a strange herd, and then milking them again early the following morning, before they too were loaded on to lorries and taken away.

We came back to work of a different kind. An Exeter Friend, Norman Yeandell, had made a generous gift to enable some of the Spiceland equipment to be made available at very reasonable cost to Semi-perms now setting up homes for the first time. Post-war prices of furniture and household items were very high, and there were no coupons available to C.Os. We were soon engaged in writing letters and making up parcels of blankets, sheet sleeping bags and the like to give effect to this gift. At the same time we were preparing an inventory of the stuff which was to be taken to a depository in Exeter for public auction. The Hostel had officially closed at the end of October, but small groups of hostellers still turned up reminding us of what one of the old tramps who regularly stopped by for rest and refreshment was wont to reply when he was told that the Wayfarers' Home was closed. "You may close a good home, but I never do."

We had not the heart to turn them away with so many hilly miles between them and a possible bed. We bought some Spiceland single beds and mattresses so that when the bulk of the furniture finally went in December, we could still provide some hospitality for the new style Wayfarers. It was just as well. We did not, as we expected, spend Christmas by ourselves in the gaunt, nearly empty, house. One or two Spicelanders, and one or two hostellers who regarded themselves as Spicelanders, including one George Umber who spent all three hostel Christmasses with us, came to celebrate the very last Spiceland Christmas in modest but traditionally true style. Our resources were stretched to the very limit of make do, but there was plenty of food and, by then, Marjorie and I had become small-scale hostel wardens in very truth.

We knew where to find sheltered spots where primroses could be found in bloom on Christmas Day, and a small bowl of these precocious harbingers of spring made a graceful tribute to Spiceland's past, and made a gesture to the future in which what had been fashioned and experienced there will remain evergreen.

Bagging and weighing potatoes

Epilogue

In January 1946 the equipment stored in Exeter was sold at a public auction. Marjorie and I acted as caretakers until the Youth Hostel wardens arrived, and then moved into part of a sixteenth century house at the foot of Ponchydown Hill. It was, in effect, a tied cottage and I worked for a local farmer. The house was made of "cob" — a West Country material consisting mainly of rammed clay. The walls were over a foot thick, but were honeycombed with rat runs, and those unwelcome occupants could frequently be heard scurrying about on their missions. Lassie, our farm dog, listened intently to their movements, quickly fathomed their points of ingress and egress, and skilfully and steadily reduced their numbers, but never eliminated them. The original, and no doubt often renewed, thatch roof, had years ago been replaced with corrugated iron which did not entirely destroy the picturesque character of the building.

The rooms were huge, the floors bare, the main living room had a vast fireplace with iron pot-hooks, and the fire a voracious appetite for wood fuel. Our kitchen had been in times past a dairy, and sported unglazed, gauze-filled windows, which together with the slate floor and slate-topped benches, ensured temperatures ranging from freezing to cool. The water supply was a stream, piped from some yards up the hill, which discharged into a prepared place in the garden and filled the relay of buckets which we carried to and fro. The toilet was organically primitive.

We bathed in front of the fire, mindful of danger, in a galvanised tin bath which we filled with buckets of hot water lifted from a copper boiler and carried from the scullery. We emptied the long narrow bath by ungainly porterage through the house, and a final great heave into the garden.

By continuous struggle with inconvenience and basic equipment we made a home; the folk who visited and stayed with us, loved it, as did the growing Adrian who explored all the exciting possibilities with frightening dexterity.

We used the months we lived there to explore various ways which would enable us to go on living in the country, preferably as farmers, so that we could try out the ideas and agricultural theories which we had explored at Spiceland, and satisfy the sheer love of working on the land with which I had been infected as a boy. We gave up the cherished desire to take part in the relief work for which we had never trained, but we were able to keep an eye on what was happening to Spiceland at the top of the hill.

There were good times and bad times. I enjoyed life in the fields, working the horses, milking the cows, and sharing sometimes incomprehensible conversations with Joe and Fritz, two German prisoners of war who also worked there; but I clashed on many matters, like dairy hygiene — the milk was emptied from the milking buckets into an open collecting bucket placed outside the cowshed, where it was subject to unwholesome invasion by the farm cats and chickens — discouraged, but not deterred, by well-aimed stones. I worked a great deal of unpaid overtime — evening milking often started well after my supposed finishing time — and this, without any calculation, was loosely set against the rent of the house which was, in any case, already deemed to be covered by Sunday morning milking.

I quickly realised that I was a difficult employee, prickly on farming matters, weak, but resentful, about wages which had not been a consideration for years; and that our lack of financial resource made it probable that a farm worker was all that I was likely to be in this area of small family farms. The run-down farms which had enabled Roland Wood to make his start no longer existed in a country where farming had become prosperous.

Once or twice I expected the sack, but my speed about the farm and my strength were to my employer saving graces. I was useful too as a reliable horse carer when he entered his hunter in a local point-to-point race, and there was a good day-out towards the end of my time there, when the farmer's car broke down, and we all piled into the old bull-nosed Morris and went on a jolly journey to Bampton fair to buy a pony for one of his children.

I became secretary of the village hall committee, and found myself organising a gymkhana to raise funds. It was a taxing exercise. The overheads were far beyond what I thought they ought to be, prizes were generously spread over the events, and donations were nothing like as generous. The horse-riding, hunting, pony club folk were not my favourite flavour, and their interests were more dominant than those of the village. Mr. Broom loaned a very good level field which had recently been cut for hay, and the Cullompton police gave their services in organising the traffic and providing a friendly presence. The most taxing part was literally the recovery of entertainment tax from a reluctant revenue department, which seriously doubted whether the overheads had not prejudiced the charitable nature of the exercise. I eventually succeeded, and a modest sum went into the village kitty.

At the height of the harvest I experienced seering pain and irritation round my neck and shoulders — an irritation which showed itself in a curving line into my scalp. I thought it must be something like the barley awn rash I had had years before, but it proved to be shingles. There was a chicken-pox epidemic in the village. Although I quickly returned to work, the illness had a depressing effect on me such as I had never before experienced, and never have done since.

My pre-war employers chose this moment of low spirit to invite me to renew my appointment with them — I had been given unpaid leave of absence for the duration of the war — and my old boss, who had kept in regular touch with me by an exchange of letters, assured me that I would be warmly received. We agonised. We had a small son, and five years of voluntary work plus six months farm labouring had created a financial base from which the invitation looked like an irresistible temptation. In December 1946 we fulfilled the War Agricultural Committee men's prophecy and returned to London.

In October the YHA had decided not to exercise their option to purchase Spiceland. Their Regional Group had shown little interest in the hostel, their wardens had not been particularly happy in what had been, for them, a completely new experience, and numbers visiting the hostel had declined. It was decided to sell the property with the help of the Land Agent, and a small committee was appointed with power to act as it deemed fit.

The property, a mansion and thirty-three acres of land, was sold for £900. and the rent of the forty acres was eventually settled by arbitration at about one half of the rent which I had originally offered to its owner! The sales of farm stock and crops, the contents of the house, and now of the house and land resulted in cash assets of about £2300 after the farm loans had been repaid.

The committee considered a number of proposals before deciding, as an interim measure, that it would spend the income on giving financial support to people who undertook "work of the nature and in the spirit of that undertaken by Spicelanders." The capital was retained in the hope that a Quaker Centre would be established in the southwest.

At sometime in 1940 Mary Cash, a Friend who lived in Devonshire, had come to Spiceland and had enthused about what she experienced during her visit. She was hopeful about proposals for a Quaker Centre, and saw potential in what was happening at Blackborough. In 1941 it was she who had enriched life in the Common Room with the gift of a Steinway Grand piano, and in the Quiet Room by the gift of an organ — which was played by special dispensation only!

In October 1946 the committee was informed that Mary Cash had died and bequeathed to Spiceland a legacy of £300 and a share in the residual value of her estate, which proved to be a substantial sum. Friends were uneasy about accepting such a gift at a time of indecision, but Counsel advised, and a Court decided, that, as long as an active Society of Friends existed, the purposes of the Spiceland Trust could not fail, and inhibitions about accepting the legacy were set aside.

It is worthwhile quoting the main clause of the Spiceland Trust Deed:

"The purposes for which the Trustees hold the property are to help and assist persons to express through service to the community the meaning and spirit of Quakerism and Christianity.

Without prejudice to the generality of the foregoing the purpose may include the training of persons for service agriculture and relief work for refugees unemployed persons adults who have not all the privileges and amenities of the wealthier sections of the population children needing inexpensive holidays and any other service for others rendered without regard for any reimbursement by them which may in the opinion of the Committee tend to promote an understanding of the Quaker way of life and any other service work or undertaking of a similar nature or incidental to the before mentioned purposes."

In 1947 I became secretary of the Spiceland Trust, and for twenty years the Committee spent its income in support of many worthwhile individual and group activities which came within the terms of the Trust. It also considered a number of worthwhile proposals for the use of the Trust capital, but none of these was considered to fulfil properly "the purposes."

The predominantly educational and recreational Centre which south western Friends thought they required to develop their spiritual and corporate life did not meet the requirement of paragraph two. Only a Centre which embraced a variety of practical and intellectual activities such as were experienced at Spiceland could truly do that. After all, the deed had been drawn up by a member of the Peace Committee, without legal help, in time of war, with little time to turn aside from the pressures of a demanding present, and at a time when Spiceland activity at Blackborough and beyond was at its height. The deed was really based on what was happening at that time. I cannot trace that the deed was ever discussed in depth. It seemed as if it just happened.

The decision to close Spiceland Training Centre in 1945 was undeniably the overwhelming "sense of the meeting." I was at the time a co-opted member of the committee. I had personal doubts about the timing — based, in part, on strong sentiment, in part on the opportunities inherent in the site, and in part by the place Spiceland then occupied in the local community. Dick and I had never been convinced about the likelihood of the building's imminent collapse, and had often said that, if it had to go, something more suitable could be built.

I had been attracted to the Society in 1937 by a host of heart-warming attitudes to religion and life, one of which was a belief that sacred and secular living could not be separated. The small scattered Quaker groups in Devon and Cornwall could never have supported a Quaker Centre such as the Selly Oak College of Woodbrooke in Birmingham. Some ongoing activity which would sustain a centre between training courses, conferences, summer schools, childrens camps and the like was essential. I was, and am, prejudiced. The farm provided a link, as well as a background which fitted into the locality, for the less permanent activities, in a way which a guest house (a recurrent suggestion) could not. I found it difficult to understand why a Society which believed in the possible sacramental nature of all life should jib at one activity and not the other. A sustainable farm would have provided a respite to postpone the decision beyond the immediate post-war period, when so much else occupied Friends' minds. The Mary Cash bequest would have postponed the need for an appeal for funds. Eventually closure may have proved inevitable but ....?

We none of us wanted to continue as a small charity spending its small income each year — however worthwhile the spending — and holding on to its capital. In the 1950s Reg Reynolds, himself an ex-Spicelander, had responded to a statement of mine that we had insufficient funds to start anything remotely like Spiceland, by saying that what was too little in Britain might be enough in Africa. In the 1960s I attended a conference at Friends House where one Friend proposed setting up a fund to bring Africans to England for further education, and another had countered by saying that money spent in Africa to serve the same ends would achieve much more. The two thoughts linked together and I suggested that we should ask the Friends Service Council whether they had an overseas project which fitted our Trust Deed, and was in need of funds.

The F.S.C. introduced us to Roy and Irene Henson who were planning a rural service centre in Southern Rhodesia. In 1966 we decided to lay down the Spiceland Trust, and to donate the funds to that project. The project started in 1967 and flourishes still, under a Zimbabwean Quaker Management Committee as "HLEKWENI." An extract from its most recent leaflet states that it provides training "in a broad variety of agricultural, rural and domestic skills to local people so that they may then practise and pass on these skills to others in their home villages. No preliminary qualifications are required of the trainees and no certificates are awarded; the emphasis is on helping trainees to maximise the potential of their home lives — to grow more food, to conserve water, to build weather-proof homes. .... "extension" courses take place in the villages. From a modest beginning Hlekweni has grown into a genuine community of its own including 400 children who attend school within its boundaries."

Spicelanders would approve and be proud of this.

In 1967 Britain was operating a policy of sanctions to try and bring down the government of Ian Smith. There were delays before permission was given to transfer our money, which formed a substantial part of the sum required to purchase, (echos from the past!) 1800 acres of sub-marginal farm land; but the multi-racial, multi-cultural project melted official hearts and all was well. £5,402.11.9d old money was handed to the F.S.C.

There was still a great deal of correspondence and tidying up to do, the mills of the Charity Commission grind slowly, but on September 21st, 1971 the Charity Commission wrote to me, thanking me for copies of final accounts and other enclosures, and stated that Spiceland Training Centre had been removed from the Central Register under Section 4 (3) of the Charities Act 1960.

POWs – see page 247

IV: *The warden of Spiceland, John Hoare, with brother Os (left), and Arthur Hewlett of Friends Service Council (right).*

V: *Margaret Hoare with David Hoare (born 1939): washing the bee-hive.*

VI: *The crumbling splendour of Spiceland.*

VII: *The warden welcomes a new batch of Spiceland trainees after their six mile uphill walk from Cullompton Station.*

VIII: *Bert Baldwin explains re-roofing techniques.*

IX: *Much of the large house was a ruin, awaiting room by room reconstruction: excellent training for future bomb-damage repair work. Peter Reddick (left), Godfrey Whitwell (right).*

X: *Margot and Bill Sessions with Basil Goodey, clearing decades of Jackdaw nesting debris from one of the lofty chimneys, in order to unblock the fireplace below.*

XI: *Under Bert Baldwin's expert guidance, this first-floor Quiet Room was reconstructed: joists, floorboards, brickwork, plastering, electrics, the lot.*

XII & XIII: *'Keep chopping: we haven't got all day!' It was out-door cooking of dinner for 70 on alternate weeks, organised by Basil Goodey, including such delicacies as spinach-like nettle-tips. Would the trainees manage to burn the soup that day?*

XIV: *Tom Burke prepares Bonny for a hard day's work.*

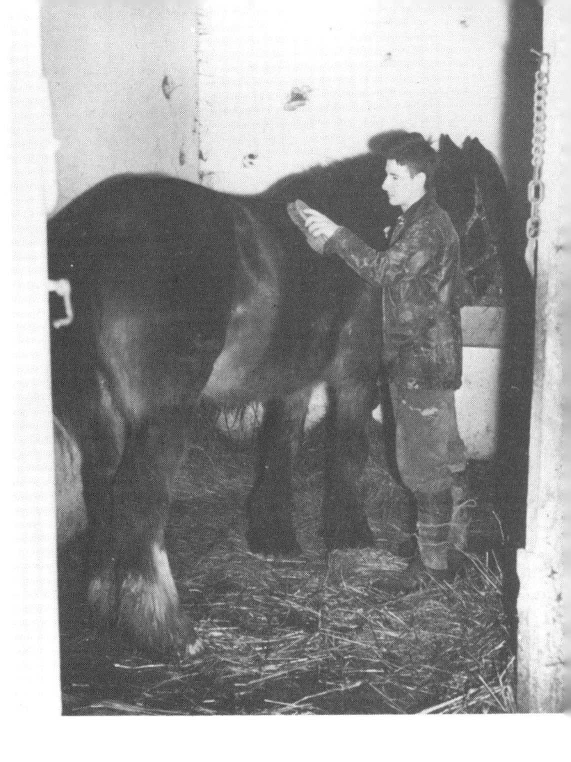

XV: *Jo Noble (o/c cooking) watches Hugh Flatt's milking lesson. (Trainees can seriously reduce the milk yield).*

XVI: *On the left Rudi Weiss, Austrian refugee gardener; on the right Hugh Flatt o/c farming, with trainee Bill Sessions and June the beloved and temperamental horse 'whose grandmother had jumped at Olympia'.*

XVII: *Anti-rabbit wiring: Rudi Weiss' newly planted vegetables.*

XVIII: *First-aid tuition. Brother Os demanding 'wrapped' attention.*

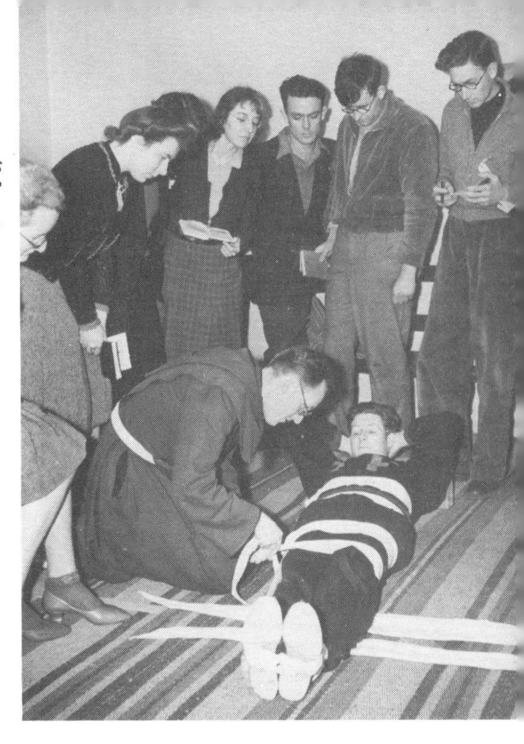

XIX: *Bert Baldwin (off-duty) gives young David Hoare a ride on Prince with mother Margaret in attendance left. Meantime 'food and pigs' trainees pause momentarily.*

XX: *The old well back into use. Marjorie Smith, John Benjamin, and Hugh Flatt.*

XXI: *Spicelanders sunning on the 'terrace'.*

XXII: *The back stairs to 'the ruins' and the nest of the resident barn-owl. (From a water-colour by Godwin Arnold).*

Editorial – Number One

Self-expression is an important part of community life; and where the machinery for producing a proper newspaper does not exist the Wall Magazine is the next best thing. Control of this one is not from above but from below, making it everyone's responsibility. If it succeeds it is because everyone in the community wishes it to succeed. If it fails, it is not the fault of any one person, but of the whole. It means that the community is intellectually dead. I do not believe this of Spiceland, so with the co-operation of several comrades, I went ahead with the scheme.

Writing is the best practice in thought organisation. Discussion is excellent, but put it down on paper, and you are getting somewhere. What you think counts, but what you do lasts longer. This board is here for the production of work of permanent value. It is not merely a diversion but, if we wish it, an essential part of our lives here. It is as important as milking a cow, making a shelf, or cooking a meal.

Tony. January 1941.

AN INGENIOUS LIBEL AGAINST SURGEONS.

(Showing their indebtedness to Procrustes. Father of Surgery.)
by
Reginald Reynolds, Gent.

Procrustes had a famous bed
    Whereon his guests he put
He measured downwards from the head
    And cut 'em down a foot.
But if the guest was short and stout
    His kindly host instead
Would stretch the wretched fellow out
    Upon that famous bed.
The surgeons when they saw the thing
    Cried out with one accord:
"Eureka!" "Cripes!" "God save the King!"
    "Beau Gests!" and "Praise the Lord!"
They said "This chopping off of legs
    Should keep us from starvation,
But let us not put all our eggs"
    (said they) "on amputation."
"We'll get Heath Robinson to make
    A sort of fracture rack
And those who seem to need a Break
    We'll give them what they lack."
They fixed the pulleys, weighed the lead
    And praised the merry jest:
"Jokes are a tonic," someone said,
    "But Leg-pulls are the best."
They said: "We grieve to see your leg
    Has tendencies to pain ---
Just place it in this rack, We beg:
    We'll put it right again,
A pity that your leg should lose
    An inch or two in length
When we can make what length we choose,
    By adding weight and strength
And stretch your left leg or your right
    Much longer than its brother
Adding a cubit to its height ---
    (Then you can break the other)."

AT THIS HOUR

At this hour,
when reason halts,
when violence
crowned by stupidity and fear
usurps dominion;
when the translucent word,
torn from the spirit's heart
or poured out in love of man,
means nothing;
when darkness breeds, and faith
makes treaties with despair ----

at this hour
let us at least control
our own kingdom,
unite those triple forces, love's contingents,
stir in the individual life no local war,
seek, each in each
the wholeness we would wish the world's ---
deny allegiance save at love's dictation,
at this hour
when fear commands.

Clive Sansom. January 1941.

A SELECTION OF CLERIHEWS

Diana
Has a charming manner
Even her chickens
Admire her like the dickens.

Tony
Is quite stony
Yet he's made his wall magazine
A free-to-all magazine.

When on rota
I always note a
Distinct strain
On the brain.

When John Naumann
Turned cowman
He took half a day
To milk May.

Philip may
go grey
He has the consolation that Perc
y's worse.

Helen
's spellin
of the rotas is
better than her other notices

It is not easy to Clerihugh
Hew
and we didn't do much better trying Winifread
insted.

SPICELAND'S FIRST BIRTHDAY

It was only the day before that someone realised that Saturday the 15th of March was the first birthday of Spiceland. What a pity — some of us had said — that we had not thought of it before, some kind of celebration could have been arranged. Alas it was too late, and so the matter dropped.

But on Saturday afternoon an idea occurred to Doris. She mentioned it to one or two of us — apologetically — for she considered it would be childish. Why not — she said — collect some primroses and stand them on the Supper table with a candle in the centre?

Childish? Perhaps; but when is man more human than when he is childish? We liked the idea, and so on Supper table duly appeared a birthday cake bearing a garland of primroses and one solitary candle. It is true that an unimaginative person might have seen only a circular wire basket on which were perched a few primroses and a domestic candle; but his lack of perception would have run away with him. We saw a cake. No fairer cake ever graced a festive board — and the fishpaste Blackborough Beacon completed the scene.

John was to light the candle. The ceremony — he said — was a surprise to him. He would not make a speech. He would simply light the candle; the Spiceland candle that would never go out. We may have been mistaken but we thought we detected a tiny catch in John's voice as he said those last words — a catch that we certainly felt in our own hearts.

After Supper it seemed only fitting that something in the nature of a birthday party should take place. Nobody arranged it, but surely it happened. And a very good party it was too. How can one describe it? Starting with a — shall we say — slightly boisterous netball match in which Marjorie's socks made an admirable ball, the celebrations advanced to community singing during which the untiring hands of Harold thumped endlessly on the piano and the no less untiring voices of the Spiceland Choir swept up through the Billiard Room — not always too melodiously — to be distributed to every nook and cranny of the building.

For a long time we shall remember the charming ballet of Geoffrey and Clive and its title of "Food and Pigs," the clever charades in which too many took part to mention names, and the uproarious sketch by Frank (Give us another tanner and we'll buy a blinking banner!!) And as though by way of contrast to such an hilarious evening there was the ghost story by Clive and the real live murder story by Stan — both told in the dark to make our flesh creep just a little.

At midnight the candle was still bravely burning, the primroses still peeping at us mischievously.

And so to bed — each of us happy that we had been privileged to see Spiceland pass the first milestone on its journey — its long and ever more fruitful journey, we fervently hoped — along life's highway.

Ted. March 1941.

LONDON LETTER

Hitler has started to put the finishing touches to the Balkans, and I am afraid we have to face a further spreading of the horrors. If the Germans are turning on a full blitz (I can't find out much today — Palm Sunday) I can't see much hope for Jugo Slavia or Greece. The optimists have one consolation in Russia's friendship with the former, but I shall be surprised if Joe Stalin ever does the British a good turn. Meanwhile in London we have dropped back to spectators with no raids to speak of. Nobody imagines that this will last for long.

The outcome of the Peoples Convention versus the B.B.C. fight has pleased everyone with any sense. Apart from this the Convention has received a lot of publicity in the national press, especially in the form of some good letters from Michael Redgrave. I have been trying to find out how they feel about pacifists but knowing the Communist Party is having a strong influence on the Convention's activities it is not hard to guess. Of course they would be all in our favour at the moment; anything so long as it opposes a capitalist war. But if they ever get power and turned it into what they want — a peoples' War, they would jug the lot of us.

The people in an East End shelter which was going to be closed protested. They wrote letters to the King, the Home Secretary and the Prime Minister. One day this week a hundred mothers with their children lobbied members in the House of Commons and wouldn't go away until they got satisfaction. The people won. The shelter is to stay open with many improvements.

This week we had the upsetting news of the deaths of two wonderful women — Virginia Wolf and Mary Hughes. I'm sure that neither of them would want anyone to mourn or feel sad, but it is difficult to avoid it. In their different ways both these women were examples of what is good in life. Mrs. Woolf's novels are full of charm and really great writing, and her essays contain a healthy exposure of hypocrisy. As a person she was kind and sensitive, and always loyal to her friends. With her passes another part of Bloomsbury life, the atmosphere of which has produced and influenced the best literature and painting of our terrifying times. Mary Hughes gave up everything to help the poor of the East End. Dewdrop Inn was open house to everyone in need. Everyone knew Mary and took their problems to her. The best way of remembering her goodness is to increase our own efforts to make up for her loss.

Tony Hyndman. April 1941.

Walls Have Ears:

Social Editor: I hear Bert's going to have a go at the hornets' nest today.

John Hoare: I dreamt about a hornets' nest last night. I wonder whether it was a revelation.

Social Editor: What happened?

John: I can't remember.

Overheard: "I did not say 'not sober' I said 'Donald Soper.'"

First Days at Ham Green.

"......reached the hospital on Monday afternoon a fortnight ago ......swept away to the ward and set to work cutting bread and butter......

During the first few days I was let loose on sweeping and scrubbing floors, cleaning the grate, washing up....... before long I was washing bottles, making meals, giving out meals...... and lately I have been taking temperatures and pulses, but there is still a considerable part of the work I have not touched.

Having been used to a weekend it takes time to get used to one day, or two half days, off at irregular intervals......we live in homely squalor, in a hut, where we have two rooms, a place to wash and a long passage lined with store rooms. Both rooms are common — one rather more common having four beds and a wireless. You ask what parts of Spiceland training I have found most useful at Ham Green. Laundry is useful — the laundry here maltreats clothes so much that we wash our own. Most essential are the "Oswald" courses in housework and home nursing; but of all the things I learnt the most necessary are cheerfulness and patience. For as we see it, besides working for them and waiting on them, it is essential to be friends with our patients. By learning their likes and dislikes, opinions and hopes, it becomes easier to understand and feel with them, and this it is which make the parts of our work which have to deal directly with them far and away the most interesting.

Godwin Arnold. September 1941."

Letter From Coventry.

"........people are still sleeping in the shelters 'we have been here for nearly a year now' some say — and are proud of it. One old lady admits that she likes talking about the terrible raids of November 14th 1940 and April 8th 1941......everyone will tell you about their experiences......I listen patiently as I cannot counter their stories......the suffering has created great cheerfulness but it is not constructive and has no depth......The only feeding arrangements at present is the Cadbury van which brings cups of cocoa to shelters nearly every night......we will soon have to prepare for the long winter nights......many well-paid workers grab their money and clear out into neighbouring villages but there are many still here......one little house has been occupied by the same family for five generations and now a large crack divides the walls in two. They love the old place but have to sleep in the shelter with their seven children.

And what do I think about A.R.P. work for pacifists? It is irrelevant to consider what other people think. It depends on the quality of one's living......unless a man has a special vocation — teaching, ministering, agriculture, engineering......I think that work for the protection of people against air raids is nearly the best work. It is civilian, it is not aggressive, it is not productive of weapons of war and one can sow the seeds of peace.

Richard Reiss. September 1941."

Journalism is a trade as much as bricklaying, and one is no more equipped to enter a newspaper office after writing for Wallpaper than one is equipped to build a house after attending Bert's lectures. But you need not be a born writer to become a contributor to Wallpaper. It is sufficient that you have something to say — and that you are here surely demonstrates that you have. So use Wallpaper to say it. And when you leave — for God's sake and for the sake of humanity, go out and live it.

Noel F. Cohen. December 1941.

Overheard at Lunch:

Arthur: "Donald keeps a bowl of Dissolute under his bed."

Oswald to Basil: "The difference between 'Dissolute' and 'Dissolite' is the difference between 'U' and 'I' "

Basil: " 'You' and 'Me' "

Stanley: "Ration of corn for a racehorse is more than that for a farm horse."

Someone: "Let's start a Spiceland stud and feed farm horses on racehorses' corn and racehorses on carrots."

Basil: "and then they'd be night mares!"

Afterthought.

Which reminds me of a profound remark by Jonathan (late lamented): "First out — best dressed."

A one-way plough

'Winston'!!

Muse at Play

Lovely fire. Quiet Room. Condition — it is necessary for me to get a place near it. Break down the barricade. There is a concerted scuffling, a mumbling of unnecessary apologies, a squeaking of castors, and lo! the furnace looms before me. I sit; in ten minutes my sandals are roasted, my finger tips iced. So heat can be polarised, as well as light. Well, here's a good yellow pencil and a white sheet of paper. I must write something for Wallpaper.

Conscience? Inspiration? Neither. It is my first free weekend and the rain lashes down, encircling the Quiet Room window. I have written all my letters and come to a dark age in the History of Mr. Polly. Moreover, Basil (or is it Jo?) has pleased me immensely with the supper sweet — apple, raspberry jam, ground nuts and bread crumbs at a rough guess, but it must be called Danish Apple Cake. The psychological reaction is rosy. I feel the urge to self-exhibition, like an awakening pork-butcher with thirty years of suburban mediocrity behind him.

What to write? Not a single idea, just incessant doodling. Must not bite my nails, I'm getting out of that habit. Yes, I can let myself pull at my chin. It was shaved this morning with a new blade, and should give inspiration. That log hisses delightfully. Like a cloud of steam issuing from a kettle. Is it the log now? Or is it olive oil making rivulets in my ears? It is the log. Getting a bit too warm now. I wonder if it would create Bedlam if I were to move my chair back a little. Worth trying anyhow.

There's Sidney, deeply engaged in Dorothy Sayers. Surprising the way this lady's criminological works, rather than her counsels for religious reform, make an appeal to Spicelandic pacifists. Look in the Library Book and witness their popularity for yourself. This bears investigation. Do we all abandon our principles in the hour of enjoyment? Even though we try to avoid it? Strange how we indulge freely in the readymade and non-stimulating pleasures which serve to amuse the public and keep it contentedly subservient.

Good topic for Wallpaper? Controversial certainly. But heavy. We Spicelanders don't like heavy stuff in Wallpaper. Either we object to it on principle, or else we like to read it written by some qualified and authoritative expert. Well! what about humour? Norman, called Dick, is begging for humour, far and wide in agonised terms. But what sort of humour? Pure wit, farce, burlesque, parody, satire, irony, buffoonery, lampoonery, or what? Really I suppose there is only one answer. Scandal.

Spiceland is a venerable institution, likes few things better than to see itself guyed. We thrive on personal imputation. Note the crowd round the Social Column each week, the lurid grins and the infinite variety of guffaws.

By Jove! John's got "Twelve Studies on Soviet Russia". Never noticed that before. This is a ripping library.

I might as well go back to Mr. Polly, for all the inspiration I receive. Anyhow I do not feel like guying unfortunate Spicelanders tonight. The hungry Philip, for instance........

Blimey, talk of the devil, he's just gone off to sleep with a Penguin on his knees. Fortunate fellow. He does not need the stimulus of a First Aid Lecture. I'm tired too. One week on the Dolly Tub, and I'm feeling like an occidental Mr. Wu.

Article for Wallpaper. Wallpaper article. Article for Wallpaper. Where was I? Dashed if I can remember, after that first class supper. Incidentally, the fire's getting pretty hot. Shouldn't have put that log on. Wonder if I dare push the circle further back. Chrysanthemums in November? Where did Helen find them?

All this worry and fuss about a few lines for Wallpaper. Such is the curse of adult humanity. There was David, this afternoon, romping happily after his ball, in blissful ignorance of war, capital accumulation, interpenetration of opposites, electrons, genes, conditional reflexes, carbohydrates, chlorophyll, and spicas. He does not have to know whether 2 plus 2 = 4, let alone whether personal contact can achieve more than political action in the way of social reform. Lucky David.

Yet how different in fact are children from the adults? They are both active parts of the experimental process: profiting by trial and error. Both have their best-laid schemes smashed by desires and impulses which they believe they have mastered or of which they take no account at all. They are only at different stations on the journey, with different amounts and qualities of experience.........'struth! I could go on all night.

But wait. The tree, ill planted though it be (Apologies Winifred), is bearing fruit. I have an idea for a short story. 88% were in favour of short stories. Maybe I shall start to write it. Maybe (but a lesser maybe) you'll see it next week. Anyway that is how inspiration comes to the weary. As an apologist for T.S.Eliot has said,

"This is not a period in which good art can be written."

John Gray. November 1941.

"IT'S A POOR MEMORY THAT ONLY WORKS BACKWARDS"

Could we but really see the oak-tree in the acorn,
the tower in the brick, the girder in the bolt;
could we but find a remedy
for dying on the image of event,
we then might save the heraldry
that makes all action cliche,
stopping the thousand deaths, the thousand memories
go bad and then be glad
to see the thing we meant a fact.
But there behind the fatal seizure in the imaging
comes all disaster, and in the secret streets
in secret towns the master carpenter
hammers the air-raid coffin 'gainst the act that fills it.

Before the world is left to worms,
leave! leave the blue print of our living,
stir out his cob-webbed womb the rust-red regent
memory and build a morning in the mind
letting the fresh winds take us forth
far from the grooves we run in blind
to take new meaning from the acts
that are our being, or else the watch stops,
the hand grasp chills, the motion of the thought
fast petrifies, the fossiled head nods nonsense
in the grass grown street;
beat! beat the madman race to hell
before the shutter falls and tell
new meaning to our being.

Glyn Richards. January 1942.

COMMUNITY

For a period of four years before coming to Spiceland, I have taken part in dozens of discussions about Community. Since coming to Spiceland I have heard the subject discussed only once — a remarkable fact. As one who is interested in the idea, I should like to hear opinions as to why communities fail — some of them dismally. Spicelanders with their experience of successful community life ought to be able to supply sound judgements on the subject. Here's a subject for Wallpaper correspondents or for Sunday evening discussion.

May I suggest, by the way, that we support the forthcoming village whist-drive. Not only is it for a good cause but will be the means of furthering reconciliation between pacifist and non-pacifist which must take place before the wider sphere of international conciliation can take place. Another thought for discussion — How can we bridge the gap between pacifist and non-pacifist? They are both guilty of intolerance.

Denis. April 1942.

Spiceland Dinner — by — David Gurney Hoare.

Lots of people.......lots of people, Daddy.......
all talking, Daddy.
All get up, Daddy....all sit down....all stop a minute...
all talking, Daddy.
All get up again.... all talking.... lovely time, Daddy.
Daddy ring bell....David ring bell.

Reported Sayings from Gerbestone Children's Home:

Johnny (aged 8) describing swans flying "and they were so low you could hear their breff."

Roy (aged 5) Soup was served at a meal which reminded him of something he had had at home "but Tom, you can't smell the taste of it."

Muriel's parents wrote and said that she didn't half have a good time at Gerbestone, to which Muriel replied: "Don't write and tell me we don't half have a good time down here because we have a hole of a good time."

Grace was said at Harry's birthday party: "Thank you for our tea and Harry's birthday." At which Harry immediately cut in: "Blimey he's put me in it."

Ministry of Cork and Sealing Wax,
Whitehall,
S.W.1.

To the Editor of Wallpaper.

Dear Sir,

Among the imponderabilia for which our whole nation, nay Empire, may be fairly said to be fighting, surely the freedom of expression may be ranked among the highest. Sir, it is with great perturbation that I have been aquainted with the impending cessation of your most valuable publication.

The mighty bastions of our free press is the most cherished facet of the many sided jewel of our heritage. You, sir, performed a most valuable service by daring to publish my adumbration of the inequities perpetrated by our outworn fiscal system on the unhappy industrialist. I refer, of course, to my communication of the 12th of January 1942 on the calamitous burdens imposed by the Excess Profits Tax. I hope that victory will put a speedy end to this so called sham of a so called National Government, masquerading as such so as to conceal its true nature of Socialism at its worst and most rampant manifestation.

I remain, dear sir,

Yours truly,

Kyle of Localsh,
January 1943.

IT'S THAT PLACE AGAIN – ITPA

Heard in the kitchen: "You have to stir for ten minutes and then beat it." "Oh I see, where do I have to go to?"

"I can't read my notes, should it be steam or scream for two and a half hours?"

"Couldn't we put in a little soya flour?"

In the Farmyard: "Look Marjorie, I have found an egg in the cockerels' pen." "That's interesting............or it would be if it were not a china egg."

In Construction: "I levelled those chair legs and it's a good stool now."

Cecile has christened the milking stool she has made "Semi-perm" – something to do with its temporary nature.

Carpentry term defined by Cecile: Mortise and Tenon = Hole and Bung.

Drenching Prince

THE LAST EDITORIAL

How very apt are the words of Shakespeare in Scene Five, Act Two, Twelfth Night. For the Editorship of Wallpaper was indeed "thrust upon me" before it was realised that this was to be the final issue of a very long and honourable line of forebears. This fact alone is responsible for the Editorial Cloak falling upon our shoulders instead of those more worthy and qualified to undertake the onerous task of writing the last Editorial.

Now that the future of Spiceland is no longer in the realm of conjecture, it is possible for us to throw off the air of dejection and gloom that has characterized several recent editorials, and to voice our extreme relief and pleasure that the answer to the burning question "Stands Spiceland where it did?" is in the affirmative — or nearly so. We shall after all be able to return either as youth hostellers, or for a holiday, or for a honeymoon, or to polish up our cooking or poultry keeping, — in fact, to the Alma Mater of the 350 Spicelanders whose lives have been so enriched by their sojourn within those cold and forbidding walls whose appearance so belies the warmth of the atmosphere within.

It is appropriate, we believe, upon this occasion, to add yet one more tribute to the multitudes that have gone before to that mysterious something known as the "Spiceland Spirit" which is to be recognised de jure, we understand, by the formation of an Association, and to all those, especially John and the Semi-perms who have done so much to make this place a centre whence pacifists have sallied forth to various spheres of service, refreshed in spirit, mind, and body. We might in fact describe it as a veritable Practical Pacifist University.

In conclusion, we express our sincerest good wishes to those in whose hands the future destinies of our home from home have been entrusted. Knowing them as we do we confidently foretell the day when the name of Spiceland will mean to Youth Hostellers and pacifists what Mecca signifies to the followers of Mahomet. If we regard the closing of the Training Centre as the end of a chapter, we can but hope that the "Book of Spiceland" will rival "Gone With The Wind or "War and Peace" in length.

Bill. January 23rd, 1943.

Names of Spicelanders

"The men and women turned out from Spiceland were among the most reliable, rescourceful, and enduring of all those who joined War Vics."
— Roger Wilson (Quaker Relief, 1952)

Absalom Harold J.
Aitken Michael M.W.
Amos Edwin
Amsden Ronald C.
Andrew Douglas
Andrew Malcolm
Ansell David
Appleyard Edward
Appleyard Marjorie
Armstrong John
Arnold Godwin
Atkin Laurence
Atkinson John
Ayliffe Lionel (FAU)
Baldwin Bert
Baldwin Hilda
Barber Godfrey
Barber Violet (Mac)
Barelli George
Barrett William
Battcock Henry
Bailey Ronald
Baynes Nan
Bazeley John
Bazeley Peggy
Bechet Rene
Bell Philip
Best Anthony
Bewley Neville
Blake J.Alan
Bland Jim
Blaxland Harold
Bolton Oliver
Braithwaite George
Braithwaite June (Baldwin)
Brammer Hugh
Brand John Henry
Bray Raymond
Brayshaw Christopher
Brook (Evans) Alfred
Brooks Ernest
Brook John
Brown Arthur
Brown Philip
Brown Wilfrid (Bill)
Browne Eleanor
Browne William
Bryan Alexander
Bubb Charles
Bubb Mary Paul (nee Quick)
Bullock Dennis
Bullock Molly (nee King)
Burke Thomas
Burnell Arnold

Burnell Norah
Burrows Reginald F.
Butlin Tony
Cain Clifford
Cain Stanley
Callender Stella
Carter Edwin (Walter)
Carter Noel
Catleugh Marjorie (Joan)
Chadwick James
Charesworth Irene
Charlesworth Philip
Claiden Alfred (Daniel)
Clark Elizabeth
Clarke Harold
Cleave Philip
Clewer H. Dorothy (Street)
Clifton Philip
Cohen Noel
Cole Leonard
Coles Ivor J.
Constable Denis
Cook Fred
Cook Elsie
Cooper Gladys
Cooper Stanley
Craven Edward
Cronshaw Thomas
Crosland Frank
Crosland Stanley
Crozier Eric
Cullum Donald
Cummings Brian
Curtis Arthur
Davie Glen
Davies Alun
Davies Cecil
Davison Bob
Dolling Clarence
Drewitt Geoffrey
Dring Basil (Charles)
Dromard Harold Ernest
Du Feu Stanley
Dyer Reginald
Eddington John
Edwards Doris
Eldridge Thomas
Ellis A. Derwent
Etherington George
Evans Elizabeth (Betty)
Evens William H. (Tim)
Everett Sidney
Eyres Cyril Nicholas
Faussett Shelley
Field Jonathan
Finney Celia
Fitton Laurence
FitzGerald Desmond N.
Flatt Doris (nee Rutter)
Flatt Hugh A.L.
Ford May (Lillian)
Ford William
Forward Norman
Fox Dorothy
Frank Harold J. (Bill)
Frimston David
Friston D. Frances
Gale William
Gayton Morley
Gilbertson Norman
Gilderdale Michael
Gold Donald
Goodey Basil
Goodey Joan
Graddon Ethel
Gray John
Green Alan
Gregory Theo C.
Gruenseld Alfred
Hadcock Marian
Hadcock Richard H.
Hadley Ronald

Hall Arthur
Hardie Leslie Charles
Harkness John
Harkness Roger
Harper William McD.
Harrington Herbert
Harrison Paul
Harrison Sidney
Harvey Sidney H.
Henderson Thomas B.
Hawkes Herbert G.
Hill Doreen
Hinton Michael
Hirst Ralph
Hitchens Ron
Hobbs John
Holliday David John (Dan)
Holliday Kathleen Ruth
Holloway Mary
Holloway Robert
Holman Philip
Alexander Holmes
Holmes Kenneth
Hopkins George
Howe Philip
Humphreys Alfred
Hyndman Tony A.R.
Ingram Eric
Ironside Donald J.
Ironside Jean
Jarvis Roy
Jefferson Derek H.
Jenkins Dafyd
Jennings Howard
Jeremiah Keith
Jessop Gordon
Johnson Kenneth
Johnson Peter
Jones Arnold
Jones David
Jones Louis
Jones Phyllis
Jorns Karl Heinz (Johnny)
Keight Harry
Kenner Lionel
Kennish Paul
King-Beer Michael
Kirby Frank
Knight Kenneth
Knowler Robin
LaMaison Alexander L.
Lambert Bert
Lambert Eric
Lascelles Douglas
Last Alfred
Layman John
Layman Paul W.R.
Le Gros John G.Le
Levy Kurt
Lewis Watkin
Linford Jack
Linsdell Frank
Little Chris
Lloyd Ben
Lovejoy Howard
Luke Frederick Davey
Lumb Thelma
Lunnon Chris
Lusby Arthur
Manning Richard William
Marder Arnold
Markham Gennifer
Martin Leslie
Martin Reginald
Massey Patricia
Masters Doris
Masters Ronald
Mather Leslie
Maw Francis
May Fred
May Heather
Mays Robert H.

McKinlay David
McQuillen Helene (nee Biller)
McQuillen Kenneth
Mellor Arthur
Mellor Hugh V.
Mellor Hugh W.
Milner John P.
Milner Wilfred
Moberly Edward
Moon Keith
Morgan David H.
Moriarty Denis
Musk Dorothy
Musk Stanley
Naish Richard
Naumann John
Neale Jessica
Nerichow Karl Heinz
Newton Robert
Nicholls Ken
Noble Josephine
Noel Tom
Norman Jim
Notcutt Frank
Nottridge Harold
Nunn Kenneth (FAU)
Ollier Hubert
Oswald Brother (S.S.F.)
Page Geoffrey
Pallett Henry (Harry)
Palmer George
Pascoe Percival (Percy)
Pechey John
Penny Victor
Perry John Wheeler
Pettet Arthur
Phibbs Richard
Pickford Denys Arthur
Pullen Hilda
Quickenden Anthony M.
Rawling Cecile
Reddick Peter
Reeves David
Reiss Richard (Henry)
Rendell Wilfred
Reynolds Reginald Arthur
Reynolds Joan
Richards Glyn
Richardson Winifred
Rieger Philipp
Roberts Diana
Robinson Arthur H.
Robinson Evan
Robinson John
Robinson Richard
Rodger Betty
Rodger Donald
Rollason Frederick
Routledge Eric
Rowntree Martin
Rowntree Reginald
Runswick Roy G.
Rutherford H.J.P. (Pat)
Sandle Walter G.
Sanger Fred
Sansom Clive
Sansom Ruth
Sayers Nigel B.H.
Sessions E. Margaret (Margot)
Sessions William Kaye (Bill)
Sharman Cecil
Sharp Denis
Sharp Leslie
Sherrington Dick
Shiner Jim
Shipley Raymond A.
Short Raymond
Siburn Arthur
Sichrovsky Harry
Slader Frances
Slader Harold
Smart Edwin

Smith Cedric A.B.
Smith Ralph
Smith Marjorie F. and
Smith Stanley
Smith Stanley (Winford)
Smith Steven
Sogan Jack
Sorensen Michael (FAU)
South Frederick
Southall Brian Henry
Sparkes Roger
Stapleton George Brian
Steel Joan
Steel Norman
Street David H.
Strevens Peter
Sutherland Ian
Sutton Dennis (FAU)
Sweetman Dallis
Sweetman Philip
Sweetman William
Sykes Eva M.
Taylor Ronald
Teague Geoffrey S.
Theobald Peter
Thom William
Thomas Alan
Thompson Alan
Townell George
Trivett Greta
Trivett John
Turner Philip
Tyldesley Alan J.
Tyldesley Eric (George)
Tyler Ken
Tyler Marie
Tyson George
Tyson Olive
Unite Jack
Unite Janet
Unite Rex
Upton Christopher
Upton Sybil
Wade Fred Allen
Walesby Jack
Walker Gerald
Wall Dennis
Wallace Bruce
Walsh Peter
Warner Roger H.M.
Watkin William F.
Watkins Michael
Weiss Rudolf
Wheatley Harold
Wheatley Janette
White Alfred (FAU)
White Edwin
Whitehouse Donald
Whiteman John (Charles Robert)
Whiting John
Whiting Roger
Whitwell Godfrey
Whitwell Catherine
Wildman Doris
Williams Eric
Wilson Andrew
Wilson Norah
Wolstenholme John (Leslie)
Wood Gilbert
Woodhouse Charles F.
Worsley Stanley (Benjamin)
Youngman Harry
Youngs Ronald E.S.

Making silage

'Tailpiece'